Data Wrangling with Python

Creating actionable data from raw sources

Dr. Tirthajyoti Sarkar and Shubhadeep Roychowdhury

Data Wrangling with Python

Authors: Dr. Tirthajyoti Sarkar and Shubhadeep Roychowdhury

Managing Editor: Steffi Monteiro

Acquisitions Editor: Kunal Sawant

Production Editor: Nitesh Thakur

Editorial Board: David Barnes, Ewan Buckingham, Shivangi Chatterji, Simon Cox, Manasa Kumar, Alex Mazonowicz, Douglas Paterson, Dominic Pereira, Shiny Poojary, Saman Siddiqui, Erol Staveley, Ankita Thakur, and Mohita Vyas.

First Published: February 2019

Production Reference: 2101121

ISBN: 978-1-78980-011-1

Published by Packt Publishing Ltd.

Livery Place, 35 Livery Street

Birmingham B3 2PB, UK

Table of Contents

Preface   i

Introduction to Data Wrangling with Python   1

Introduction 2

Importance of Data Wrangling 2

Python for Data Wrangling 4

Lists, Sets, Strings, Tuples, and Dictionaries 6

Lists 6

Exercise 1: Accessing the List Members 7

Exercise 2: Generating a List 9

Exercise 3: Iterating over a List and Checking Membership 12

Exercise 4: Sorting a List 14

Exercise 5: Generating a Random List 16

Activity 1: Handling Lists 17

Sets 17

Introduction to Sets 17

Union and Intersection of Sets 18

Creating Null Sets 20

Dictionary 20

Exercise 6: Accessing and Setting Values in a Dictionary 21

Exercise 7: Iterating Over a Dictionary 22

Exercise 8: Revisiting the Unique Valued List Problem 22

Exercise 9: Deleting Value from Dict 24

Exercise 10: Dictionary Comprehension 24

Tuples 25

Creating a Tuple with Different Cardinalities 26

Unpacking a Tuple 26

Exercise 11: Handling Tuples 27

Strings 27

Exercise 12: Accessing Strings 28

Exercise 13: String Slices 29

String Functions 29

Exercise 14: Split and Join 30

Activity 2: Analyze a Multiline String and Generate the
Unique Word Count 31

Summary 32

Advanced Data Structures and File Handling   35

Introduction 36

Advanced Data Structures 36

Iterator 37

Exercise 15: Introduction to the Iterator 37

Stacks 39

Exercise 16: Implementing a Stack in Python 39

Exercise 17: Implementing a Stack Using User-Defined Methods 41

Exercise 18: Lambda Expression 44

Exercise 19: Lambda Expression for Sorting 45

Exercise 20: Multi-Element Membership Checking 46

Queue 47

Exercise 21: Implementing a Queue in Python 48

Activity 3: Permutation, Iterator, Lambda, List 49

Basic File Operations in Python 51

Exercise 22: File Operations 51

File Handling 52

Exercise 23: Opening and Closing a File 54

The with Statement 54

Opening a File Using the with Statement 55

Exercise 24: Reading a File Line by Line 56

Exercise 25: Write to a File 57

Activity 4: Design Your Own CSV Parser 59

Summary 60

Introduction to NumPy, Pandas,and Matplotlib   63

Introduction 64

NumPy Arrays 64

NumPy Array and Features 64

Exercise 26: Creating a NumPy Array (from a List) 65

Exercise 27: Adding Two NumPy Arrays 66

Exercise 28: Mathematical Operations on NumPy Arrays 67

Exercise 29: Advanced Mathematical Operations on NumPy Arrays 68

Exercise 30: Generating Arrays Using arange and linspace 69

Exercise 31: Creating Multi-Dimensional Arrays 70

Exercise 32: The Dimension, Shape, Size, and Data Type of the
Two-dimensional Array 71

Exercise 33: Zeros, Ones, Random, Identity Matrices, and Vectors 72

Exercise 34: Reshaping, Ravel, Min, Max, and Sorting 74

Exercise 35: Indexing and Slicing 76

Conditional Subsetting 79

Exercise 36: Array Operations (array-array, array-scalar, and
universal functions) 80

Stacking Arrays 82

Pandas DataFrames 83

Exercise 37: Creating a Pandas Series 84

Exercise 38: Pandas Series and Data Handling 86

Exercise 39: Creating Pandas DataFrames 87

Exercise 40: Viewing a DataFrame Partially 89

Indexing and Slicing Columns 91

Indexing and Slicing Rows 93

Exercise 41: Creating and Deleting a New Column or Row 96

Statistics and Visualization with NumPy and Pandas 98

Refresher of Basic Descriptive Statistics (and the Matplotlib
Library for Visualization) 99

Exercise 42: Introduction to Matplotlib Through a Scatter Plot 99

Definition of Statistical Measures – Central Tendency and Spread 102

Random Variables and Probability Distribution 104

What Is a Probability Distribution? 104

Discrete Distributions 105

Continuous Distributions 105

Data Wrangling in Statistics and Visualization 106

Using NumPy and Pandas to Calculate Basic Descriptive
Statistics on the DataFrame 107

Random Number Generation Using NumPy 107

Exercise 43: Generating Random Numbers from a
Uniform Distribution 108

Exercise 44: Generating Random Numbers from a
Binomial Distribution and Bar Plot 109

Exercise 45: Generating Random Numbers from Normal
Distribution and Histograms 110

Exercise 46: Calculation of Descriptive Statistics from a
DataFrame 112

Exercise 47: Built-in Plotting Utilities 115

Activity 5: Generating Statistics from a CSV File 116

Summary 117

Introduction 122

Subsetting, Filtering, and Grouping 122

    Exercise 48: Loading and Examining a Superstore's Sales Data
from an Excel File 123

    Subsetting the DataFrame 124

    An Example Use Case: Determining Statistics on Sales and Profit 125

    Exercise 49: The unique Function 126

    Conditional Selection and Boolean Filtering 128

    Exercise 50: Setting and Resetting the Index 133

    Exercise 51: The GroupBy Method 136

Detecting Outliers and Handling Missing Values 139

    Missing Values in Pandas 141

    Exercise 52: Filling in the Missing Values with fillna 143

    Exercise 53: Dropping Missing Values with dropna 147

    Outlier Detection Using a Simple Statistical Test 148

Concatenating, Merging, and Joining 150

    Exercise 54: Concatenation 151

    Exercise 55: Merging by a Common Key 152

    Exercise 56: The join Method 156

Useful Methods of Pandas 159

    Exercise 57: Randomized Sampling 159

    The value_counts Method 162

    Pivot Table Functionality 162

    Exercise 58: Sorting by Column Values – the sort_values Method 163

    Exercise 59: Flexibility for User-Defined Functions with the
apply Method 166

    Activity 6: Working with the Adult Income Dataset (UCI) 170

Summary 172

Getting Comfortable with Different Kinds of Data Sources   175

Introduction 176

Reading Data from Different Text-Based (and Non-Text-Based) Sources 176

Data Files Provided with This Chapter 176

Libraries to Install for This Chapter 177

Exercise 60: Reading Data from a CSV File Where Headers Are Missing 177

Exercise 61: Reading from a CSV File where Delimiters are not Commas 179

Exercise 62: Bypassing the Headers of a CSV File 180

Exercise 63: Skipping Initial Rows and Footers when Reading a CSV File 182

Reading Only the First N Rows (Especially Useful for Large Files) 184

Exercise 64: Combining Skiprows and Nrows to Read Data in Small Chunks 185

Setting the skip_blank_lines Option 185

Read CSV from a Zip file 186

Reading from an Excel File Using sheet_name and Handling a Distinct sheet_name 187

Exercise 65: Reading a General Delimited Text File 187

Reading HTML Tables Directly from a URL 189

Exercise 66: Further Wrangling to Get the Desired Data 190

Exercise 67: Reading from a JSON File 191

Reading a Stata File 192

Exercise 68: Reading Tabular Data from a PDF File 193

Introduction to Beautiful Soup 4 and Web Page Parsing 196

Structure of HTML 197

Exercise 69: Reading an HTML file and Extracting its Contents
Using BeautifulSoup 198

Exercise 70: DataFrames and BeautifulSoup 204

Exercise 71: Exporting a DataFrame as an Excel File 206

Exercise 72: Stacking URLs from a Document using bs4 206

Activity 7: Reading Tabular Data from a Web Page and Creating
DataFrames 207

Summary 208

Learning the Hidden Secrets of Data Wrangling 211

Introduction 212

Additional Software Required for This Section 212

Advanced List Comprehension and the zip Function 212

Introduction to Generator Expressions 213

Exercise 73: Generator Expressions 213

Exercise 74: One-Liner Generator Expression 215

Exercise 75: Extracting a List with Single Words 215

Exercise 76: The zip Function 218

Exercise 77: Handling Messy Data 219

Data Formatting 220

The % operator 220

Using the format Function 223

Exercise 78: Data Representation Using {} 225

Identify and Clean Outliers 226

Exercise 79: Outliers in Numerical Data 227

Z-score 229

Exercise 80: The Z-Score Value to Remove Outliers 230

Exercise 81: Fuzzy Matching of Strings 231

Activity 8: Handling Outliers and Missing Data 233

Summary 234

Advanced Web Scraping and Data Gathering   237

Introduction 238

The Basics of Web Scraping and the Beautiful Soup Library 238

    Libraries in Python 239

    Exercise 81: Using the Requests Library to Get a Response from
    the Wikipedia Home Page 239

    Exercise 82: Checking the Status of the Web Request 241

    Checking the Encoding of the Web Page 242

    Exercise 83: Creating a Function to Decode the Contents of the
    Response and Check its Length 242

    Exercise 84: Extracting Human-Readable Text From a
    BeautifulSoup Object 244

    Extracting Text from a Section 245

    Extracting Important Historical Events that Happened
    on Today's Date 247

    Exercise 85: Using Advanced BS4 Techniques to Extract
    Relevant Text 250

    Exercise 86: Creating a Compact Function to Extract the
    "On this Day" Text from the Wikipedia Home Page 254

Reading Data from XML 255

    Exercise 87: Creating an XML File and Reading XML
    Element Objects 255

    Exercise 88: Finding Various Elements of Data within a
    Tree (Element) 257

    Reading from a Local XML File into an ElementTree Object 258

    Exercise 89: Traversing the Tree, Finding the Root, and Exploring
    all Child Nodes and their Tags and Attributes 259

    Exercise 90: Using the text Method to Extract Meaningful Data 260

Extracting and Printing the GDP/Per Capita Information Using a Loop 261

Exercise 91: Finding All the Neighboring Countries for each Country and Printing Them 262

Exercise 92: A Simple Demo of Using XML Data Obtained by Web Scraping 263

Reading Data from an API 266

Defining the Base URL (or API Endpoint) 267

Exercise 93: Defining and Testing a Function to Pull Country Data from an API 268

Using the Built-In JSON Library to Read and Examine Data 269

Printing All the Data Elements 270

Using a Function that Extracts a DataFrame Containing Key Information 272

Exercise 94: Testing the Function by Building a Small Database of Countries' Information 274

Fundamentals of Regular Expressions (RegEx) 276

Regex in the Context of Web Scraping 276

Exercise 95: Using the match Method to Check Whether a Pattern matches a String/Sequence 277

Using the Compile Method to Create a Regex Program 277

Exercise 96: Compiling Programs to Match Objects 278

Exercise 97: Using Additional Parameters in Match to Check for Positional Matching 279

Finding the Number of Words in a List That End with "ing" 280

Exercise 98: The search Method in Regex 281

Exercise 99: Using the span Method of the Match Object to Locate the Position of the Matched Pattern 281

Exercise 100: Examples of Single Character Pattern Matching with search 282

Exercise 101: Examples of Pattern Matching at the Start or End of a String 284

Exercise 102: Examples of Pattern Matching with
Multiple Characters 285

Exercise 103: Greedy versus Non-Greedy Matching 287

Exercise 104: Controlling Repetitions to Match 288

Exercise 105: Sets of Matching Characters 290

Exercise 106: The use of OR in Regex using the OR Operator 292

The `findall` Method 293

Activity 9: Extracting the Top 100 eBooks from Gutenberg 294

Activity 10: Building Your Own Movie Database by
Reading an API 295

Summary 297

RDBMS and SQL — 299

Introduction 300

Refresher of RDBMS and SQL 301

How is an RDBMS Structured? 301

SQL 302

Using an RDBMS (MySQL/PostgreSQL/SQLite) 304

Exercise 107: Connecting to Database in SQLite 305

Exercise 108: DDL and DML Commands in SQLite 306

Reading Data from a Database in SQLite 307

Exercise 109: Sorting Values that are Present in the Database 308

Exercise 110: Altering the Structure of a Table and Updating
the New Fields 309

Exercise 111: Grouping Values in Tables 310

Relation Mapping in Databases 311

Adding Rows in the comments Table 313

Joins 314

Retrieving Specific Columns from a JOIN query 316

Exercise 112: Deleting Rows 317

Updating Specific Values in a Table 318

Exercise 113: RDBMS and DataFrames 319

Activity 11: Retrieving Data Correctly From Databases 320

Summary 322

Application of Data Wrangling in Real Life   325

Introduction 326

Applying Your Knowledge to a Real-life Data Wrangling Task 326

Activity 12: Data Wrangling Task – Fixing UN Data 328

Activity 13: Data Wrangling Task – Cleaning GDP Data 329

Activity 14: Data Wrangling Task – Merging UN Data and
GDP Data 331

Activity 15: Data Wrangling Task – Connecting the New Data to
the Database 331

An Extension to Data Wrangling 332

Additional Skills Required to Become a Data Scientist 332

Basic Familiarity with Big Data and Cloud Technologies 333

What Goes with Data Wrangling? 334

Tips and Tricks for Mastering Machine Learning 336

Summary 337

Appendix   339

Index   425

Preface

About the Book

For data to be useful and meaningful, it must be curated and refined. *Data Wrangling with Python* teaches you all the core ideas behind these processes and equips you with knowledge about the most popular tools and techniques in the domain.

The book starts with the absolute basics of Python, focusing mainly on data structures, and then quickly jumps into the NumPy and pandas libraries as the fundamental tools for data wrangling. We emphasize why you should stay away from the traditional way of data cleaning, as done in other languages, and take advantage of the specialized pre-built routines in Python. Thereafter, you will learn how, using the same Python backend, you can extract and transform data from a diverse array of sources, such as the internet, large database vaults, or Excel financial tables. Then, you will also learn how to handle missing or incorrect data, and reformat it based on the requirements from the downstream analytics tool. You will learn about these concepts through real-world examples and datasets.

By the end of this book, you will be confident enough to handle a myriad of sources to extract, clean, transform, and format your data efficiently.

About the Authors

Dr. Tirthajyoti Sarkar works as a senior principal engineer in the semiconductor technology domain, where he applies cutting-edge data science/machine learning techniques to design automation and predictive analytics. He writes regularly about Python programming and data science topics. He holds a Ph.D. from the University of Illinois, and certifications in artificial intelligence and machine learning from Stanford and MIT.

Shubhadeep Roychowdhury works as a senior software engineer at a Paris-based cybersecurity start-up, where he is applying state-of-the-art computer vision and data engineering algorithms and tools to develop cutting-edge products. He often writes about algorithm implementation in Python and similar topics. He holds a master's degree in computer science from West Bengal University of Technology and certifications in machine learning from Stanford.

Learning Objectives

- Use and manipulate complex and simple data structures

- Harness the full potential of DataFrames and numpy.array at run time

- Perform web scraping with BeautifulSoup4 and html5lib

- Execute advanced string search and manipulation with RegEX

- Handle outliers and perform data imputation with Pandas

- Use descriptive statistics and plotting techniques

- Practice data wrangling and modeling using data generation techniques

Approach

Data Wrangling with Python takes a practical approach to equip beginners with the most essential data analysis tools in the shortest possible time. It contains multiple activities that use real-life business scenarios for you to practice and apply your new skills in a highly relevant context.

Audience

Data Wrangling with Python is designed for developers, data analysts, and business analysts who are keen to pursue a career as a full-fledged data scientist or analytics expert. Although, this book is for beginners, prior working knowledge of Python is necessary to easily grasp the concepts covered here. It will also help to have rudimentary knowledge of relational database and SQL.

Minimum Hardware Requirements

For the optimal student experience, we recommend the following hardware configuration:

- Processor: Intel Core i5 or equivalent

- Memory: 8 GB RAM

- Storage: 35 GB available space

Software Requirements

You'll also need the following software installed in advance:

- OS: Windows 7 SP1 64-bit, Windows 8.1 64-bit or Windows 10 64-bit, Ubuntu Linux, or the latest version of macOS

- version of OS X

- Processor: Intel Core i5 or equivalent

- Memory: 4 GB RAM (8 GB Preferred)

- Storage: 35 GB available space

Conventions

Code words in text, database table names, folder names, filenames, file extensions, pathnames, dummy URLs, user input, and Twitter handles are shown as follows: " This will return the value associated with it- **["list_element1", 34]**"

A block of code is set as follows:

```
list_1 = []
    for x in range(0, 10):
    list_1.append(x)
list_1
```

New terms and important words are shown in bold. Words that you see on the screen, for example, in menus or dialog boxes, appear in the text like this: "Click on **New** and choose **Python 3**."

Installation and Setup

Each great journey begins with a humble step. Our upcoming adventure in the land of data wrangling is no exception. Before we can do awesome things with data, we need to be prepared with the most productive environment. In this short section, we shall see how to do that.

The only prerequisite regarding the environment for this book is to have Docker installed. If you have never heard of Docker or you have only a very faint idea what it is, then fear not. All you need to know about Docker for the purpose of this book is this: Docker is a lightweight containerization engine that runs on all three major platforms (Linux, Windows, and macOS). The main idea behind Docker is give you safe, easy, and lightweight virtualization on top of your native OS.

Install Docker

1. To install Docker on a Mac or Windows machine, create an account on Docker and download the latest version. It's easy to install and set up.

2. Once you have set up Docker, open a shell (or Terminal if you are a Mac user) and type the following command to verify that the installation has been successful:

   ```
   docker version
   ```

   If the output shows you the server and client version of Docker, then you are all set up.

Pull the image

1. Pull the image and you will have all the necessary packages (including Python 3.6.6) installed and ready for you to start working. Type the following command in a shell:

   ```
   docker pull rcshubhadeep/packt-data-wrangling-base
   ```

2. If you want to know the full list of all the packages and their versions included in this image, you can check out the **requirements.txt** file in the **setup** folder of the source code repository of this book. Once the image is there, you are ready to roll. Downloading it may take time, depending on your connection speed.

Run the environment

1. Run the image using the following command:

   ```
   docker run -p 8888:8888 -v 'pwd':/notebooks -it rcshubhadeep/packt-data-
   wrangling-base
   ```

   This will give you a ready-to-use environment.

2. Open a browser tab in Chrome or Firefox and go to **http://localhost:8888**. You will be prompted to enter a token. The token is **dw_4_all**.

3. Before you run the image, create a new folder and navigate there from the shell using the **cd** command.

   Once you create a notebook and save it as **ipynb** file. You can use *Ctrl* +C to stop running the image.

Introduction to Jupyter notebook

Project Jupyter is open source, free software that gives you the ability to run code, written in Python and some other languages, interactively from a special notebook, similar to a browser interface. It was born in 2014 from the **IPython** project and has since become the default choice for the entire data science workforce.

1. Once you are running the Jupyter server, click on **New** and choose **Python 3**. A new browser tab will open with a new and empty notebook. Rename the Jupyter file:

Figure 0.1: Jupyter server interface

The main building blocks of Jupyter notebooks are cells. There are two types of cells: **In** (short for input) and **Out** (short for output). You can write code, normal text, and Markdown in **In** cells, press *Shift + Enter* (or *Shift + Return*), and the code written in that particular **In** cell will be executed. The result will be shown in an **Out** cell, and you will land in a new **In** cell, ready for the next block of code. Once you get used to this interface, you will slowly discover the power and flexibility it offers.

2. One final thing you should know about Jupyter cells is that when you start a new cell, by default, it is assumed that you will write code in it. However, if you want to write text, then you have to change the type. You can do that using the following sequence of keys: *Escape->m->Enter*:

```
In [1]:  import numpy as np
         import pandas as pd

In [2]:  a = np.random.randn(5, 3)

In [3]:  a

Out[3]:  array([[ 8.37235095e-01, -5.37907860e-01,  9.10259320e-01],
                [ 3.25343803e+00, -1.36313039e+00,  1.66336086e-01],
                [ 2.08849405e-01,  1.44449165e+00,  1.28198815e-01],
                [ 4.31214651e-01,  3.24061116e-01, -2.80120534e-03],
                [-2.52064176e-01,  3.17086224e-01,  7.28020973e-02]])
```

Hey There! I am a Markdown cell

```
In [ ]:
```

Figure 0.2: Jupyter notebook

3. And when you are done with writing the text, execute it using *Shift + Enter*. Unlike the code cells, the result of the compiled Markdown will be shown in the same place as the "**In**" cell.

> **Note**
>
> To have a "Cheat sheet" of all the handy key shortcuts in Jupyter, you can bookmark this Gist: https://gist.github.com/kidpixo/f4318f8c8143adee5b40. With this basic introduction and the image ready to be used, we are ready to embark on the exciting and enlightening journey that awaits us!

Installing the Code Bundle

Copy the code bundle for the class to the `C:/Code` folder.

Additional Resources

The code bundle for this book is also hosted on GitHub at: https://github.com/TrainingByPackt/Data-Wrangling-with-Python.

We also have other code bundles from our rich catalog of books and videos available at https://github.com/PacktPublishing/. Check them out!

Introduction to Data Wrangling with Python

Learning Objectives

By the end of this chapter, you will be able to do the following:

- Define the importance of data wrangling in data science
- Manipulate the data structures that are available in Python
- Compare the different implementations of the inbuilt Python data structures

This chapter describes the importance of data wrangling, identifies the important tasks to be performed in data wrangling, and introduces basic Python data structures.

Introduction

Data science and analytics are taking over the whole world and the job of a data scientist is routinely being called the coolest job of the 21st century. But for all the emphasis on data, it is the science that makes you – the practitioner – truly valuable.

To practice high-quality science with data, you need to make sure it is properly sourced, cleaned, formatted, and pre-processed. This book teaches you the most essential basics of this invaluable component of the data science pipeline: data wrangling. In short, data wrangling is the process that ensures that the data is in a format that is clean, accurate, formatted, and ready to be used for data analysis.

A prominent example of data wrangling with a large amount of data is the one conducted at the Supercomputer Center of University of California San Diego (UCSD). The problem in California is that wildfires are very common, mainly because of the dry weather and extreme heat, especially during the summers. Data scientists at the UCSD Supercomputer Center gather data to predict the nature and spread direction of the fire. The data that comes from diverse sources such as weather stations, sensors in the forest, fire stations, satellite imagery, and Twitter feeds might still be incomplete or missing. This data needs to be cleaned and formatted so that it can be used to predict future occurrences of wildfires.

This is an example of how data wrangling and data science can prove to be helpful and relevant.

Importance of Data Wrangling

Oil does not come in its final form from the rig; it has to be refined. Similarly, data must be curated, massaged, and refined to be used in intelligent algorithms and consumer products. This is known as wrangling. Most data scientists spend the majority of their time data wrangling.

Data wrangling is generally done at the very first stage of a data science/analytics pipeline. After the data scientists identify useful data sources for solving the business problem (for instance, in-house database storage or internet or streaming sensor data), they then proceed to extract, clean, and format the necessary data from those sources.

Generally, the task of data wrangling involves the following steps:

- Scraping raw data from multiple sources (including web and database tables)
- Imputing, formatting, and transforming – basically making it ready to be used in the modeling process (such as advanced machine learning)
- Handling read/write errors
- Detecting outliers
- Performing quick visualizations (plotting) and basic statistical analysis to judge the quality of your formatted data

This is an illustrative representation of the positioning and essential functional role of data wrangling in a typical data science pipeline:

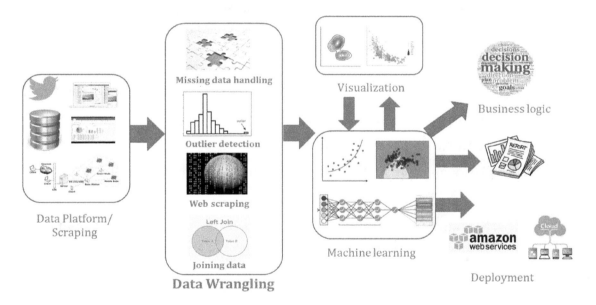

Figure 1.1: Process of data wrangling

The process of data wrangling includes first finding the appropriate data that's necessary for the analysis. This data can be from one or multiple sources, such as tweets, bank transaction statements in a relational database, sensor data, and so on. This data needs to be cleaned. If there is missing data, we will either delete or substitute it, with the help of several techniques. If there are outliers, we need to first detect them and then handle them appropriately. If data is from multiple sources, we will have to perform join operations to combine it.

In an extremely rare situation, data wrangling may not be needed. For example, if the data that's necessary for a machine learning task is already stored in an acceptable format in an in-house database, then a simple SQL query may be enough to extract the data into a table, ready to be passed on to the modeling stage.

Python for Data Wrangling

There is always a debate on whether to perform the wrangling process using an enterprise tool or by using a programming language and associated frameworks. There are many commercial, enterprise-level tools for data formatting and pre-processing that do not involve much coding on the part of the user. These examples include the following:

- General purpose data analysis platforms such as Microsoft Excel (with add-ins)
- Statistical discovery package such as **JMP** (from SAS)
- Modeling platforms such as **RapidMiner**
- Analytics platforms from niche players focusing on data wrangling, such as **Trifacta**, **Paxata**, and **Alteryx**

However, programming languages such as Python provide more flexibility, control, and power compared to these off-the-shelf tools.

As the volume, velocity, and variety (the three Vs of **big data**) of data undergo rapid changes, it is always a good idea to develop and nurture a significant amount of in-house expertise in data wrangling using fundamental programming frameworks so that an organization is not beholden to the whims and fancies of any enterprise platform for as basic a task as data wrangling:

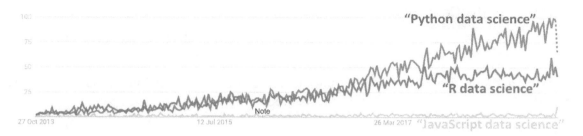

Figure 1.2: Google trend worldwide over the last Five years

A few of the obvious advantages of using an open source, free programming paradigm such as Python for data wrangling are the following:

- General purpose open source paradigm putting no restriction on any of the methods you can develop for the specific problem at hand

- Great ecosystem of fast, optimized, open source libraries, focused on data analytics

- Growing support to connect Python to every conceivable data source type

- Easy interface to basic statistical testing and quick visualization libraries to check data quality

- Seamless interface of the data wrangling output with advanced machine learning models

Python is the most popular language of choice of machine learning and artificial intelligence these days.

Lists, Sets, Strings, Tuples, and Dictionaries

Now that we have learned the importance of Python, we will start by exploring various basic data structures in Python. We will learn techniques to handle data. This is invaluable for a data practitioner.

We can issue the following command to start a new Jupyter server by typing the following in to the Command Prompt window:

```
docker run -p 8888:8888 -v 'pwd':/notebooks -it rcshubhadeep/packt-data-
wrangling-base:latest ipython
```

This will start a jupyter server and you can visit it at **http://localhost:8888** and use the passcode **dw_4_all** to access the main interface.

Lists

Lists are fundamental Python data structures that have continuous memory locations, can host different data types, and can be accessed by the index.

We will start with a list and list comprehension. We will generate a list of numbers, and then examine which ones among them are even. We will sort, reverse, and check for duplicates. We will also see how many different ways we can access the list elements, iterating over them and checking the membership of an element.

The following is an example of a simple list:

```
list_example = [51, 27, 34, 46, 90, 45, -19]
```

The following is also an example of a list:

```
list_example2 = [15, "Yellow car", True, 9.456, [12, "Hello"]]
```

As you can see, a list can contain any number of the allowed datatype, such as **int**, **float**, **string**, and **Boolean**, and a list can also be a mix of different data types (including nested lists).

If you are coming from a strongly typed language, such as C, C++, or Java, then this will probably be strange as you are not allowed to mix different kinds of data types in a single array in those languages. Lists are somewhat like arrays, in the sense that they are both based on continuous memory locations and can be accessed using indexes. But the power of Python lists come from the fact that they can host different data types and you are allowed to manipulate the data.

> **Note**
>
> Be careful, though, as the very power of lists, and the fact that you can mix different data types in a single list, can actually create subtle bugs that can be very difficult to track.

Exercise 1: Accessing the List Members

In the following exercise, we will be creating a list and then observing the different ways of accessing the elements:

1. Define a list called **list_1** with four integer members, using the following command:

   ```
   list_1 = [34, 12, 89, 1]
   ```

   The indices will be automatically assigned, as follows:

List_1

	34	12	89	1
Indices (Forward)	0	1	2	3
Indices (Backward)	-4	-3	-2	-1

Figure 1.3: List showing the forward and backward indices

2. Access the first element from **list_1** using its forward index:

```
list_1[0]  #34
```

3. Access the last element from **list_1** using its forward index:

```
list_1[3]  #1
```

4. Access the last element from **list_1** using the **len** function:

```
list_1[len(list_1) - 1]  #1
```

The **len** function in Python returns the length of the specified list.

5. Access the last element from **list_1** using its backward index:

```
list_1[-1]  #1
```

6. Access the first three elements from **list_1** using forward indices:

```
list_1[1:3]  # [12, 89]
```

This is also called list slicing, as it returns a smaller list from the original list by extracting only, a part of it. To slice a list, we need two integers. The first integer will denote the start of the slice and the second integer will denote the end-1 element.

> **Note**
>
> Notice that slicing did not include the third index or the end element. This is how list slicing works.

7. Access the last two elements from **list_1** by slicing:

```
list_1[-2:]  # [89, 1]
```

8. Access the first two elements using backward indices:

```
list_1[:-2]  # [34, 12]
```

When we leave one side of the colon (:) blank, we are basically telling Python either to go until the end or start from the beginning of the list. It will automatically apply the rule of list slices that we just learned.

9. Reverse the elements in the string:

```
list_1[-1::-1] # [1, 89, 12, 34]
```

> **Note**
>
> The last bit of code is not very readable, meaning it is not obvious just by looking at it what it is doing. It is against Python's philosophy. So, although this kind of code may look clever, we should resist the temptation to write code like this.

Exercise 2: Generating a List

We are going to examine various ways of generating a list:

1. Create a list using the **append** method:

```
list_1 = []
for x in range(0, 10):
    list_1.append(x)
list_1
```

The output will be as follows:

```
[0, 1, 2, 3, 4, 5, 6, 7, 8, 9]
```

Here, we started by declaring an empty list and then we used a **for** loop to append values to it. The **append** method is a method that's given to us by the Python list data type.

2. Generate a list using the following command:

```
list_2 = [x for x in range(0, 100)]
list_2
```

The partial output is as follows:

```
[0,
 1,
 2,
 3,
 4,
 5,
 6,
 7,
 8,
 9,
 10,
 11,
 12,
 13,
 14,
 15,
 16,
 17,
 18,
```

Figure 1.4: List comprehension

This is list comprehension, which is a very powerful tool that we need to master. The power of list comprehension comes from the fact that we can use conditionals inside the comprehension itself.

3. Use a **while** loop to iterate over a list to understand the difference between a **while** loop and a **for** loop:

```
i = 0
while i < len(list_1) :
    print(list_1[i])
    i += 1
```

The partial output will be as follows:

```
0
1
2
3
4
5
6
7
8
9
```

Figure 1.5: Output showing the contents of list_1 using a while loop

4. Create **list_3** with numbers that are divisible by **5**:

    ```
    list_3 = [x for x in range(0, 100) if x % 5 == 0]
    list_3
    ```

    The output will be a list of numbers up to 100 in increments of 5:

    ```
    [0, 5, 10, 15, 20, 25, 30, 35, 40, 45, 50, 55, 60, 65, 70, 75, 80, 85, 90,
    95]
    ```

5. Generate a list by adding the two lists:

    ```
    list_1 = [1, 4, 56, -1]
    list_2 = [1, 39, 245, -23, 0, 45]
    list_3 = list_1 + list_2
    list_3
    ```

    The output is as follows:

    ```
    [1, 4, 56, -1, 1, 39, 245, -23, 0, 45]
    ```

6. Extend a string using the extend keyword:

    ```
    list_1.extend(list_2)
    list_1
    ```

The partial output is as follows:

```
[1, 4, 56, -1, 1, 39, 245, -23, 0, 45]
```

Figure 1.6: Contents of list_1

The second operation changes the original list (list_1) and appends all the elements of list_2 to it. So, be careful when using it.

Exercise 3: Iterating over a List and Checking Membership

We are going to iterate over a list and test whether a certain value exists in it:

1. Iterate over a list:

```
list_1 = [x for x in range(0, 100)]
for i in range(0, len(list_1)):
    print(list_1[i])
```

The output is as follows:

```
0
1
2
3
4
5
6
7
8
9
10
11
12
13
14
15
16
17
18
19
20
21
22
23
24
25
26
27
```

Figure 1.7: Section of list_1

2. However, it is not very Pythonic. Being Pythonic is to follow and conform to a set of best practices and conventions that have been created over the years by thousands of very able developers, which in this case means to use the **in** keyword, because Python does not have index initialization, bounds checking, or index incrementing, unlike traditional languages. The Pythonic way of iterating over a list is as follows:

```
for i in list_1:
    print(i)
```

The output is as follows:

```
0
1
2
3
4
5
6
7
8
9
10
11
12
13
14
15
16
17
18
19
20
21
22
23
24
25
26
27
28
29
30
31
32
33
34
```

Figure 1.8: A section of list_1

Notice that, in the second method, we do not need a counter anymore to access the list index; instead, Python's **in** operator gives us the element at the *i* th position directly.

3. Check whether the integers 25 and -45 are in the list using the **in** operator:

```
25 in list_1
```

The output is **True.**

```
-45 in list_1
```

The output is **False.**

Exercise 4: Sorting a List

We generated a list called **list_1** in the previous exercise. We are going to sort it now:

1. As the list was originally a list of numbers from **0** to **99**, we will sort it in the reverse direction. To do that, we will use the **sort** method with **reverse=True**:

```
list_1.sort(reverse=True)
list_1
```

The partial output is as follows:

```
[99,
 98,
 97,
 96,
 95,
 94,
 93,
 92,
 91,
 90,
 89,
 88,
 87,
 86,
 85,
 84,
 83,
 82,
 81,
 80,
 79,
 78,
 77,
 76,
 75,
 74,
 73,
 72,
 71,
 70,
 69,
 68,
 67,
 66,
 65,
 64,
 63,
```

Figure 1.9: Section of output showing the reversed list

2. We can use the **reverse** method directly to achieve this result:

```
list_1.reverse()
list_1
```

The output is as follows:

```
[0,
 1,
 2,
 3,
 4,
 5,
 6,
 7,
 8,
 9,
 10,
 11,
 12,
 13,
 14,
 15,
 16,
 17,
 18,
 19,
 20,
 21,
 22,
 23,
 24,
 25,
 26,
 27,
 28,
 29,
 30,
 31,
 32,
 33,
 34,
 35,
 36,
 37,
 38,
 39,
 40,
 41,
 42,
```

Figure 1.10: Section of output after reversing the string

> **Note**
>
> The difference between the sort function and the reverse function is the fact that we can use sort with custom sorting functions to do custom sorting, whereas we can only use reverse to reverse a list. Here also, both the functions work in-place, so be aware of this while using them.

Exercise 5: Generating a Random List

In this exercise, we will be generating a **list** with random numbers:

1. Import the **random** library:

   ```
   import random
   ```

2. Use the **randint** function to generate random integers and add them to a list:

   ```
   list_1 = [random.randint(0, 30) for x in range (0, 100)]
   ```

3. Print the list using **print(list_1)**. Note that there will be duplicate values in **list_1**:

   ```
   list_1
   ```

   The sample output is as follows:

```
[6,
 5,
 18,
 22,
 16,
 15,
 8,
 19,
 0,
 5,
 11,
 4,
 13,
 0,
 6,
 13,
 28,
 13,
 28,
 7,
 7,
 28,
 7,
 23,
 14,
 17,
 12,
 8,
 28,
 25,
 29,
 1,
```

Figure 1.11: Section of the sample output for list_1

There are many ways to get a list of unique numbers, and while you may be able to write a few lines of code using a for loop and another list (you should actually try doing it!), let's see how we can do this without a for loop and with a single line of code. This will bring us to the next data structure, sets.

Activity 1: Handling Lists

In this activity, we will generate a **list** of random numbers and then generate another **list** from the first one, which only contains numbers that are divisible by three. Repeat the experiment three times. Then, we will calculate the average difference of length between the two lists.

These are the steps for completing this activity:

1. Create a **list** of 100 random numbers.

2. Create a new **list** from this random **list**, with numbers that are divisible by 3.

3. Calculate the length of these two lists and store the difference in a new variable.

4. Using a loop, perform steps 2 and 3 and find the difference variable three times.

5. Find the arithmetic mean of these three difference values.

> **Note**
>
> The solution for this activity can be found on page 282.

Sets

A set, mathematically speaking, is just a collection of well-defined distinct objects. Python gives us a straightforward way to deal with them using its **set** datatype.

Introduction to Sets

With the last list that we generated, we are going to revisit the problem of getting rid of duplicates from it. We can achieve that with the following line of code:

```
list_12 = list(set(list_1))
```

If we print this, we will see that it only contains unique numbers. We used the **set** data type to turn the first list into a set, thus getting rid of all duplicate elements, and then we used the **list** function on it to turn it into a list from a set once more:

```
list_12
```

The output will be as follows:

```
[0,
 1,
 2,
 3,
 4,
 5,
 6,
 7,
 8,
 9,
 11,
 12,
 13,
 14,
 15,
 16,
 17,
 18,
 19,
 20,
 21,
 22,
 23,
 24,
 25,
 27,
 28,
 29,
 30]
```

Figure 1.12: Section of output for list_21

Union and Intersection of Sets

This is what a union between two sets looks like:

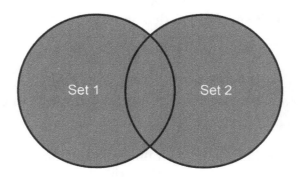

Figure 1.13: Venn diagram showing the union of two sets

This simply means take everything from both sets but take the common elements only once.

We can create this using the following code:

```
set1 = {"Apple", "Orange", "Banana"}

set2 = {"Pear", "Peach", "Mango", "Banana"}
```

To find the union of the two sets, the following instructions should be used:

```
set1 | set2
```

The output would be as follows:

```
{'Apple', 'Banana', 'Mango', 'Orange', 'Peach', 'Pear'}
```

Notice that the common element, Banana, appears only once in the resulting set. The common elements between two sets can be identified by obtaining the intersection of the two sets, as follows:

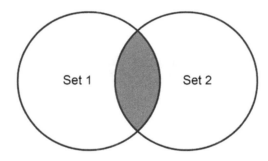

Figure 1.14: Venn diagram showing the intersection of two sets

We get the intersection of two sets in Python as follows:

```
set1 & set2
```

This will give us a set with only one element. The output is as follows:

```
{'Banana'}
```

> **Note**
>
> You can also calculate the difference between sets (also known as complements). To find out more, refer to this link: https://docs.python.org/3/tutorial/datastructures.html#sets.

Creating Null Sets

You can create a null set by creating a set containing no elements. You can do this by using the following code:

```
null_set_1 = set({})
null_set_1
```

The output is as follows:

```
set()
```

However, to create a dictionary, use the following command:

```
null_set_2 = {}
null_set_2
```

The output is as follows:

```
{}
```

We are going to learn about this in detail in the next topic.

Dictionary

A dictionary is like a list, which means it is a collection of several elements. However, with the dictionary, it is a collection of key-value pairs, where the key can be anything that can be hashed. Generally, we use numbers or strings as keys.

To create a dictionary, use the following code:

```
dict_1 = {"key1": "value1", "key2": "value2"}
dict_1
```

The output is as follows:

```
{'key1': 'value1', 'key2': 'value2'}
```

This is also a valid dictionary:

```
dict_2 = {"key1": 1, "key2": ["list_element1", 34], "key3": "value3",
          "key4": {"subkey1": "v1"}, "key5": 4.5}
dict_2
```

The output is as follows:

```
{'key1': 1,
 'key2': ['list_element1', 34],
 'key3': 'value3',
 'key4': {'subkey1': 'v1'},
 'key5': 4.5}
```

The keys must be unique in a dictionary.

Exercise 6: Accessing and Setting Values in a Dictionary

In this exercise, we are going to access and set values in a dictionary:

1. Access a particular key in a dictionary:

    ```
    dict_2["key2"]
    ```

    This will return the value associated with it as follows:

    ```
    ['list_element1', 34]
    ```

2. Assign a new value to the key:

    ```
    dict_2["key2"] = "My new value"
    ```

3. Define a blank dictionary and then use the key notation to assign values to it:

    ```
    dict_3 = {}  # Not a null set. It is a dict
    dict_3["key1"] = "Value1"
    dict_3
    ```

    The output is as follows:

    ```
    {'key1': 'Value1'}
    ```

Exercise 7: Iterating Over a Dictionary

In this exercise, we are going to iterate over a dictionary:

1. Create **dict_1**:

```
dict_1 = {"key1": 1, "key2": ["list_element1", 34], "key3": "value3",
"key4": {"subkey1": "v1"}, "key5": 4.5}
```

2. Use the looping variables **k** and **v**:

```
for k, v in dict_1.items():
    print("{} - {}".format(k, v))
```

The output is as follows:

```
key1 - 1
key2 - ['list_element1', 34]
key3 - value3
key4 - {'subkey1': 'v1'}
key5 - 4.5
```

Note

Notice the difference between how we did the iteration on the list and how we are doing it here.

Exercise 8: Revisiting the Unique Valued List Problem

We will use the fact that dictionary keys cannot be duplicated to generate the unique valued list:

1. First, generate a random list with duplicate values:

```
list_1 = [random.randint(0, 30) for x in range (0, 100)]
```

2. Create a unique valued list from **list_1**:

```
list(dict.fromkeys(list_1).keys())
```

The sample output is as follows:

```
[6,
 30,
 25,
 26,
 14,
 15,
 29,
 18,
 10,
 1,
 0,
 20,
 28,
 19,
 11,
 16,
 27,
 22,
 4,
 21,
 24,
 9,
 5,
 23,
 7,
 2,
 17,
 13,
 12,
 8]
```

Figure 1.15: Output showing the unique valued list

Here, we have used two useful functions on the dict data type in Python, **fromkeys** and **keys**. **fromkeys** creates a dict where the keys come from the **iterable** (in this case, which is a list), values default to None, and **keys** give us the keys of a dict.

Exercise 9: Deleting Value from Dict

In this exercise, we are going to delete a value from a **dict**:

1. Create **list_1** with five elements:

   ```
   dict_1 = {"key1": 1, "key2": ["list_element1", 34], "key3": "value3",
             "key4": {"subkey1": "v1"}, "key5": 4.5}
   dict_1
   ```

   The output is as follows:

   ```
   {'key1': 1,
    'key2': ['list_element', 34],
    'key3': 'value3',
    'key4': {'subkey1': 'v1'},
    'key5': 4.5}
   ```

2. We will use the **del** function and specify the element:

   ```
   del dict_1["key2"]
   ```

   The output is as follows:

   ```
   {'key3': 'value3', 'key4': {'subkey1': 'v1'}, 'key5': 4.5}
   ```

   > **Note**
   >
   > The **del** operator can be used to delete a specific index from a list as well.

Exercise 10: Dictionary Comprehension

In this final exercise on **dict**, we will go over a less used comprehension than the list one: dictionary comprehension. We will also examine two other ways to create a **dict**, which will be useful in the future.

A dictionary comprehension works exactly the same way as the list one, but we need to specify both the keys and values:

1. Generate a dict that has **0** to **9** as the keys and the square of the key as the values:

   ```
   list_1 = [x for x in range(0, 10)]
   dict_1 = {x : x**2 for x in list_1}
   dict_1
   ```

The output is as follows:

```
{0: 0, 1: 1, 2: 4, 3: 9, 4: 16, 5: 25, 6: 36, 7: 49, 8: 64, 9: 81}
```

Can you generate a **dict** using **dict** comprehension where the keys are from **0** to **9** and the values are the square root of the keys? This time, we won't use a list.

2. Generate a **dictionary** using the **dict** function:

```
dict_2 = dict([('Tom', 100), ('Dick', 200), ('Harry', 300)])
dict_2
```

The output is as follows:

```
{'Tom': 100, 'Dick': 200, 'Harry': 300}
```

You can also generate **dictionary** using the **dict** function, as follows:

```
dict_3 = dict(Tom=100, Dick=200, Harry=300)
dict_3
```

The output is as follows:

```
{'Tom': 100, 'Dick': 200, 'Harry': 300}
```

It is pretty versatile. So, both the preceding commands will generate valid dictionaries.

The strange looking pair of values that we had just noticed ('Harry', 300) is called a **tuple**. This is another important fundamental data type in Python. We will learn about tuples in the next topic.

Tuples

A tuple is another data type in Python. It is sequential in nature and similar to lists.

A tuple consists of values separated by commas, as follows:

```
tuple_1 = 24, 42, 2.3456, "Hello"
```

Notice that, unlike lists, we did not open and close square brackets here.

Creating a Tuple with Different Cardinalities

This is how we create an empty tuple:

```
tuple_1 = ()
```

And this is how we create a tuple with only one value:

```
tuple_1 = "Hello",
```

Notice the trailing comma here.

We can nest tuples, similar to list and dicts, as follows:

```
tuple_1 = "hello", "there"
tuple_12 = tuple_1, 45, "Sam"
```

One special thing about tuples is the fact that they are an immutable data type. So, once created, we cannot change their values. We can just access them, as follows:

```
tuple_1 = "Hello", "World!"
tuple_1[1] = "Universe!"
```

The last line of code will result in a **TypeError** as a tuple does not allow modification.

This makes the use case for tuples a bit different than lists, although they look and behave very similarly in a few aspects.

Unpacking a Tuple

The term unpacking a tuple simply means to get the values contained in the tuple in different variables:

```
tuple_1 = "Hello", "World"
hello, world = tuple_1
print(hello)
print(world)
```

The output is as follows:

```
Hello
World
```

Of course, as soon as we do that, we can modify the values contained in those variables.

Exercise 11: Handling Tuples

1. Create a tuple to demonstrate how tuples are immutable. Unpack it to read all elements, as follows:

```
tupleE = "1", "3", "5"
tupleE
```

The output is as follows:

```
('1', '3', '5')
```

2. Try to override a variable from the **tupleE** tuple:

```
tupleE[1] = "5"
```

This step will result in **TypeError** as the tuple does not allow modification.

3. Try to assign a series to the **tupleE** tuple:

```
1, 3, 5 = tupleE
```

4. Print the output:

```
print(1)
print(3)
```

The output is as follows:

```
1
3
```

We have mainly seen two different types of data so far. One is represented by numbers; another is represented by textual data. Whereas numbers have their own tricks, which we will see later, it is time to look into textual data in a bit more detail.

Strings

In the final section of this section, we will learn about strings. Strings in Python are similar to any other programming language.

This is a string:

```
string1 = 'Hello World!'
```

A string can also be declared in this manner:

```
string2 = "Hello World 2!"
```

You can use single quotes and double quotes to define a string.

Exercise 12: Accessing Strings

Strings in Python behave similar to lists, apart from one big caveat. Strings are immutable, whereas lists are mutable data structures:

1. Create a string called **str_1**:

    ```
    str_1 = "Hello World!"
    ```

    Access the elements of the string by specifying the location of the element, like we did in lists.

2. Access the first member of the string:

    ```
    str_1[0]
    ```

    The output is as follows:

    ```
    'H'
    ```

3. Access the fourth member of the string:

    ```
    str_1[4]
    ```

    The output is as follows:

    ```
    'o'
    ```

4. Access the last member of the string:

    ```
    str_1[len(str_1) - 1]
    ```

    The output is as follows:

    ```
    '!'
    ```

5. Access the last member of the string:

    ```
    str_1[-1]
    ```

    The output is as follows:

    ```
    '!'
    ```

    Each of the preceding operations will give you the character at the specific index.

> **Note**
>
> The method for accessing the elements of a string is like accessing a list.

Exercise 13: String Slices

Just like lists, we can slice strings:

1. Create a string, **str_1**:

   ```
   str_1 = "Hello World! I am learning data wrangling"
   ```

2. Specify the slicing values and slice the string:

   ```
   str_1[2:10]
   ```

   The output is this:

   ```
   'llo Worl'
   ```

3. Slice a string by skipping a slice value:

   ```
   str_1[-31:]
   ```

   The output is as follows:

   ```
   'd! I am learning data wrangling'
   ```

4. Use negative numbers to slice the string:

   ```
   str_1[-10:-5]
   ```

   The output is as follows:

   ```
   ' wran'
   ```

String Functions

To find out the length of a string, we simply use the **len** function:

```
str_1 = "Hello World! I am learning data wrangling"
len(str_1)
```

The length of the string is 41. To convert a string's case, we can use the **lower** and **upper** methods:

```
str_1 = "A COMPLETE UPPER CASE STRING"
str_1.lower()
str_1.upper()
```

The output is as follows:

```
'A COMPLETE UPPER CASE STRING'
```

To search for a string within a string, we can use the **find** method:

```
str_1 = "A complicated string looks like this"

str_1.find("complicated")

str_1.find("hello")# This will return -1
```

The output is -1. Can you figure out whether the find method is case-sensitive or not? Also, what do you think the find method returns when it actually finds the string?

To replace one string with another, we have the **replace** method. Since we know that a string is an immutable data structure, replace actually returns a new string instead of replacing and returning the actual one:

```
str_1 = "A complicated string looks like this"

str_1.replace("complicated", "simple")
```

The output is as follows:

```
'A simple string looks like this'
```

You should look up string methods in the standard documentation of Python 3 to discover more about these methods.

Exercise 14: Split and Join

These two string methods need separate introductions, as they enable you to convert a string into a list and vice versa:

1. Create a string and convert it to a list using the **split** method:

    ```
    str_1 = "Name, Age, Sex, Address"
    list_1 = str_1.split(",")
    list_1
    ```

    The preceding code will give you a list similar to the following:

    ```
    ['Name', ' Age', ' Sex', ' Address']
    ```

2. Combine this list into another string using the **join** method:

    ```
    " | ".join(list_1)
    ```

    This code will give you a string like this:

    ```
    'Name | Age | Sex | Address'
    ```

With these, we are at the end of our second topic of this chapter. We now have the motivation to learn data wrangling and have a solid introduction to the fundamentals of data structures using Python. There is more to this topic, which will be covered in a future chapters.

We have designed an activity for you so that you can practice all the skills you just learned. This small activity should take around 30 to 45 minutes to finish.

Activity 2: Analyze a Multiline String and Generate the Unique Word Count

This section will ensure that you have understood the various basic data structures and their manipulation. We will do that by going through an activity that has been designed specifically for this purpose.

In this activity, we will do the following:

- Get multiline text and save it in a Python variable

- Get rid of all new lines in it using string methods

- Get all the unique words and their occurrences from the string

- Repeat the step to find all unique words and occurrences, without considering case sensitivity

> **Note**
>
> For the sake of simplicity for this activity, the original text (which can be found at https://www.gutenberg.org/files/1342/1342-h/1342-h.htm) has been pre-processed a bit.

These are the steps to guide you through solving this activity:

1. Create a `mutliline_text` variable by copying the text from the first chapter of *Pride and Prejudice*.

> **Note**
>
> The first chapter of Pride and Prejudice by Jane Austen has been made available on the GitHub repository at https://github.com/TrainingByPackt/Data-Wrangling-with-Python/blob/master/Chapter01/Activity02/.

2. Find the type and length of the `multiline_text` string using the commands `type` and `len`.

3. Remove all new lines and symbols using the `replace` function.

4. Find all of the words in `multiline_text` using the `split` function.

5. Create a list from this list that will contain only the unique words.

6. Count the number of times the unique word has appeared in the list using the `key` and `value` in `dict`.

7. Find the top 25 words from the unique words that you have found using the `slice` function.

You just created, step by step, a unique word counter using all the neat tricks that you learned about in this chapter.

> **Note**
>
> The solution for this activity can be found on page 285.

Summary

In this chapter, we learned what the term data wrangling means. We also got examples from various real-life data science situations where data wrangling is very useful and is used in industry. We moved on to learn about the different built-in data structures that Python has to offer. We got our hands dirty by exploring lists, sets, dictionaries, tuples, and strings. They are the fundamental building blocks in Python data structures, and we need them all the time while working and manipulating data in Python. We did several small hands-on exercises to learn more about them. We finished this chapter with a carefully designed activity, which let us combine a lot of different tricks from all the different data structures into a real-life situation and let us observe the interplay between all of them.

In the next chapter, we will learn about the data structures in Python and utilize them to solve real-world problems.

Advanced Data Structures and File Handling

Learning Objectives

By the end of this chapter, you will be able to:

- Compare Python's advanced data structures
- Utilize data structures to solve real-world problems
- Make use of OS file-handling operations

This chapter emphasizes the data structures in Python and the operating system functions that are the foundation of this book.

Introduction

We were introduced to the basic concepts of different fundamental data structures in the last chapter. We learned about the list, set, dict, tuple, and string. They are the building blocks of future chapters and are essential for data science.

However, what we have covered so far were only basic operations on them. They have much more to offer once you learn how to utilize them effectively. In this chapter, we will venture further into the land of data structures. We will learn about advanced operations and manipulations and use these fundamental data structures to represent more complex and higher-level data structures; this is often handy while wrangling data in real life.

In real life, we deal with data that comes from different sources and generally read data from a file or a database. We will be introduced to operations related to files. We will see how to open a file and how many ways there are to do it, how to read data from it, how to write data to it, and how to safely close it once we are done. The last part, which many people tend to ignore, is super important. We often run into very strange and hard-to-track-down bugs in a real-world system just because a process opened a file and did not close it properly. Without further ado, let's begin our journey.

Advanced Data Structures

We will start this chapter by discussing advanced data structures. We will do that by revisiting lists. We will construct a stack and a queue, explore multiple element membership checking, and throw a bit of functional programming in for good measure. If all of this sounds intimidating, then do not worry. We will get to things step by step, like in the previous chapter, and you will feel confident once you have finished this chapter.

To start this chapter, you have to open an empty notebook. To do that, you can simply input the following command in a shell. It is advised that you first navigate to an empty directory using **cd** before you enter the command:

```
docker run -p 8888:8888 -v 'pwd':/notebooks -it rcshubhadeep/packt-data-
wrangling-base:latest
```

Once the Docker container is running, point your browser to http://localhost:8888 and use **dw_4_all** as the passcode to access the notebook interface.

Iterator

We will start off this topic with lists. However, before we get into lists, we will introduce the concept of an iterator. An iterator is an object that implements the **next** method, meaning an iterator is an object that can iterate over a collection (lists, tuples, dicts, and so on). It is stateful, which means that each time we call the **next** method, it gives us the next element from the collection. And if there is no further element, then it raises a **StopIteration** exception.

> **Note**
>
> A **StopIteration** exception occurs with the iterator's next method when there are no further values to iterate.

If you are familiar with a programming language like C, C++, Java, JavaScript, or PHP, you may have noticed the difference between the **for loop** implementation in those languages, which consists of three distinct parts, precisely the initiation, the increment, and the termination condition, and the **for loop** in Python. In Python, we do not use that kind of for loop. What we use in Python is more like a **foreach** loop: **for i in list_1**. This is because, under the hood, the for loop is using an iterator, and thus we do not need to do all the extra steps. The iterator does this for us.

Exercise 15: Introduction to the Iterator

To generate lists of numbers, we can use different methods:

1. Generate a list that will contain 10000000: ones:

   ```
   big_list_of_numbers = [1 for x in range(0, 10000000)]
   ```

2. Check the size of this variable:

   ```
   from sys import getsizeof
   getsizeof(big_list_of_numbers)
   ```

   The value it will show you will be something around **81528056** (it is in bytes). This is a lot of memory! And the **big_list_of_numbers** variable is only available once the list comprehension is over. It can also overflow the available system memory if you try too big a number.

3. Use an iterator to reduce memory utilization:

```
from itertools import repeat
small_list_of_numbers = repeat(1, times=10000000)
getsizeof(small_list_of_numbers)
```

The last line shows that our **small_list_of_numbers** is only **56** bytes in size. Also, it is a lazy method, as it did not generate all the elements. It will generate them one by one when asked, thus saving us time. In fact, if you omit the **times** keyword argument, then you can practically generate an infinite number of 1s.

4. Loop over the newly generated iterator:

```
for i, x in enumerate(small_list_of_numbers):
    print(x)
    if i > 10:
        break
```

We use the **enumerate** function so that we get the loop counter, along with the values. This will help us break once we reach a certain number of the counter (10 for example).

The output will be a list of 10 ones.

5. To look up the definition of any function, type the function name, followed by a ? and press *Shift + Enter* in a Jupyter notebook. Run the following code to understand how we can use permutations and combinations with itertools:

```
from itertools import (permutations, combinations, dropwhile, repeat,
zip_longest)
permutations?
combinations?
dropwhile?
repeat?
zip_longest?
```

Stacks

A stack is a very useful data structure. If you know a bit about CPU internals and how a program gets executed, then you have an idea that a stack is present in many such cases. It is simply a list with one restriction, Last In First Out (LIFO), meaning an element that comes in last goes out first when a value is read from a stack. The following illustration will make this a bit clearer:

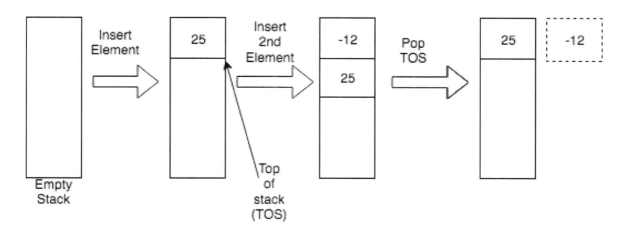

Figure 2.1: A stack with two insert elements and one pop operation

As you can see, we have a LIFO strategy to read values from a stack. We will implement a stack using a Python list. Python's lists have a method called **pop**, which does the exact same pop operation that you can see in the preceding illustration. We will use that to implement a stack.

Exercise 16: Implementing a Stack in Python

1. First, define an empty stack:

   ```
   stack = []
   ```

2. Use the append method to add an element in the stack. Thanks to append, the element will be always appended at the end of the list:

   ```
   stack.append(25)
   stack
   ```

   The output is as follows:

   ```
   [25]
   ```

3. Append another value to the stack:

```
stack.append(-12)
stack
```

The output is as follows:

```
[25, -12]
```

4. Read a value from our stack using the **pop** method. This method reads at the current last index of the list and returns it to us. It also deletes the index once the read is done:

```
tos = stack.pop()
tos
```

The output is as follows:

```
-12
```

After we execute the preceding code, we will have -12 in **tos** and the stack will have only one element in it, **25**.

5. Append hello to the stack:

```
stack.append("Hello")
stack
```

The output is as follows:

```
[25, 'Hello']
```

Imagine you are scraping a web page and you want to follow each URL that is present there. If you insert (append) them one by one in a stack, while you read the web page, and then pop them one by one and follow the link, then you have a clean and extendable solution to the problem. We will examine part of this task in the next exercise.

Exercise 17: Implementing a Stack Using User-Defined Methods

We will continue the topic of the stack from the last exercise. But this time, we will implement the **append** and **pop** functions by ourselves. The aim of this exercise is twofold. On one hand, we will implement the stack, and this time with a real-life example, which also involves knowledge of string methods and thus serves as a reminder of the last chapter and activity. On the other hand, it will show us a subtle feature of Python and how it handles passing list variables to functions, and will bring us to the next exercise, functional programming:

1. First, we will define two functions, **stack_push** and **stack_pop**. We renamed them so that we do not have a namespace conflict. Also, create a stack called **url_stack** for later use:

```
def stack_push(s, value):
    return s + [value]

def stack_pop(s):
    tos = s[-1]
    del s[-1]
    return tos

url_stack = []
```

2. The first function takes the already existing stack and adds the value at the end of it.

> **Note**
>
> Notice the square brackets around the value to convert it in to a one-element list for the sake of the + operation.

3. The second one reads the value that's currently at the **-1** index of the stack and then uses the **del** operator to delete that index, and finally returns the value it read earlier.

4. Now, we are going to have a string with a few URLs in it. Our job is to analyze the string so that we push the URLs in the stack one by one as we encounter them, and then finally use a for loop to pop them one by one. Let's take the first line from the Wikipedia article about data science:

```
wikipedia_datascience = "Data science is an interdisciplinary field that
uses scientific methods, processes, algorithms and systems to extract
knowledge [https://en.wikipedia.org/wiki/Knowledge] and insights from data
[https://en.wikipedia.org/wiki/Data] in various forms, both structured and
unstructured,similar to data mining [https://en.wikipedia.org/wiki/Data_
mining]"
```

5. For the sake of the simplicity of this exercise, we have kept the links in square brackets beside the target words.

6. Find the length of the string:

```
len(wikipedia_datascience)
```

The output is as follows:

```
347
```

7. Convert this string into a list by using the **split** method from the string and then calculate its length:

```
wd_list = wikipedia_datascience.split()
len(wd_list)
```

The output is as follows:

```
34
```

8. Use a for loop to go over each word and check whether it is a URL. To do that, we will use the **startswith** method from the string, and if it is a URL, then we push it into the stack:

```
for word in wd_list:
    if word.startswith("[https://"):
        url_stack = stack_push(url_stack, word[1:-1])
    # Notice the clever use of string slicing
```

9. Print the value in **url_stack**:

```
url_stack
```

The output is as follows:

```
['https://en.wikipedia.org/wiki/Knowledge',
 'https://en.wikipedia.org/wiki/Data',
 'https://en.wikipedia.org/wiki/Data_mining']
```

10. Iterate over the list and print the URLs one by one by using the **stack_pop** function:

```
for i in range(0, len(url_stack)):
    print(stack_pop(url_stack))
```

The output is as follows:

```
https://en.wikipedia.org/wiki/Data_mining
https://en.wikipedia.org/wiki/Data
https://en.wikipedia.org/wiki/Knowledge
```

Figure 2.2: Output of the URLs that are printed using a stack

11. Print it again to make sure that the stack is empty after the final for loop:

```
print(url_stack)
```

The output is as follows:

```
[]
```

We have noticed a strange phenomenon in the **stack_pop** method. We passed the list variable there, and we used the **del** operator inside the function, but it changed the original variable by deleting the last index each time we call the function. If you are coming from a language like C, C++, and Java, then this is a completely unexpected behavior, as in those languages this can only happen if we pass the variable by reference and it can lead to subtle bugs in Python code. So be careful. In general, it is not a good idea to change a variable's value in place, meaning inside a function. Any variable that's passed to the function should be considered and treated as immutable. This is close to the principles of functional programming. A lambda expression in Python is a way to construct one-line, nameless functions that are, by convention, side effect-free.

Exercise 18: Lambda Expression

In this exercise, we will use a lambda expression to prove the famous trigonometric identity:

$$sin^2(x) + cos^2(x) = 1$$

Figure 2.3 Trigonometric identity

1. Import the **math** package:

   ```
   import math
   ```

2. Define two functions, **my_sine** and **my_cosine**. The reason we are declaring these functions is because the original **sin** and **cos** functions from the math package take radians as input, but we are more familiar with degrees. So, we will use a lambda expression to define a nameless one-line function and use it. This lambda function will automatically convert our degree input to radians and then apply **sin** or **cos** on it and return the value:

   ```
   def my_sine():
       return lambda x: math.sin(math.radians(x))


   def my_cosine():
       return lambda x: math.cos(math.radians(x))
   ```

3. Define **sine** and **cosine** for our purpose:

   ```
   sine = my_sine()
   cosine = my_cosine()
   math.pow(sine(30), 2) + math.pow(cosine(30), 2)
   ```

   The output is as follows:

   ```
   1.0
   ```

   Notice that we have assigned the return value from both **my_sine** and **my_cosine** to two variables, and then used them directly as the functions. It is a much cleaner approach than using them explicitly. Notice that we did not explicitly write a **return** statement inside the lambda function. It is assumed.

Exercise 19: Lambda Expression for Sorting

The lambda expression will take an input and sort it according to the values in tuples. A lambda can take one or more inputs. A lambda expression can also be used to reverse sort by using the parameter of **reverse** as **True**:

1. Imagine you're in a data wrangling job where you are confronted with the following list of tuples:

   ```
   capitals = [("USA", "Washington"), ("India", "Delhi"), ("France", "Paris"),
   ("UK", "London")]
   capitals
   ```

   The output will be as follows:

   ```
   [('USA', 'Washington'),
    ('India', 'Delhi'),
    ('France', 'Paris'),
    ('UK', 'London')]
   ```

2. Sort this list by the name of the capitals of each country, using a simple lambda expression. Use the following code:

   ```
   capitals.sort(key=lambda item: item[1])
   capitals
   ```

   The output will be as follows:

   ```
   [('India', 'Delhi'),
    ('UK', 'London'),
    ('France', 'Paris'),
    ('USA', 'Washington')]
   ```

As we can see, lambda expressions are powerful if we master them and use them in our data wrangling jobs. They are also side effect-free, meaning that they do not change the values of the variables that are passed to them in place.

Exercise 20: Multi-Element Membership Checking

Here is an interesting problem. Let's imagine a list of a few words scraped from a text corpus you are working with:

1. Create a **list_of_words** list with words scraped from a text corpus:

   ```
   list_of_words = ["Hello", "there.", "How", "are", "you", "doing?"]
   ```

2. Find out whether this list contains all the elements from another list:

   ```
   check_for = ["How", "are"]
   ```

   There exists an elaborate solution, which involves a **for loop** and few if-else conditions (and you should try to write it!), but there also exists an elegant Pythonic solution to this problem, which takes one line and uses the **all** function. The **all** function returns **True** if all elements of the iterable are true.

3. Using the **in** keyword to check membership in the list **list_of_words**:

   ```
   all(w in list_of_words for w in check_for)
   ```

   The output is as follows:

   ```
   True
   ```

   It is indeed elegant and simple to reason about, and this neat trick is very important when dealing with lists.

Queue

Apart from stacks, another high-level data structure that we are interested in is queue. A queue is like a stack, meaning that you continue adding elements one by one. With a queue, the reading of elements obeys a FIFO (First In First Out) strategy. Check out the following diagram to understand this better:

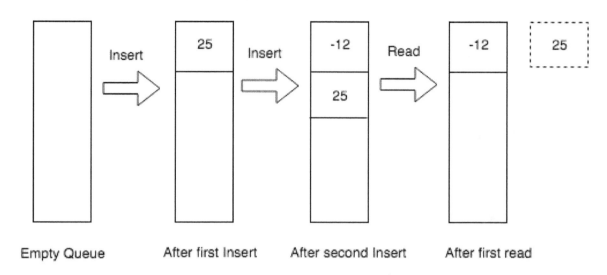

Figure 2.4: Pictorial representation of a queue

We will accomplish this first using list methods and we will show you that for this purpose, it is inefficient. Then, we will learn about the **dequeue** data structure from the collection module of Python.

Exercise 21: Implementing a Queue in Python

1. Create a Python queue with the plain list methods:

```
%%time
queue = []
for i in range(0, 100000):
    queue.append(i)
print("Queue created")
```

The output is as follows:

```
Queue created
Wall time: 11 ms
```

2. Use the **pop** function to empty the queue and check items in it:

```
for i in range(0, 100000):
    queue.pop(0)
print("Queue emptied")
```

The output is as follows:

```
Queue emptied
```

If we use the **%%time** magic command while executing the preceding code, we will see that it takes a while to finish. In a modern MacBook, with a quad-core processor and 8 GB RAM, it took around 1.20 seconds to finish. This time is taken because of the **pop(0)** operation, which means every time we pop a value from the left of the list (which is the current 0 index), Python has to rearrange all the other elements of the list by shifting them one space left. Indeed, it is not a very optimized implementation.

3. Implement the same queue using the **deque** data structure from Python's collection package:

```
%%time
from collections import deque
queue2 = deque()
for i in range(0, 100000):
    queue2.append(i)
print("Queue created")
for i in range(0, 100000):
    queue2.popleft()
print("Queue emptied")
```

The output is as follows:

```
Queue created
Queue emptied
Wall time: 23 ms
```

4. With the specialized and optimized queue implementation from Python's standard library, the time that's taken for this operation is only in the range of 28 milliseconds! This is a huge improvement on the previous one.

A queue is a very important data structure. To give one example from real life, we can think about a producer-consumer system design. While doing data wrangling, you will often come across a problem where you must process very big files. One of the ways to deal with this problem is to chunk the contents of the file in to smaller parts and then push them in to a queue while creating small, dedicated worker processes, which reads off the queue and processes one small chunk at a time. This is a very powerful design, and you can even use it efficiently to design huge multi-node data wrangling pipelines.

We will end the discussion on data structures here. What we discussed here is just the tip of the iceberg. Data structures are a fascinating subject. There are many other data structures that we did not touch and which, when used efficiently, can offer enormous added value. We strongly encourage you to explore data structures more. Try to learn about linked lists, tree, graph, trie, and all the different variations of them as much as you can. Not only do they offer the joy of learning, but they are also the secret mega weapons in the arsenal of a data practitioner that you can bring out every time you are challenged with a difficult data wrangling job.

Activity 3: Permutation, Iterator, Lambda, List

In this activity, we will be using **permutations** to generate all possible three-digit numbers that can be generated using 0, 1, and 2. Then, loop over this iterator, and also use **isinstance** and **assert** to make sure that the return types are tuples. Also, use a single line of code involving **dropwhile** and **lambda** expressions to convert all the tuples to lists while dropping any leading zeros (for example, (0, 1, 2) becomes [1, 2]). Finally, write a function that takes a list like before and returns the actual number contained in it.

These steps will guide you to solve this activity:

1. Look up the definition of **permutations** and **dropwhile** from **itertools**.

2. Write an expression to generate all the possible three-digit numbers using **0**, **1**, and **2**.

3. Loop over the iterator expression you generated before. Print each element that's returned by the iterator. Use **assert** and **isinstance** to make sure that the elements are of the tuple type.

4. Write the loop again using **dropwhile** with a lambda expression to drop any leading zeros from the tuples. As an example, **(0, 1, 2)** will become **[0, 2]**. Also, cast the output of **dropwhile** to a list.

5. Check the actual type that **dropwhile** returns.

6. Combine the preceding code into one block, and this time write a separate function where you will pass the list generated from **dropwhile**, and the function will return the whole number contained in the list. As an example, if you pass **[1, 2]** to the function, it will return **12**. Make sure that the return type is indeed a number and not a string. Although this task can be achieved using other tricks, we require that you treat the incoming list as a stack in the function and generate the number by reading the individual digits from the stack.

With this activity, we have finished this topic and we will head over to the next topic, which involves basic file-level operations. But before we leave this topic, we encourage you to think about a solution to the preceding problem without using all the advanced operations and data structures we have used here. You will soon realize how complex the naive solution is, and how much value these data structures and operations bring.

> **Note**
>
> The solution for this activity can be found on page 289.

Basic File Operations in Python

In the previous topic, we investigated a few advanced data structures and also learned neat and useful functional programming methods to manipulate them without side effects. In this topic, we will learn about a few operating system (OS)-level functions in Python. We will concentrate mainly on file-related functions and learn how to open a file, read the data line by line or all at once, and finally how to cleanly close the file we opened. We will apply a few of the techniques we have learned about on a file that we will read to practice our data wrangling skills further.

Exercise 22: File Operations

In this exercise, we will learn about the OS module of Python, and we will also see two very useful ways to write and read environment variables. The power of writing and reading environment variables is often very important while designing and developing data wrangling pipelines.

> **Note**
>
> In fact, one of the factors of the famous 12-factor app design is the very idea of storing configuration in the environment. You can check it out at this URL: https://12factor.net/config.

The purpose of the OS module is to give you ways to interact with operating system-dependent functionalities. In general, it is pretty low-level and most of the functions from there are not useful on a day-to-day basis, however, some are worth learning. **os.environ** is the collection Python maintains with all the present environment variables in your OS. It gives you the power to create new ones. The **os.getenv** function gives you the ability to read an environment variable:

1. Import the **os** module.

   ```
   import os
   ```

2. Set few environment variables:

   ```
   os.environ['MY_KEY'] = "MY_VAL"
   os.getenv('MY_KEY')
   ```

The output is as follows:

```
'MY_VAL'
```

Print the environment variable when it is not set:

```
print(os.getenv('MY_KEY_NOT_SET'))
```

The output is as follows:

```
None
```

3. Print the **os** environment:

```
print(os.environ)
```

> **Note**
>
> The output has not been added for security reasons.

After executing the preceding code, you will be able to see that you have successfully printed the value of **MY_KEY**, and when you tried to print **MY_KEY_NOT_SET**, it printed None.

File Handling

In this exercise, we will learn about how to open a file in Python. We will learn about the different modes that we can use and what they stand for. Python has a built-in **open** function that we will use to open a file. The **open** function takes few arguments as input. Among them, the first one, which stands for the name of the file you want to open, is the only one that's mandatory. Everything else has a default value. When you call **open**, Python uses underlying system-level calls to open a file handler and will return it to the caller.

Usually, a file can be opened either for reading or for writing. If we open a file in one mode, the other operation is not supported. Whereas reading usually means we start to read from the beginning of an existing file, writing can mean either starting a new file and writing from the beginning or opening an existing file and appending to it. Here is a table showing you all the different modes Python supports for opening a file:

Character	Meaning of the character
'r'	Open for reading
'w'	Open for writing
'x'	Create a new file and open it for writing
'a'	Open for writing in append mode, if it exists
'b'	Binary mode
't'	Text mode (default)
'+'	Update mode (both write and read)

Figure 2.5 Modes to read a file

There also exists a deprecated mode, **U**, which in a Python3 environment does nothing. One thing we must remember here is that Python will always differentiate between **t** and **b** modes, even if the underlying OS doesn't. This is because in **b** mode, Python does not try to decode what it is reading and gives us back the bytes object instead, whereas in **t** mode, it does try to decode the stream and gives us back the string representation.

You can open a file for reading like so:

```
fd = open("Alice's Adventures in Wonderland, by Lewis Carroll")
```

This is opened in **rt** mode. You can open the same file in binary mode if you want. To open the file in binary mode, use the **rb** mode:

```
fd = open("Alice's Adventures in Wonderland, by Lewis Carroll",
        "rb")

fd
```

The output is as follows:

```
<_io.BufferedReader name='Alice's Adventures in Wonderland, by Lewis Carroll'>
```

This is how we open a file for writing:

```
fd = open("interesting_data.txt", "w")

fd
```

The output is as follows:

```
<_io.TextIOWrapper name='interesting_data.txt' mode='w' encoding='cp1252'>
```

Exercise 23: Opening and Closing a File

In this exercise, we will learn how to close an open file. It is very important that we close a file once we open it. A lot of system-level bugs can occur due to a dangling file handler. Once we close a file, no further operations can be performed on that file using that specific file handler:

1. Open a file in binary mode:

    ```
    fd = open("Alice's Adventures in Wonderland, by Lewis Carroll",
              "rb")
    ```

2. Close a file using **close()**:

    ```
    fd.close()
    ```

3. Python also gives us a **closed** flag with the file handler. If we print it before closing, then we will see **False**, whereas if we print it after closing, then we will see **True**. If our logic checks whether a file is properly closed or not, then this is the flag we want to use.

The with Statement

In this exercise, we will learn about the **with** statement in Python and how we can effectively use it in the context of opening and closing files.

The **with** command is a compound statement in Python. Like any compound statement, **with** also affects the execution of the code enclosed by it. In the case of **with**, it is used to wrap a block of code in the scope of what we call a **Context Manager** in Python. A detailed discussion of the context manager is out of the scope of this exercise and this topic in general, but it is sufficient to say that thanks to a context manager implemented inside the **open** call for opening a file in Python, it is guaranteed that a close call will automatically happen if we wrap it inside a **with** statement.

> **Note**
>
> There is an entire PEP for with at https://www.python.org/dev/peps/pep-0343/. We encourage you to look into it.

Opening a File Using the **with** Statement

Open a file using the with statement:

```
with open("Alice's Adventures in Wonderland, by Lewis Carroll")as fd:
    print(fd.closed)
print(fd.closed)
```

The output is as follows:

```
False
True
```

If we execute the preceding code, we will see that the first print will end up printing **False**, whereas the second one will print **True**. This means that as soon as the control goes out of the **with** block, the file descriptor is automatically closed.

> **Note**
>
> This is by far the cleanest and most Pythonic way to open a file and obtain a file descriptor for it. We encourage you to use this pattern whenever you need to open a file by yourself.

Exercise 24: Reading a File Line by Line

1. Open a file and then read the file line by line and print it as we read it:

```
with open("Alice's Adventures in Wonderland, by Lewis Carroll",
        encoding="utf8") as fd:
    for line in fd:
            print(line)
```

The output is as follows:

```
CHAPTER I. Down the Rabbit-Hole


Alice was beginning to get very tired of sitting by her sister on the

bank, and of having nothing to do: once or twice she had peeped into the

book her sister was reading, but it had no pictures or conversations in

it, 'and what is the use of a book,' thought Alice 'without pictures or

conversations?'


So she was considering in her own mind (as well as she could, for the

hot day made her feel very sleepy and stupid), whether the pleasure
```

Figure 2.6: Screenshot from the Jupyter notebook

2. Looking at the preceding code, we can really see why it is important. With this small snippet of code, you can even open and read files that are many GBs in size, line by line, and without flooding or overrunning the system memory!

    There is another explicit method in the file descriptor object called **readline**, which reads one line at a time from a file.

3. Duplicate the same for loop, just after the first one:

```
with open("Alice's Adventures in Wonderland, by Lewis Carroll",
        encoding="utf8") as fd:
    for line in fd:
        print(line)
    print("Ended first loop")
    for line in fd:
        print(line)
```

The output is as follows:

```
CHAPTER I. Down the Rabbit-Hole

Alice was beginning to get very tired of sitting by her sister on the

bank, and of having nothing to do: once or twice she had peeped into the

book her sister was reading, but it had no pictures or conversations in

it, 'and what is the use of a book,' thought Alice 'without pictures or

conversations?'


So she was considering in her own mind (as well as she could, for the

hot day made her feel very sleepy and stupid), whether the pleasure
```

Figure 2.7: Section of the open file

Exercise 25: Write to a File

We will end this topic on file operations by showing you how to write to a file. We will write a few lines to a file and read the file:

1. Use the **write** function from the file descriptor object:

    ```
    data_dict = {"India": "Delhi", "France": "Paris", "UK": "London",
                "USA": "Washington"}
    with open("data_temporary_files.txt", "w") as fd:
        for country, capital in data_dict.items():
            fd.write("The capital of {} is {}\n".format(
                country, capital))
    ```

2. Read the file using the following command:

    ```
    with open("data_temporary_files.txt", "r") as fd:
        for line in fd:
            print(line)
    ```

    The output is as follows:

    ```
    The capital of India is Delhi

    The capital of France is Paris

    The capital of UK is London

    The capital of USA is Washington
    ```

3. Use the print function to write to a file using the following command:

```
data_dict_2 = {"China": "Beijing", "Japan": "Tokyo"}
with open("data_temporary_files.txt", "a") as fd:
    for country, capital in data_dict_2.items():
        print("The capital of {} is {}".format(
            country, capital), file=fd)
```

4. Read the file using the following command:

```
with open("data_temporary_files.txt", "r") as fd:
    for line in fd:
        print(line)
```

The output is as follows:

```
The capital of India is Delhi

The capital of France is Paris

The capital of UK is London

The capital of USA is Washington

The capital of China is Beijing

The capital of Japan is Tokyo
```

> **Note:**
>
> In the second case, we did not add an extra newline character, \n, at the end of the string to be written. The print function does that automatically for us.

With this, we will end this topic. Just like the previous topics, we have designed an activity for you to practice your newly acquired skills.

Activity 4: Design Your Own CSV Parser

A CSV file is something you will encounter a lot in your life as a data practitioner. A CSV is a comma-separated file where data from a tabular format is generally stored and separated using commas, although other characters can also be used.

In this activity, we will be tasked with building our own CSV reader and parser. Although it is a big task if we try to cover all use cases and edge cases, along with escape characters and all, for the sake of this small activity, we will keep our requirements small. We will assume that there is no escape character, meaning that if you use a comma at any place in your row, it means you are starting a new column. We will also assume that the only function we are interested in is to be able to read a CSV file line by line where each read will generate a new dict with the column names as keys and row names as values.

Here is an example:

Name	Age	Location
Bob	24	California

Figure 2.8 Table with sample data

We can convert the data in the preceding table into a Python dictionary, which would look as follows: `{"Name": "Bob", "Age": "24", "Location": "California"}`:

1. Import **zip_longest** from **itertools**. Create a function to zip **header**, **line** and **fillvalue=None**.

2. Open the accompanying **sales_record.csv** file from the GitHub link by using **r** mode inside a with block and first check that it is opened.

3. Read the first line and use string methods to generate a list of all the column names.

4. Start reading the file. Read it line by line.

5. Read each line and pass that line to a function, along with the list of the headers. The work of the function is to construct a dict out of these two and fill up the **key:values**. Keep in mind that a missing value should result in **None**.

> **Note**
>
> The solution for this activity can be found on page 291.

Summary

In this chapter, we learned about the workings of advanced data structures such as stacks and queues. We implemented and manipulated both stacks and queues. We then focused on different methods of functional programming, including iterators, and combined lists and functions together. After this, we looked at the **OS**-level functions and the management of environment variables and files. We also examined a clean way to deal with files, and we created our own CSV parser in the last activity.

In the next chapter, we will be dealing with the three most important libraries, namely NumPy, pandas, and matplotlib.

3

Introduction to NumPy, Pandas, and Matplotlib

Learning Objectives

By the end of the chapter, you will be able to:

- Create and manipulate one-dimensional and multi-dimensional arrays
- Create and manipulate pandas DataFrames and series objects
- Plot and visualize numerical data using the Matplotlib library
- Apply matplotlib, NumPy, and pandas to calculate descriptive statistics from a DataFrame/matrix

In this chapter, you will learn about the fundamentals of the NumPy, pandas, and matplotlib libraries.

Introduction

In the preceding chapters, we have covered some advanced data structures, such as stack, queue, iterator, and file operations in Python. In this section, we will cover three essential libraries, namely NumPy, pandas, and matplotlib.

NumPy Arrays

In the life of a data scientist, reading and manipulating arrays is of prime importance, and it is also the most frequently encountered task. These arrays could be a one-dimensional list or a multi-dimensional table or a matrix full of numbers.

The array could be filled with integers, floating-point numbers, Booleans, strings, or even mixed types. However, in the majority of cases, numeric data types are predominant.

Some example scenarios where you will need to handle numeric arrays are as follows:

- To read a list of phone numbers and postal codes and extract a certain pattern

- To create a matrix with random numbers to run a Monte Carlo simulation on some statistical process

- To scale and normalize a sales figure table, with lots of financial and transactional data

- To create a smaller table of key descriptive statistics (for example, mean, median, min/max range, variance, inter-quartile ranges) from a large raw data table

- To read in and analyze time series data in a one-dimensional array daily, such as the stock price of an organization over a year or daily temperature data from a weather station

In short, arrays and numeric data tables are everywhere. As a data wrangling professional, the importance of the ability to read and process numeric arrays cannot be overstated. In this regard, NumPy arrays will be the most important object in Python that you need to know about.

NumPy Array and Features

NumPy and **SciPy** are open source add-on modules for Python that provide common mathematical and numerical routines in pre-compiled, fast functions. These have grown into highly mature libraries that provide functionality that meets, or perhaps exceeds, what is associated with common commercial software such as **MATLAB** or **Mathematica**.

One of the main advantages of the NumPy module is to handle or create one-dimensional or multi-dimensional arrays. This advanced data structure/class is at the heart of the NumPy package and it serves as the fundamental building block of more advanced classes such as **pandas** and **DataFrame**, which we will cover shortly in this chapter.

NumPy arrays are different than common Python lists, since Python lists can be thought as simple array. NumPy arrays are built for **vectorized** operations that process a lot of numerical data with just a single line of code. Many built-in mathematical functions in NumPy arrays are written in low-level languages such as C or Fortran and pre-compiled for real, fast execution.

> **Note**
>
> NumPy arrays are optimized data structures for numerical analysis, and that's why they are so important to data scientists.

Exercise 26: Creating a NumPy Array (from a List)

In this exercise, we will create a NumPy array from a list:

1. To work with NumPy, we must import it. By convention, we give it a short name, **np**, while importing:

    ```
    import numpy as np
    ```

2. Create a list with three elements, 1, 2, and 3:

    ```
    list_1 = [1,2,3]
    ```

3. Use the **array** function to convert it into an array:

    ```
    array_1 = np.array(list_1)
    ```

    We just created a NumPy array object called **array_1** from the regular Python list object, **list_1**.

4. Create an array of floating type elements 1.2, 3.4, and 5.6:

    ```
    import array as arr
    a = arr.array('d', [1.2, 3.4, 5.6])
    print(a)
    ```

The output is as follows:

```
array('d', [1.2, 3.4, 5.6])
```

5. Let's check the type of the newly created object by using the **type** function:

```
type(array_1)
```

The output is as follows:

```
numpy.ndarray
```

6. Use **type** on **list_1**:

```
type (list_1)
```

The output is as follows:

```
list
```

So, this is indeed different from the regular **list** object.

Exercise 27: Adding Two NumPy Arrays

This simple exercise will demonstrate the addition of two NumPy arrays, and thereby show the key difference between a regular Python list/array and a NumPy array:

1. Consider **list_1** and **array_1** from the preceding exercise. If you have changed the Jupyter notebook, you will have to declare them again.

2. Use the **+** notation to add two **list_1** object and save the results in **list_2**:

```
list_2 = list_1 + list_1
print(list_2)
```

The output is as follows:

```
[1, 2, 3, 1, 2, 3]
```

3. Use the same **+** notation to add two **array_1** objects and save the result in **array_2**:

```
array_2 = array_1 + array_1
print(array_2)
```

The output is as follows:

```
[2, ,4, 6]
```

Did you notice the difference? The first print shows a list with 6 elements [1, 2, 3, 1, 2, 3]. But the second print shows another NumPy array (or vector) with the elements [2, 4, 6], which are just the sum of the individual elements of **array_1**.

NumPy arrays are like mathematical objects – **vectors**. They are built for element-wise operations, that is, when we add two NumPy arrays, we add the first element of the first array to the first element of the second array – there is an element-to-element correspondence in this operation. This is in contrast to Python lists, where the elements are simply appended and there is no element-to-element relation. This is the real power of a NumPy array: they can be treated just like mathematical vectors.

A vector is a collection of numbers that can represent, for example, the coordinates of points in a three-dimensional space or the color of numbers (RGB) in a picture. Naturally, relative order is important for such a collection and as we discussed previously, a NumPy array can maintain such order relationships. That's why they are perfectly suitable to use in numerical computations.

Exercise 28: Mathematical Operations on NumPy Arrays

Now that you know that these arrays are like vectors, we will try some mathematical operations on arrays.

NumPy arrays even support element-wise exponentiation. For example, suppose there are two arrays – the elements of the first array will be raised to the power of the elements in the second array:

1. Multiply two arrays using the following command:

   ```
   print("array_1 multiplied by array_1: ",array_1*array_1)
   ```

   The output is as follows:

   ```
   array_1 multiplied by array_1:  [1 4 9]
   ```

2. Divide two arrays using the following command:

   ```
   print("array_1 divided by array_1: ",array_1/array_1)
   ```

   The output is as follows:

   ```
   array_1 divided by array_1:  [1. 1. 1.]
   ```

3. Raise one array to the second arrays power using the following command:

```
print("array_1 raised to the power of array_1: ",array_1**array_1)
```

The output is as follows:

```
array_1 raised to the power of array_1:  [ 1  4 27]
```

Exercise 29: Advanced Mathematical Operations on NumPy Arrays

NumPy has all the built-in mathematical functions that you can think of. Here, we are going to be creating a list and converting it into a NumPy array. Then, we will perform some advanced mathematical operations on that array.

Here, we are creating a list and then converting that into a NumPy array. We will then show you how to perform some advanced mathematical operations on that array:

1. Create a list with five elements:

```
list_5=[i for i in range(1,6)]
print(list_5)
```

The output is as follows:

```
[1, 2, 3, 4, 5]
```

2. Convert the list into a NumPy array by using the following command:

```
array_5=np.array(list_5)
array_5
```

The output is as follows:

```
array([1, 2, 3, 4, 5])
```

3. Find the **sine** value of the array by using the following command:

```
# sine function
print("Sine: ",np.sin(array_5))
```

The output is as follows:

```
Sine:  [ 0.84147098  0.90929743  0.14112001 -0.7568025  -0.95892427]
```

4. Find the logarithmic value of the array by using the following command:

```
# logarithm
print("Natural logarithm: ",np.log(array_5))
print("Base-10 logarithm: ",np.log10(array_5))
print("Base-2 logarithm: ",np.log2(array_5))
```

The output is as follows:

```
Natural logarithm:    [0.          0.69314718 1.09861229 1.38629436
1.60943791]
Base-10 logarithm:    [0.          0.30103    0.47712125 0.60205999 0.69897
]
Base-2 logarithm:    [0.          1.          1.5849625  2.          2.32192809]
```

5. Find the exponential value of the array by using the following command:

```
# Exponential
print("Exponential: ",np.exp(array_5))
```

The output is as follows:

```
Exponential:    [  2.71828183    7.3890561    20.08553692   54.59815003
148.4131591 ]
```

Exercise 30: Generating Arrays Using arange and linspace

Generation of numerical arrays is a fairly common task. So far, we have been doing this by creating a Python list object and then converting that into a NumPy array. However, we can bypass that and work directly with native NumPy methods.

The **arange** function creates a series of numbers based on the minimum and maximum bounds you give and the step size you specify. Another function, `linspace`, creates a series of the fixed numbers of intermediate points between two extremes:

1. Create a series of numbers using the **arange** method, by using the following command:

```
print("A series of numbers:",np.arange(5,16))
```

The output is as follows:

```
A series of numbers: [ 5  6  7  8  9 10 11 12 13 14 15]
```

2. Print numbers using the **arange** function by using the following command:

```
print("Numbers spaced apart by 2: ",np.arange(0,11,2))
print("Numbers spaced apart by a floating point number: ",np.
arange(0,11,2.5))
print("Every 5th number from 30 in reverse order\n",np.arange(30,-1,-5))
```

The output is as follows:

```
Numbers spaced apart by 2:  [ 0  2  4  6  8 10]
Numbers spaced apart by a floating point number:  [ 0.   2.5  5.   7.5 10. ]
Every 5th number from 30 in reverse order
 [30 25 20 15 10  5  0]
```

3. For linearly spaced numbers, we can use the **linspace** method, as follows:

```
print("11 linearly spaced numbers between 1 and 5: ",np.linspace(1,5,11))
```

The output is as follows:

```
11 linearly spaced numbers between 1 and 5:  [1.   1.4 1.8 2.2 2.6 3.   3.4
3.8 4.2 4.6 5. ]
```

Exercise 31: Creating Multi-Dimensional Arrays

So far, we have created only one-dimensional arrays. Now, let's create some multi-dimensional arrays (such as a matrix in linear algebra). Just like we created the one-dimensional array from a simple flat list, we can create a two-dimensional array from a list of lists:

1. Create a list of lists and convert it into a two-dimensional NumPy array by using the following command:

```
list_2D = [[1,2,3],[4,5,6],[7,8,9]]
mat1 = np.array(list_2D)
print("Type/Class of this object:",type(mat1))
print("Here is the matrix\n----------\n",mat1,"\n----------")
```

The output is as follows:

```
Type/Class of this object: <class 'numpy.ndarray'>
Here is the matrix
----------
[[1 2 3]
 [4 5 6]
 [7 8 9]]
----------
```

2. Tuples can be converted into multi-dimensional arrays by using the following code:

```
tuple_2D = np.array([(1.5,2,3), (4,5,6)])
mat_tuple = np.array(tuple_2D)
print (mat_tuple)
```

The output is as follows:

```
[[1.5 2.  3. ]
 [4.  5.  6. ]]
```

Thus, we have created multi-dimensional arrays using Python lists and tuples.

Exercise 32: The Dimension, Shape, Size, and Data Type of the Two-dimensional Array

The following methods let you check the dimension, shape, and size of the array. Note that if it's a 3x2 matrix, that is, it has 3 rows and 2 columns, then the shape will be (3,2), but the size will be 6, as 6 = 3x2:

1. Print the dimension of the matrix using **ndim** by using the following command:

```
print("Dimension of this matrix: ",mat1.ndim,sep='')
```

The output is as follows:

```
Dimension of this matrix: 2
```

2. Print the size using **size**:

```
print("Size of this matrix: ", mat1.size,sep='')
```

The output is as follows:

```
Size of this matrix: 9
```

3. Print the shape of the matrix using **shape**:

```
print("Shape of this matrix: ", mat1.shape,sep='')
```

The output is as follows:

```
Shape of this matrix: (3, 3)
```

4. Print the dimension type using **dtype**:

```
print("Data type of this matrix: ", mat1.dtype,sep='')
```

The output is as follows:

```
Data type of this matrix: int32
```

Exercise 33: Zeros, Ones, Random, Identity Matrices, and Vectors

Now that we are familiar with basic vector (one-dimensional) and matrix data structures in NumPy, we will take a look how to create special matrices easily. Often, you may have to create matrices filled with zeros, ones, random numbers, or ones in the diagonal:

1. Print the vector of zeros by using the following command:

```
print("Vector of zeros: ",np.zeros(5))
```

The output is as follows:

```
Vector of zeros:  [0. 0. 0. 0. 0.]
```

2. Print the matrix of zeros by using the following command:

```
print("Matrix of zeros: ",np.zeros((3,4)))
```

The output is as follows:

```
Matrix of zeros:  [[0. 0. 0. 0.]
 [0. 0. 0. 0.]
 [0. 0. 0. 0.]]
```

3. Print the matrix of fives by using the following command:

```
print("Matrix of 5's: ",5*np.ones((3,3)))
```

The output is as follows:

```
Matrix of 5's:   [[5. 5. 5.]
 [5. 5. 5.]
 [5. 5. 5.]]
```

4. Print an identity matrix by using the following command:

```
print("Identity matrix of dimension 2:",np.eye(2))
```

The output is as follows:

```
Identity matrix of dimension 2: [[1. 0.]
 [0. 1.]]
```

5. Print an identity matrix with a dimension of 4x4 by using the following command:

```
print("Identity matrix of dimension 4:",np.eye(4))
```

The output is as follows:

```
Identity matrix of dimension 4: [[1. 0. 0. 0.]
 [0. 1. 0. 0.]
 [0. 0. 1. 0.]
 [0. 0. 0. 1.]]
```

6. Print a matrix of random shape using the **randint** function:

```
print("Random matrix of shape (4,3):\n",np.random.
randint(low=1,high=10,size=(4,3)))
```

The sample output is as follows:

```
Random matrix of shape (4,3):
 [[6 7 6]
 [5 6 7]
 [5 3 6]
 [2 9 4]]
```

> **Note**
>
> When creating matrices, you need to pass on tuples of integers as arguments.

Random number generation is a very useful utility and needs to be mastered for data science/data wrangling tasks. We will look at the topic of random variables and distributions again in the section on statistics and see how NumPy and pandas have built-in random number and series generation, as well as manipulation functions.

Exercise 34: Reshaping, Ravel, Min, Max, and Sorting

Reshaping an array is a very useful operation for vectors as machine learning algorithms may demand input vectors in various formats for mathematical manipulation. In this section, we will be looking at how reshaping can take be done on an array. The opposite of **reshape** is the **ravel** function, which flattens any given array into a one-dimensional array. It is a very useful action in many machine learning and data analytics tasks.

The following functions reshape the function. We will first generate a random one-dimensional vector of 2-digit numbers and then reshape the vector into multi-dimensional vectors:

1. Create an array of 30 random integers (sampled from 1 to 99) and reshape it into two different forms using the following code:

```
a = np.random.randint(1,100,30)
b = a.reshape(2,3,5)
c = a.reshape(6,5)
```

2. Print the shape using the **shape** function by using the following code:

```
print ("Shape of a:", a.shape)
print ("Shape of b:", b.shape)
print ("Shape of c:", c.shape)
```

The output is as follows:

```
Shape of a: (30,)
Shape of b: (2, 3, 5)
Shape of c: (6, 5)
```

3. Print the arrays a, b, and c using the following code:

```
print("\na looks like\n",a)
print("\nb looks like\n",b)
print("\nc looks like\n",c)
```

The sample output is as follows:

```
a looks like
 [ 7 82  9 29 50 50 71 65 33 84 55 78 40 68 50 15 65 55 98 38 23 75 50 57
 32 69 34 59 98 48]

b looks like
 [[[ 7 82  9 29 50]
  [50 71 65 33 84]
  [55 78 40 68 50]]

 [[15 65 55 98 38]
  [23 75 50 57 32]
  [69 34 59 98 48]]]

c looks like
 [[ 7 82  9 29 50]
  [50 71 65 33 84]
  [55 78 40 68 50]
  [15 65 55 98 38]
  [23 75 50 57 32]
  [69 34 59 98 48]]
```

> **Note**
>
> "b" is a three-dimensional array – a kind of list of a list of a list.

4. Ravel file b using the following code:

```
b_flat = b.ravel()
print(b_flat)
```

The sample output is as follows:

```
[ 7 82  9 29 50 50 71 65 33 84 55 78 40 68 50 15 65 55 98 38 23 75 50 57
 32 69 34 59 98 48]
```

Exercise 35: Indexing and Slicing

Indexing and **slicing** of NumPy arrays is very similar to regular list indexing. We can even step through a vector of elements with a definite step size by providing it as an additional argument in the format (start, step, end). Furthermore, we can pass a list as the argument to select specific elements.

In this exercise, we will learn about indexing and slicing on one-dimensional and multi-dimensional arrays:

> **Note**
>
> In multi-dimensional arrays, you can use two numbers to denote the position of an element. For example, if the element is in the third row and second column, its indices are 2 and 1 (because of Python's zero-based indexing).

1. Create an array of 10 elements and examine its various elements by slicing and indexing the array with slightly different syntaxes. Do this by using the following command:

   ```
   array_1 = np.arange(0,11)
   print("Array:",array_1)
   ```

   The output is as follows:

   ```
   Array: [ 0  1  2  3  4  5  6  7  8  9 10]
   ```

2. Print the element in the seventh position by using the following command:

   ```
   print("Element at 7th index is:", array_1[7])
   ```

   The output is as follows:

   ```
   Element at 7th index is: 7
   ```

3. Print the elements between the third and sixth positions by using the following command:

   ```
   print("Elements from 3rd to 5th index are:", array_1[3:6])
   ```

   The output is as follows:

   ```
   Elements from 3rd to 5th index are: [3 4 5]
   ```

4. Print the elements until the fourth position by using the following command:

```
print("Elements up to 4th index are:", array_1[:4])
```

The output is as follows:

```
Elements up to 4th index are: [0 1 2 3]
```

5. Print the elements backwards by using the following command:

```
print("Elements from last backwards are:", array_1[-1::-1])
```

The output is as follows:

```
Elements from last backwards are: [10  9  8  7  6  5  4  3  2  1  0]
```

6. Print the elements using their backward index, skipping three values, by using the following command:

```
print("3 Elements from last backwards are:", array_1[-1:-6:-2])
```

The output is as follows:

```
3 Elements from last backwards are: [10  8  6]
```

7. Create a new array called **array_2** by using the following command:

```
array_2 = np.arange(0,21,2)
print("New array:",array_2)
```

The output is as follows:

```
New array: [ 0  2  4  6  8 10 12 14 16 18 20]
```

8. Print the second, fourth, and ninth elements of the array:

```
print("Elements at 2nd, 4th, and 9th index are:", array_2[[2,4,9]])
```

The output is as follows:

```
Elements at 2nd, 4th, and 9th index are: [ 4  8 18]
```

9. Create a multi-dimensional array by using the following command:

```
matrix_1 = np.random.randint(10,100,15).reshape(3,5)
print("Matrix of random 2-digit numbers\n ",matrix_1)
```

The sample output is as follows:

```
Matrix of random 2-digit numbers
  [[21 57 60 24 15]
 [53 20 44 72 68]
 [39 12 99 99 33]]
```

10. Access the values using double bracket indexing by using the following command:

```
print("\nDouble bracket indexing\n")
print("Element in row index 1 and column index 2:", matrix_1[1][2])
```

The sample output is as follows:

```
Double bracket indexing

Element in row index 1 and column index 2: 44
```

11. Access the values using single bracket indexing by using the following command:

```
print("\nSingle bracket with comma indexing\n")
print("Element in row index 1 and column index 2:", matrix_1[1,2])
```

The sample output is as follows:

```
Single bracket with comma indexing

Element in row index 1 and column index 2: 44
```

12. Access the values in a multi-dimensional array using a row or column by using the following command:

```
print("\nRow or column extract\n")
print("Entire row at index 2:", matrix_1[2])
print("Entire column at index 3:", matrix_1[:,3])
```

The sample output is as follows:

```
Row or column extract

Entire row at index 2: [39 12 99 99 33]
Entire column at index 3: [24 72 99]
```

13. Print the matrix with the specified row and column indices by using the following command:

```
print("\nSubsetting sub-matrices\n")
print("Matrix with row indices 1 and 2 and column indices 3 and 4\n",
matrix_1[1:3,3:5])
```

The sample output is as follows:

```
Subsetting sub-matrices
Matrix with row indices 1 and 2 and column indices 3 and 4
 [[72 68]
 [99 33]]
```

14. Print the matrix with the specified row and column indices by using the following command:

```
print("Matrix with row indices 0 and 1 and column indices 1 and 3\n",
matrix_1[0:2,[1,3]])
```

The sample output is as follows:

```
Matrix with row indices 0 and 1 and column indices 1 and 3
 [[57 24]
 [20 72]]
```

Conditional Subsetting

Conditional subsetting is a way to select specific elements based on some numeric condition. It is almost like a shortened version of a SQL query to subset elements. See the following example:

```
matrix_1 = np.array(np.random.randint(10,100,15)).reshape(3,5)

print("Matrix of random 2-digit numbers\n",matrix_1)

print ("\nElements greater than 50\n", matrix_1[matrix_1>50])
```

The sample output is as follows (note that the exact output will be different for you as it is random):

```
Matrix of random 2-digit numbers

 [[71 89 66 99 54]

 [28 17 66 35 85]

 [82 35 38 15 47]]


Elements greater than 50

 [71 89 66 99 54 66 85 82]
```

Exercise 36: Array Operations (array-array, array-scalar, and universal functions)

NumPy arrays operate just like mathematical matrices, and the operations are performed element-wise.

Create two matrices (multi-dimensional arrays) with random integers and demonstrate element-wise mathematical operations such as addition, subtraction, multiplication, and division. Show the exponentiation (raising a number to a certain power) operation, as follows:

> **Note**
>
> Due to random number generation, your specific output could be different to what is shown here.

1. Create two matrices:

```
matrix_1 = np.random.randint(1,10,9).reshape(3,3)
matrix_2 = np.random.randint(1,10,9).reshape(3,3)
print("\n1st Matrix of random single-digit numbers\n",matrix_1)
print("\n2nd Matrix of random single-digit numbers\n",matrix_2)
```

The sample output is as follows (note that the exact output will be different for you as it is random):

```
1st Matrix of random single-digit numbers
 [[6 5 9]
 [4 7 1]
 [3 2 7]]

2nd Matrix of random single-digit numbers
 [[2 3 1]
 [9 9 9]
 [9 9 6]]
```

2. Perform addition, subtraction, division, and linear combination on the matrices:

```
print("\nAddition\n", matrix_1+matrix_2)
print("\nMultiplication\n", matrix_1*matrix_2)
print("\nDivision\n", matrix_1/matrix_2)
print("\nLinear combination: 3*A - 2*B\n", 3*matrix_1-2*matrix_2)
```

The sample output is as follows (note that the exact output will be different for you as it is random):

```
Addition
 [[ 8  8 10]
 [13 16 10]
 [12 11 13]] ^

Multiplication
 [[12 15  9]
 [36 63  9]
 [27 18 42]]

Division
 [[3.         1.66666667 9.        ]
 [0.44444444 0.77777778 0.11111111]
 [0.33333333 0.22222222 1.16666667]]

Linear combination: 3*A - 2*B
 [[ 14   9  25]
 [ -6   3 -15]
 [ -9 -12   9]]
```

3. Perform the addition of a scalar, exponential matrix cube, and exponential square root:

```
print("\nAddition of a scalar (100)\n", 100+matrix_1)

print("\nExponentiation, matrix cubed here\n", matrix_1**3)
print("\nExponentiation, square root using 'pow' function\
n",pow(matrix_1,0.5))
```

The sample output is as follows (note that the exact output will be different for you as it is random):

```
Addition of a scalar (100)
 [[106 105 109]
 [104 107 101]
 [103 102 107]]

Exponentiation, matrix cubed here
 [[216 125 729]
 [ 64 343   1]
 [ 27   8 343]]

Exponentiation, square root using 'pow' function
 [[2.44948974 2.23606798 3.         ]
 [2.         2.64575131 1.         ]
 [1.73205081 1.41421356 2.64575131]]
```

Stacking Arrays

Stacking arrays on top of each other (or side by side) is a useful operation for data wrangling. Here is the code:

```
a = np.array([[1,2],[3,4]])
b = np.array([[5,6],[7,8]])
print("Matrix a\n",a)
print("Matrix b\n",b)
print("Vertical stacking\n",np.vstack((a,b)))
print("Horizontal stacking\n",np.hstack((a,b)))
```

The output is as follows:

```
Matrix a
  [[1 2]
  [3 4]]
Matrix b
  [[5 6]
  [7 8]]
Vertical stacking
  [[1 2]
  [3 4]
  [5 6]
  [7 8]]
Horizontal stacking
  [[1 2 5 6]
  [3 4 7 8]]
```

NumPy has many other advanced features, mainly related to statistics and linear algebra functions, which are used extensively in machine learning and data science tasks. However, not all of that is directly useful for beginner level data wrangling, so we won't cover it here.

Pandas DataFrames

The pandas library is a Python package that provides fast, flexible, and expressive data structures that are designed to make working with relational or labeled data both easy and intuitive. It aims to be the fundamental high-level building block for doing practical, real-world data analysis in Python. Additionally, it has the broader goal of becoming the most powerful and flexible open source data analysis/manipulation tool that's available in any language.

The two primary data structures of pandas, **Series** (one-dimensional) and **DataFrame** (two-dimensional), handle the vast majority of typical use cases. Pandas is built on top of NumPy and is intended to integrate well within a scientific computing environment with many other third-party libraries.

Exercise 37: Creating a Pandas Series

In this exercise, we will learn about how to create a pandas series object from the data structures that we created previously. If you have imported pandas as **pd**, then the function to create a series is simply **pd.Series**:

1. Initialize labels, lists, and a dictionary:

   ```
   labels = ['a','b','c']
   my_data = [10,20,30]
   array_1 = np.array(my_data)
   d = {'a':10,'b':20,'c':30}

   print ("Labels:", labels)
   print("My data:", my_data)
   print("Dictionary:", d)
   ```

   The output is as follows:

   ```
   Labels: ['a', 'b', 'c']
   My data: [10, 20, 30]
   Dictionary: {'a': 10, 'b': 20, 'c': 30}
   ```

2. Import pandas as **pd** by using the following command:

   ```
   import pandas as pd
   ```

3. Create a series from the **my_data** list by using the following command:

   ```
   series_1=pd.Series(data=my_data)
   print(series_1)
   ```

The output is as follows:

```
0    10
1    20
2    30
dtype: int64
```

4. Create a series from the **my_data** list along with the **labels** as follows:

```
series_2=pd.Series(data=my_data, index = labels)
print(series_2)
```

The output is as follows:

```
a    10
b    20
c    30
dtype: int64
```

5. Then, create a series from the NumPy array, as follows:

```
series_3=pd.Series(array_1,labels)
print(series_3)
```

The output is as follows:

```
a    10
b    20
c    30
dtype: int32
```

6. Create a series from the dictionary, as follows:

```
series_4=pd.Series(d)
print(series_4)
```

The output is as follows:

```
a    10
b    20
c    30
dtype: int64
```

Exercise 38: Pandas Series and Data Handling

The pandas series object can hold many types of data. This is the key to constructing a bigger table where multiple series objects are stacked together to create a database-like entity:

1. Create a pandas series with numerical data by using the following command:

```
print ("\nHolding numerical data\n",'-'*25, sep='')
print(pd.Series(array_1))
```

The output is as follows:

```
Holding numerical data
-------------------------
0    10
1    20
2    30
dtype: int32
```

2. Create a pandas series with labels by using the following command:

```
print ("\nHolding text labels\n",'-'*20, sep='')
print(pd.Series(labels))
```

The output is as follows:

```
Holding text labels
--------------------
0    a
1    b
2    c
dtype: object
```

3. Create a pandas series with functions by using the following command:

```
print ("\nHolding functions\n",'-'*20, sep='')
print(pd.Series(data=[sum,print,len]))
```

The output is as follows:

```
Holding functions
--------------------
0        <built-in function sum>
1      <built-in function print>
2        <built-in function len>
dtype: object
```

4. Create a pandas series with a dictionary by using the following command:

```
print ("\nHolding objects from a dictionary\n",'-'*40, sep='')
print(pd.Series(data=[d.keys, d.items, d.values]))
```

The output is as follows:

```
Holding objects from a dictionary
--------------------------------------
0    <built-in method keys of dict object at 0x0000...
1    <built-in method items of dict object at 0x000...
2    <built-in method values of dict object at 0x00...
dtype: object
```

Exercise 39: Creating Pandas DataFrames

The pandas DataFrame is similar to an Excel table or relational database (SQL) table that consists of three main components: the data, the index (or rows), and the columns. Under the hood, it is a stack of pandas series objects, which are themselves built on top of NumPy arrays. So, all of our previous knowledge of NumPy array applies here:

1. Create a simple DataFrame from a two-dimensional matrix of numbers. First, the code draws 20 random integers from the uniform distribution. Then, we need to reshape it into a (5,4) NumPy array – 5 rows and 4 columns:

```
matrix_data = np.random.randint(1,10,size=20).reshape(5,4)
```

2. Define the rows labels as ('A','B','C','D','E') and column labels as ('W','X','Y','Z'):

```
row_labels = ['A','B','C','D','E']
column_headings = ['W','X','Y','Z']

df = pd.DataFrame(data=matrix_data, index=row_labels,
                  columns=column_headings)
```

3. The function to create a DataFrame is **pd.DataFrame** and it is called in next:

```
print("\nThe data frame looks like\n",'-'*45, sep='')
print(df)
```

The sample output is as follows:

```
The data frame looks like
---------------------------------------------
    W   X   Y   Z
A   6   3   3   3
B   1   9   9   4
C   4   3   6   9
D   4   8   6   7
E   6   6   9   1
```

4. Create a DataFrame from a Python dictionary of some lists of integers by using the following command:

```
d={'a':[10,20],'b':[30,40],'c':[50,60]}
```

5. Pass this dictionary as the data argument to the **pd.DataFrame** function. Pass on a list of rows or indices. Notice how the dictionary keys became the column names and that the values were distributed among multiple rows:

```
df2=pd.DataFrame(data=d,index=['X','Y'])
print(df2)
```

The output is as follows:

```
    a    b    c
X   10   30   50
Y   20   40   60
```

Note

The most common way that you will encounter to create a pandas DataFrame will be to read tabular data from a file on your local disk or over the internet – CSV, text, JSON, HTML, Excel, and so on. We will cover some of these in the next chapter.

Exercise 40: Viewing a DataFrame Partially

In the previous section, we used **print(df)** to print the whole DataFrame. For a large dataset, we would like to print only sections of data. In this exercise, we will read a part of the DataFrame:

1. Execute the following code to create a DataFrame with 25 rows and fill it with random numbers:

    ```
    # 25 rows and 4 columns
    matrix_data = np.random.randint(1,100,100).reshape(25,4)
    column_headings = ['W','X','Y','Z']
    df = pd.DataFrame(data=matrix_data,columns=column_headings)
    ```

2. Run the following code to view only the first five rows of the DataFrame:

    ```
    df.head()
    ```

    The sample output is as follows (note that your output could be different due to randomness):

	W	X	Y	Z
0	70	96	7	77
1	96	73	15	74
2	50	52	61	33
3	62	4	10	37
4	3	54	59	8

    Figure 3.1: First five rows of the DataFrame

By default, **head** shows only five rows. If you want to see any specific number of rows just pass that as an argument.

3. Print the first eight rows by using the following command:

```
df.head(8)
```

The sample output is as follows:

	W	X	Y	Z
0	70	96	7	77
1	96	73	15	74
2	50	52	61	33
3	62	4	10	37
4	3	54	59	8
5	49	57	41	94
6	21	24	48	23
7	7	2	53	2

Figure 3.2: First eight rows of the DataFrame

Just like **head** shows the first few rows, **tail** shows the last few rows.

4. Print the DataFrame using the **tail** command, as follows:

```
df.tail(10)
```

The sample output is as follows:

	W	X	Y	Z
17	27	21	88	63
18	58	50	35	66
19	50	77	14	10
20	29	54	68	26
21	13	61	89	84
22	11	37	42	16
23	83	22	12	43
24	13	58	13	27

Figure 3.3: Last ten rows of the DataFrame

Indexing and Slicing Columns

There are two methods for indexing and slicing columns from a DataFrame. They are as follows:

- **DOT method**
- **Bracket method**

The DOT method is good to find specific element. The bracket method is intuitive and easy to follow. In this method, you can access the data by the generic name/header of the column.

The following code illustrates these concepts. Execute them in your Jupyter notebook:

```
print("\nThe 'X' column\n",'-'*25, sep='')

print(df['X'])

print("\nType of the column: ", type(df['X']), sep='')

print("\nThe 'X' and 'Z' columns indexed by passing a list\n",'-'*55, sep='')

print(df[['X','Z']])

print("\nType of the pair of columns: ", type(df[['X','Z']]), sep='')
```

The output is as follows (a screenshot is shown here because the actual column is long):

```
The 'X' column
-------------------------
0       60
1       48
2       13
3       33
4        6
5       49
6       43
7       48
```

Figure 3.4: Rows of the 'X' columns

This is the output showing the type of column:

```
Type of the column: <class 'pandas.core.series.Series'>
```

Figure 3.5: Type of 'X' column

This is the output showing the X and Z column indexed by passing a list:

```
The 'X' and 'Z' columns indexed by passing a list
-----------------------------------------------------
     X    Z
0   60   53
1   48    9
2   13   53
3   33   61
4    6   40
5   49   74
6   43   41
7   48   22
```

Figure 3.6: Rows of the 'Y' columns

This is the output showing the type of the pair of column:

```
Type of the pair of columns: <class 'pandas.core.frame.DataFrame'>
```

Figure 3.7: Type of 'Y' column

Note

For more than one column, the object turns into a DataFrame. But for a single column, it is a pandas series object.

Indexing and Slicing Rows

Indexing and slicing rows in a DataFrame can also be done using following methods:

- **Label-based 'loc' method**
- **Index based 'iloc' method**

The **loc** method is intuitive and easy to follow. In this method, you can access the data by the generic name of the row. On the other hand, the **iloc** method allows you to access the rows by their numerical index. It can be very useful for a large table with thousands of rows, especially when you want to iterate over the table in a loop with a numerical counter. The following code illustrate the concepts of **iloc**:

```
matrix_data = np.random.randint(1,10,size=20).reshape(5,4)

row_labels = ['A','B','C','D','E']

column_headings = ['W','X','Y','Z']


df = pd.DataFrame(data=matrix_data, index=row_labels,
                      columns=column_headings)


print("\nLabel-based 'loc' method for selecting row(s)\n",'-'*60, sep='')

print("\nSingle row\n")

print(df.loc['C'])

print("\nMultiple rows\n")

print(df.loc[['B','C']])

print("\nIndex position based 'iloc' method for selecting row(s)\n",'-'*70, sep='')

print("\nSingle row\n")

print(df.iloc[2])

print("\nMultiple rows\n")

print(df.iloc[[1,2]])
```

The sample output is as follows:

```
Label-based 'loc' method can be used for selecting row(s)
-----------------------------------------------------------

Single row

W    8
X    7
Y    9
Z    3
Name: C, dtype: int32

Multiple rows

   W  X  Y  Z
B  2  1  7  9
C  8  7  9  3

Index position based 'iloc' method can be used for selecting row(s)
-----------------------------------------------------------

Single row

W    8
X    7
Y    9
Z    3
Name: C, dtype: int32

Multiple rows

   W  X  Y  Z
B  2  1  7  9
C  8  7  9  3
```

Figure 3.8: Output of the loc and iloc methods

Exercise 41: Creating and Deleting a New Column or Row

One of the most common tasks in data wrangling is creating or deleting columns or rows of data from your DataFrame. Sometimes, you want to create a new column based on some mathematical operation or transformation involving the existing columns. This is similar to manipulating database records and inserting a new column based on simple transformations. We show some of these concepts in the following code blocks:

1. Create a new column using the following snippet:

```
print("\nA column is created by assigning it in relation\n",'-'*75, sep='')
df['New'] = df['X']+df['Z']
df['New (Sum of X and Z)'] = df['X']+df['Z']
print(df)
```

The sample output is as follows:

```
A column is created by assigning it in relation to an existing column
------------------------------------------------------------------------
    W  X  Y  Z  New  New (Sum of X and Z)
A   2  1  7  1   2                    2
B   4  2  2  3   5                    5
C   9  2  3  6   8                    8
D   5  5  2  5  10                   10
E   7  8  4  9  17                   17
```

Figure 3.9: Output after adding a new column

2. Drop a column using the **df.drop** method:

```
print("\nA column is dropped by using df.drop() method\n",'-'*55, sep='')
df = df.drop('New', axis=1) # Notice the axis=1 option, axis = 0 is
#default, so one has to change it to 1
print(df)
```

The sample output is as follows:

```
A column is dropped by using df.drop() method
------------------------------------------------------------
    W   X   Y   Z   New (Sum of X and Z)
A   2   1   7   1                      2
B   4   2   2   3                      5
C   9   2   3   6                      8
D   5   5   2   5                     10
E   7   8   4   9                     17
```

Figure 3.10: Output after dropping a column

3. Drop a specific row using the **df.drop** method:

```
df1=df.drop('A')
print("\nA row is dropped by using df.drop method and axis=0\n",'-'*65,
sep='')
print(df1)
```

The sample output is as follows:

```
A row (index) is dropped by using df.drop() method and axis=0
------------------------------------------------------------------
    W   X   Y   Z   New (Sum of X and Z)
B   4   2   2   3                      5
C   9   2   3   6                      8
D   5   5   2   5                     10
E   7   8   4   9                     17
```

Figure 3.11: Output after dropping a row

Dropping methods creates a copy of the DataFrame and does not change the original DataFrame.

4. Change the original DataFrame by setting the **inplace** argument to **True**:

```
print("\nAn in-place change can be done by making inplace=True in the drop
method\n",'-'*75, sep='')
df.drop('New (Sum of X and Z)', axis=1, inplace=True)
print(df)
```

A sample output is as follows:

```
An in-place change can be done by making inplace=True in the drop method
---------------------------------------------------------------------------
   W  X  Y  Z
A  2  1  7  1
B  4  2  2  3
C  9  2  3  6
D  5  5  2  5
E  7  8  4  9
```

Figure 3.12: Output after using the inplace argument

> **Note**
>
> All the normal operations are not in-place, that is, they do not impact the original DataFrame object but return a copy of the original with addition (or deletion). The last bit of code shows how to make a change in the existing DataFrame with the **inplace=True** argument. Please note that this change is irreversible and should be used with caution.

Statistics and Visualization with NumPy and Pandas

One of the great advantages of using libraries such as NumPy and pandas is that a plethora of built-in statistical and visualization methods are available, for which we don't have to search for and write new code. Furthermore, most of these subroutines are written using C or Fortran code (and pre-compiled), making them extremely fast to execute.

Refresher of Basic Descriptive Statistics (and the Matplotlib Library for Visualization)

For any data wrangling task, it is quite useful to extract basic descriptive statistics from the data and create some simple visualizations/plots. These plots are often the first step in identifying fundamental patterns as well as oddities (if present) in the data. In any statistical analysis, descriptive statistics is the first step, followed by inferential statistics, which tries to infer the underlying distribution or process from which the data might have been generated.

As the inferential statistics are intimately coupled with the machine learning/predictive modeling stage of a data science pipeline, descriptive statistics naturally becomes associated with the data wrangling aspect.

There are two broad approaches for descriptive statistical analysis:

- Graphical techniques: Bar plots, scatter plots, line charts, box plots, histograms, and so on

- Calculation of central tendency and spread: Mean, median, mode, variance, standard deviation, range, and so on

In this topic, we will demonstrate how you can accomplish both of these tasks using Python. Apart from NumPy and pandas, we will need to learn the basics of another great package – **matplotlib** – which is the most powerful and versatile visualization library in Python.

Exercise 42: Introduction to Matplotlib Through a Scatter Plot

In this exercise, we will demonstrate the power and simplicity of matplotlib by creating a simple scatter plot from some data about the age, weight, and height of a few people:

1. First, we define simple lists of names, age, weight (in kgs), and height (in centimeters):

```
people = ['Ann','Brandon','Chen','David','Emily','Farook',
          'Gagan','Hamish','Imran','Joseph','Katherine','Lily']
age = [21,12,32,45,37,18,28,52,5,40,48,15]
weight = [55,35,77,68,70,60,72,69,18,65,82,48]
height = [160,135,170,165,173,168,175,159,105,171,155,158]
```

2. Import the most important module from matplotlib, called **pyplot**:

    ```
    import matplotlib.pyplot as plt
    ```

3. Create simple scatter plots of age versus weight:

    ```
    plt.scatter(age,weight)
    plt.show()
    ```

    The output is as follows:

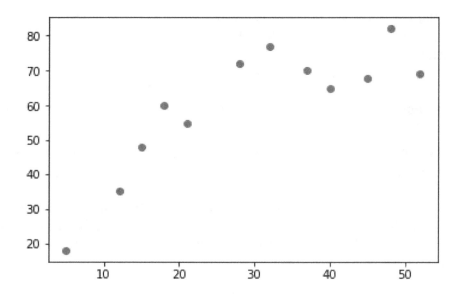

Figure 3.13: A screenshot of a scatter plot containing age and weight

The plot can be improved by enlarging the figure size, customizing the aspect ratio, adding a title with a proper font size, adding X-axis and Y-axis labels with a customized font size, adding grid lines, changing the Y-axis limit to be between 0 and 100, adding X and Y-tick marks, customizing the scatter plot's color, and changing the size of the scatter dots.

4. The code for the improved plot is as follows:

```
plt.figure(figsize=(8,6))
plt.title("Plot of Age vs. Weight (in kgs)",fontsize=20)
plt.xlabel("Age (years)",fontsize=16)
plt.ylabel("Weight (kgs)",fontsize=16)
plt.grid (True)
plt.ylim(0,100)
plt.xticks([i*5 for i in range(12)],fontsize=15)
plt.yticks(fontsize=15)
plt.scatter(x=age,y=weight,c='orange',s=150,edgecolors='k')
plt.text(x=20,y=85,s="Weights after 18-20 years of age",fontsize=15)
plt.vlines(x=20,ymin=0,ymax=80,linestyles='dashed',color='blue',lw=3)
plt.legend(['Weight in kgs'],loc=2,fontsize=12)
plt.show()
```

The output is as follows:

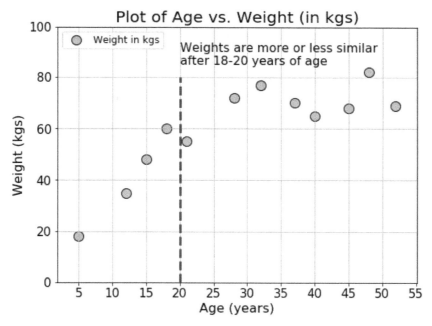

Figure 3.14: A screenshot of a scatter plot showing age versus weight

Observe the following:

- A `tuple (8,6)` is passed as an argument for the figure size.

- A list comprehension is used inside `Xticks` to create a customized list of 5-10-15-...-55.

- A newline (`\n`) character is used inside the `plt.text()` function to break up and distribute the text in two lines.

- The `plt.show()` function is used at the very end. The idea is to keep on adding various graphics properties (font, color, axis limits, text, legend, grid, and so on) until you are satisfied and then show the plot with one function. The plot will not be displayed without this last function call.

Definition of Statistical Measures – Central Tendency and Spread

A measure of central tendency is a single value that attempts to describe a set of data by identifying the central position within that set of data. They are also categorized as summary statistics:

- **Mean**: Mean is the sum of all values divided by the total number of values.

- **Median**: The median is the middle value. It is the value that splits the dataset in half. To find the median, order your data from smallest to largest, and then find the data point that has an equal amount of values above it and below it.

- **Mode**: The mode is the value that occurs the most frequently in your dataset. On a bar chart, the mode is the highest bar.

Generally, the mean is a better measure to use for symmetric data and median is a better measure for data with a skewed (left or right heavy) distribution. For categorical data, you have to use the mode:

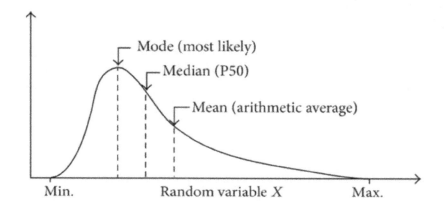

Figure 3.15: A screenshot of a curve showing the mean, median, and mode

The spread of the data is a measure of by how much the values in the dataset are likely to differ from the mean of the values. If all the values are close together then the spread is low; on the other hand, if some or all of the values differ by a large amount from the mean (and each other), then there is a large spread in the data:

- **Variance**: This is the most common measure of spread. Variance is the average of the squares of the deviations from the mean. Squaring the deviations ensures that negative and positive deviations do not cancel each other out.

- **Standard Deviation**: Because variance is produced by squaring the distance from the mean, its unit does not match that of the original data. Standard deviation is a mathematical trick to bring back the parity. It is the positive square root of the variance.

Random Variables and Probability Distribution

A **random variable** is defined as the value of a given variable that represents the outcome of a statistical experiment or process.

Although it sounds very formal, pretty much everything around us that we can measure can be thought of as a random variable.

The reason behind this is that almost all natural, social, biological, and physical processes are the final outcome of a large number of complex processes, and we cannot know the details of those fundamental processes. All we can do is observe and measure the final outcome.

Typical examples of random variables that are around us are as follows:

- The economic output of a nation
- The blood pressure of a patient
- The temperature of a chemical process in a factory
- Number of friends of a person on Facebook
- The stock market price of a company

These values can take any discrete or continuous value and they follow a particular pattern (although the pattern may vary over time). Therefore, they can all be classified as random variables.

What Is a Probability Distribution?

A **probability distribution** is a function that describes the likelihood of obtaining the possible values that a random variable can assume. In other words, the values of a variable vary based on the underlying probability distribution.

Suppose you go to a school and measure the heights of students who have been selected randomly. Height is an example of a random variable here. As you measure height, you can create a distribution of height. This type of distribution is useful when you need to know which outcomes are most likely, the spread of potential values, and the likelihood of different results.

The concepts of central tendency and spread are applicable to a distribution and are used to describe the properties and behavior of a distribution.

Statisticians generally divide all distributions into two broad categories:

- Discrete distributions
- Continuous distributions

Discrete Distributions

Discrete probability functions are also known as **probability mass functions** and can assume a discrete number of values. For example, coin tosses and counts of events are discrete functions. You can have only heads or tails in a coin toss. Similarly, if you're counting the number of trains that arrive at a station per hour, you can count 11 or 12 trains, but nothing in-between.

Some prominent discrete distributions are as follows:

- **Binomial distribution** to model binary data, such as coin tosses
- **Poisson distribution** to model count data, such as the count of library book checkouts per hour
- **Uniform distribution** to model multiple events with the same probability, such as rolling a die

Continuous Distributions

Continuous probability functions are also known as **probability density functions**. You have a continuous distribution if the variable can assume an infinite number of values between any two values. Continuous variables are often measurements on a real number scale, such as height, weight, and temperature.

The most well-known continuous distribution is the **normal distribution**, which is also known as the **Gaussian distribution** or the **bell curve**. This symmetric distribution fits a wide variety of phenomena, such as human height and IQ scores.

The normal distribution is linked to the famous **68-95-99.7 rule**, which describes the percentage of data that falls within 1, 2, or 3 standard deviations away from the mean if the data follows a normal distribution. This means that you can quickly look at some sample data, calculate the mean and standard deviation, and can have a confidence (a statistical measure of uncertainty) that any future incoming data will fall within those 68%-95%-99.7% boundaries. This rule is widely used in industries, medicine, economics, and social science:

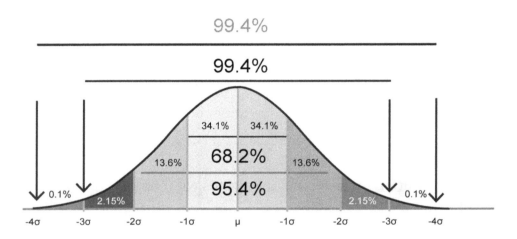

Figure 3.16: Curve showing the normal distribution of the famous 68-95-99.7 rule

Data Wrangling in Statistics and Visualization

A good data wrangling professional is expected to encounter a dizzying array of diverse data sources each day. As we explained previously, due to a multitude of complex sub-processes and mutual interactions that give rise to such data, they all fall into the category of discrete or continuous random variables.

It will be extremely difficult and confusing to the data wrangler or data science team if all of this data continues to be treated as completely random and without any shape or pattern. A formal statistical basis must be given to such random data streams, and one of the simplest ways to start that process is to measure their descriptive statistics.

Assigning a stream of data to a particular distribution function (or a combination of many distributions) is actually part of **inferential statistics**. However, inferential statistics starts only when descriptive statistics is done alongside measuring all the important parameters of the pattern of the data.

Therefore, as the front line of a data science pipeline, data wrangling must deal with measuring and quantifying such descriptive statistics of the incoming data. Along with the formatted and cleaned-up data, the primary job of a data wrangler is to hand over these measures (and sometimes accompanying plots) to the next team member of analytics.

Plotting and **visualization** also help a data wrangling team identify potential outliers and misfits in the incoming data stream and help them to take appropriate action. We will see some examples of such tasks in the next chapter, where we will identify odd data points by creating scatter plots or histograms and either impute or omit the data point.

Using NumPy and Pandas to Calculate Basic Descriptive Statistics on the DataFrame

Now that we have some basic knowledge of NumPy, pandas, and matplotlib under our belt, we can explore a few additional topics related to these libraries, such as how we can bring them together for advanced data generation, analysis, and visualization.

Random Number Generation Using NumPy

NumPy offers a dizzying array of random number generation utility functions, all of which correspond to various statistical distributions, such as uniform, binomial, Gaussian normal, Beta/Gamma, and chi-square. Most of these functions are extremely useful and appear countless times in advanced statistical data mining and machine learning tasks. Having a solid knowledge of them is strongly encouraged for all the students taking this book.

Here, we will discuss three of the most important distributions that may come in handy for data wrangling tasks – uniform, binomial, and gaussian normal. The goal here is to show an example of simple function calls that can generate one or more random numbers/arrays whenever the user needs them.

> **Note**
>
> The results will be different for each student when they use these functions as they are supposed to be random.

Exercise 43: Generating Random Numbers from a Uniform Distribution

In this exercise, we will be generating random numbers from a uniform distribution:

1. Generate a random integer between 1 and **10**:

    ```
    x = np.random.randint(1,10)
    print(x)
    ```

    The sample output is as follows (your output could be different):

    ```
    1
    ```

2. Generate a random integer between 1 and 10 but with size=1 as an argument. It generates a NumPy array of size 1:

    ```
    x = np.random.randint(1,10,size=1)
    print(x)
    ```

    The sample output is as follows (your output could be different due to random draw):

    ```
    [8]
    ```

    Therefore, we can easily write the code to generate the outcome of a dice being thrown (a normal 6-sided dice) for 10 trials.

    How about moving away from the integers and generating some real numbers? Let's say that we want to generate artificial data for weights (in kgs) of 20 adults and we can measure the accurate weights up to two decimal places.

3. Generate decimal data using the following command:

    ```
    x = 50+50*np.random.random(size=15)
    x= x.round(decimals=2)
    print(x)
    ```

    The sample output is as follows:

    ```
    [56.24 94.67 50.66 94.36 77.37 53.81 61.47 71.13 59.3  65.3  63.02 65.
     58.21 81.21 91.62]
    ```

    We are not only restricted to one-dimensional arrays.

4. Generate and show a 3x3 matrix with random numbers between 0 and 1:

```
x = np.random.rand(3,3)
print(x)
```

The sample output is as follows (note that your specific output could be different due to randomness):

```
[[0.99240105 0.9149215  0.04853315]
 [0.8425871  0.11617792 0.77983995]
 [0.82769081 0.57579771 0.11358125]]
```

Exercise 44: Generating Random Numbers from a Binomial Distribution and Bar Plot

A binomial distribution is the probability distribution of getting a specific number of successes in a specific number of trials of an event with a pre-determined chance or probability.

The most obvious example of this is a coin toss. A fair coin may have an equal chance of heads or tails, but an unfair coin may have more chances of the head coming up or vice versa. We can simulate a coin toss in NumPy in the following manner.

Suppose we have a biased coin where the probability of heads is 0.6. We toss this coin ten times and note down the number of heads turning up each time. That is one trial or experiment. Now, we can repeat this experiment (10 coin tosses) any number of times, say 8 times. Each time, we record the number of heads:

1. The experiment can be simulated using the following code:

```
x = np.random.binomial(10,0.6,size=8)
print(x)
```

The sample output is as follows (note your specific output could be different due to randomness):

```
[6 6 5 6 5 8 4 5]
```

2. Plot the result using a bar chart:

```
plt.figure(figsize=(7,4))
plt.title("Number of successes in coin toss",fontsize=16)
plt.bar(left=np.arange(1,9),height=x)
plt.xlabel("Experiment number",fontsize=15)
plt.ylabel("Number of successes",fontsize=15)
plt.show()
```

The sample output is as follows:

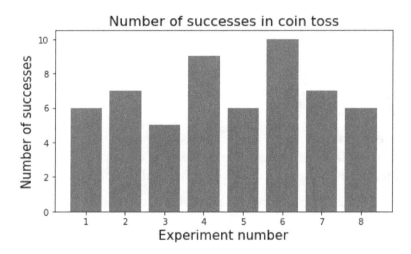

Figure 3.17: A screenshot of a graph showing the binomial distribution and the bar plot

Exercise 45: Generating Random Numbers from Normal Distribution and Histograms

We discussed the normal distribution in the last topic and mentioned that it is the most important probability distribution because many pieces of natural, social, and biological data follow this pattern closely when the number of samples is large. NumPy provides an easy way to generate random numbers corresponding to this distribution:

1. Draw a single sample from a normal distribution by using the following command:

```
x = np.random.normal()
print(x)
```

The sample output is as follows (note that your specific output could be different due to randomness):

```
-1.2423774071573694
```

We know that normal distribution is characterized by two parameters – mean (μ) and standard deviation (σ). In fact, the default values for this particular function are $\mu = 0.0$ and $\sigma = 1.0$.

Suppose we know that the heights of the teenage (12-16 years) students in a particular school is distributed normally with a mean height of 155 cm and a standard deviation of 10 cm.

2. Generate a histogram of 100 students by using the following command:

```
# Code to generate the 100 samples (heights)
heights = np.random.normal(loc=155,scale=10,size=100)
# Plotting code
#-----------------------
plt.figure(figsize=(7,5))
plt.hist(heights,color='orange',edgecolor='k')
plt.title("Histogram of teen aged students's height",fontsize=18)
plt.xlabel("Height in cm",fontsize=15)
plt.xticks(fontsize=15)
plt.yticks(fontsize=15)
plt.show()
```

The sample output is as follows:

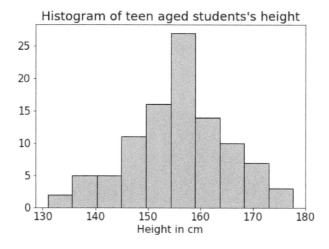

Figure 3.18: Histogram of teenage student's height

Note the use of the **loc** parameter for the mean (=155) and the **scale** parameter for standard deviation (=10). The size parameter is set to 100 for that may samples' generation.

Exercise 46: Calculation of Descriptive Statistics from a DataFrame

Recollect the **age**, **weight**, and **height** parameters that we defined for the plotting exercise. Let's put that data in a DataFrame to calculate various descriptive statistics about them.

The best part of working with a pandas DataFrame is that it has a built-in utility function to show all of these descriptive statistics with a single line of code. It does this by using the **describe** method:

1. Construct a dictionary with the available series data by using the following command:

    ```
    people_dict={'People':people,'Age':age,'Weight':weight,'Height':height}
    people_df=pd.DataFrame(data=people_dict)
    people_df
    ```

    The output is as follows:

	People	Age	Weight	Height
0	Ann	21	55	160
1	Brandon	12	35	135
2	Chen	32	77	170
3	David	45	68	165
4	Emily	37	70	173
5	Farook	18	60	168
6	Gagan	28	72	175
7	Hamish	52	69	159
8	Imran	5	18	105
9	Joseph	40	65	171
10	Katherine	48	82	155
11	Lily	15	48	158

    Figure 3.19: Output of the created dictionary

2. Find the number of rows and columns of the DataFrame by executing the following command:

    ```
    print(people_df.shape)
    ```

    The output is as follows:

    ```
    (12, 4)
    ```

3. Obtain a simple **count** (any column can be used for this purpose) by executing the following command:

    ```
    print(people_df['Age'].count())
    ```

    The output is as follows:

    ```
    12
    ```

4. Calculate the **sum** total of age by using the following command:

    ```
    print(people_df['Age'].sum())
    ```

    The output is as follows:

    ```
    353
    ```

5. Calculate the **mean** age by using the following command:

    ```
    print(people_df['Age'].mean())
    ```

    The output is as follows:

    ```
    29.416666666666668
    ```

6. Calculate the **median** weight by using the following command:

    ```
    print(people_df['Weight'].median())
    ```

    The output is as follows:

    ```
    66.5
    ```

7. Calculate the **maximum** height by using the following command:

    ```
    print(people_df['Height'].max())
    ```

    The output is as follows:

    ```
    175
    ```

8. Calculate the **standard deviation** of the weights by using the following command:

```
print(people_df['Weight'].std())
```

The output is as follows:

```
18.45120510148239
```

Note how we are calling the statistical functions directly from a DataFrame object.

9. To calculate **percentile**, we can call a function from NumPy and pass on the particular column (a pandas series). For example, to calculate the 75th and 25th percentiles of age distribution and their difference (called the inter-quartile range), use the following code:

```
pcnt_75 = np.percentile(people_df['Age'],75)
pcnt_25 = np.percentile(people_df['Age'],25)
print("Inter-quartile range: ",pcnt_75-pcnt_25)
```

The output is as follows:

```
Inter-quartile range:   24.0
```

10. Use the **describe** command to find a detailed description of the DataFrame:

```
print(people_df.describe())
```

The output is as follows:

```
              Age         Height       Weight
count   12.000000    12.000000    12.000000
mean    29.416667   157.833333    59.916667
std     15.329463    19.834925    18.451205
min      5.000000   105.000000    18.000000
25%     17.250000   157.250000    53.250000
50%     30.000000   162.500000    66.500000
75%     41.250000   170.250000    70.500000
max     52.000000   175.000000    82.000000
```

Figure 3.20: Output of the DataFrame using the describe method

Note

This function works only on the columns where numeric data is present. It has no impact on the non-numeric columns, for example, People in this DataFrame.

Exercise 47: Built-in Plotting Utilities

DataFrame also has built-in plotting utilities that wrap around matplotlib functions and create basic plots of numeric data:

1. Find the histogram of the weights by using the **hist** function:

```
people_df['Weight'].hist()
plt.show()
```

The output is as follows:

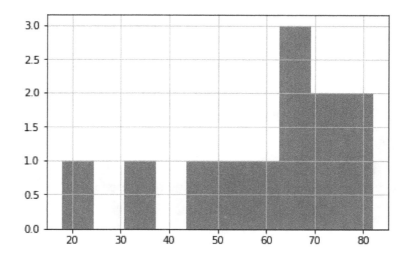

Figure 3.21: Histogram of the weights

2. Create a simple scatter plot directly from the DataFrame to plot the relationship between weight and heights by using the following command:

```
people_df.plot.scatter('Weight','Height',s=150,
c='orange',edgecolor='k')
plt.grid(True)
plt.title("Weight vs. Height scatter plot",fontsize=18)
plt.xlabel("Weight (in kg)",fontsize=15)
plt.ylabel("Height (in cm)",fontsize=15)
plt.show()
```

The output is as follows:

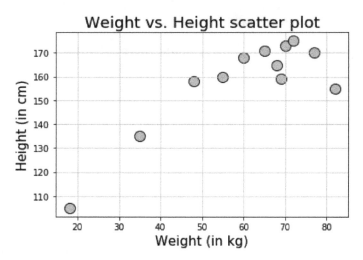

Figure 3.22: Weight versus Height scatter plot

> **Note**
>
> You can try regular matplotlib methods around this function call to make your plot pretty.

Activity 5: Generating Statistics from a CSV File

Suppose you are working with the famous Boston housing price (from 1960) dataset. This dataset is famous in the machine learning community. Many regression problems can be formulated, and machine learning algorithms can be run on this dataset. You will do perform a basic data wrangling activity (including plotting some trends) on this dataset by reading it as a pandas DataFrame.

> **Note**
>
> The pandas function for reading a CSV file is **read_csv**.

These steps will help you complete this activity:

1. Load the necessary libraries.

2. Read in the Boston housing dataset (given as a `.csv` file) from the local directory.

3. Check the first 10 records. Find the total number of records.

4. Create a smaller DataFrame with columns that do not include **CHAS**, **NOX**, **B**, and **LSTAT**.

5. Check the last seven records of the new DataFrame you just created.

6. Plot the histograms of all the variables (columns) in the new DataFrame.

7. Plot them all at once using a **for** loop. Try to add a unique title to a plot.

8. Create a scatter plot of crime rate versus price.

9. Plot using **log10(crime)** versus **price**.

10. Calculate some useful statistics, such as mean rooms per dwelling, median age, mean distances to five Boston employment centers, and the percentage of houses with a low price (< $20,000).

> **Note**
>
> The solution for this activity can be found on page 292.

Summary

In this chapter, we started with the basics of NumPy arrays, including how to create them and their essential properties. We discussed and showed how a NumPy array is optimized for vectorized element-wise operations and differs from a regular Python list. Then, we moved on to practicing various operations on NumPy arrays such as indexing, slicing, filtering, and reshaping. We also covered special one-dimensional and two-dimensional arrays, such as zeros, ones, identity matrices, and random arrays.

In the second major topic of this chapter, we started with pandas series objects and quickly moved on to a critically important object – pandas DataFrames. It is analogous to Excel or MATLAB or a database tab, but with many useful properties for data wrangling. We demonstrated some basic operations on DataFrames, such as indexing, subsetting, row and column addition, and deletion.

Next, we covered the basics of plotting with matplotlib, the most widely used and popular Python library for visualization. Along with plotting exercises, we touched upon refresher concepts of descriptive statistics (such as central tendency and measure of spread) and probability distributions (such as uniform, binomial, and normal).

In the next chapter, we will cover more advanced operation with pandas DataFrames that will come in very handy for day-to-day working in a data wrangling job.

A Deep Dive into Data Wrangling with Python

Learning Objectives

By the end of this chapter, you will be able to:

- Perform subsetting, filtering, and grouping on pandas DataFrames

- Apply Boolean filtering and indexing from a DataFrame to choose specific elements

- Perform JOIN operations in pandas that are analogous to the SQL command

- Identify missing or corrupted data and choose to drop or apply imputation techniques on missing or corrupted data

In this chapter, we will learn about pandas DataFrames in detail.

Introduction

In this chapter, we will learn about several advanced operations involving pandas DataFrames and NumPy arrays. On completing the detailed activity for this chapter, you will have handled real-life datasets and understood the process of data wrangling.

Subsetting, Filtering, and Grouping

One of the most important aspects of data wrangling is to curate the data carefully from the deluge of streaming data that pours into an organization or business entity from various sources. Lots of data is not always a good thing; rather, data needs to be useful and of high-quality to be effectively used in downstream activities of a data science pipeline such as machine learning and predictive model building. Moreover, one data source can be used for multiple purposes and this often requires different subsets of data to be processed by a data wrangling module. This is then passed on to separate analytics modules.

For example, let's say you are doing data wrangling on US State level economic output. It is a fairly common scenario that one machine learning model may require data for large and populous states (such as California, Texas, and so on), while another model demands processed data for small and sparsely populated states (such as Montana or North Dakota). As the frontline of the data science process, it is the responsibility of the data wrangling module to satisfy the requirements of both these machine learning models. Therefore, as a data wrangling engineer, you have to filter and group data accordingly (based on the population of the state) before processing them and producing separate datasets as the final output for separate machine learning models.

Also, in some cases, data sources may be biased, or the measurement may corrupt the incoming data occasionally. It is a good idea to try to filter only the error-free, good data for downstream modeling. From these examples and discussions, it is clear that filtering and grouping/bucketing data is an essential skill to have for any engineer that's engaged in the task of data wrangling. Let's proceed to learn about a few of these skills with pandas.

Exercise 48: Loading and Examining a Superstore's Sales Data from an Excel File

In this exercise, we will load and examine an Excel file.

1. To read an Excel file into pandas, you will need a small package called **xlrd** to be installed on your system. If you are working from inside this book's Docker container, then this package may not be available next time you start your container, and you have to follow the same step. Use the following code to install the xlrd package:

```
!pip install xlrd
```

2. Load the Excel file from GitHub by using the simple pandas method **read_excel**:

```
import numpy as np
import pandas as pd
import matplotlib.pyplot as plt
df = pd.read_excel("Sample - Superstore.xls")
df.head()
```

Examine all the columns and check if they are useful for analysis:

	Row ID	Order ID	Order Date	Ship Date	Ship Mode	Customer ID	Customer Name	Segment	Country	
0	1	CA-2016-152156	2016-11-08	2016-11-11	Second Class	CG-12520	Knox Ware	Consumer	United States	H
1	2	CA-2016-152156	2016-11-08	2016-11-11	Second Class	CG-12520	Phoebe Riley	Consumer	United States	H
2	3	CA-2016-138688	2016-06-12	2016-06-16	Second Class	DV-13045	Lareina Ballard	Corporate	United States	

Figure 4.1 Output of the Excel file in a DataFrame

On examining the file, we can see that the first column, called **Row ID**, is not very useful.

3. Drop this column altogether from the DataFrame by using the **drop** method:

```
df.drop('Row ID',axis=1,inplace=True)
```

4. Check the number of rows and columns in the newly created dataset. We will use the **shape** function here:

```
df.shape
```

The output is as follows:

```
(9994, 20)
```

We can see that the dataset has 9,994 rows and 20 columns.

Subsetting the DataFrame

Subsetting involves the extraction of partial data based on specific columns and rows, as per business needs. Suppose we are interested only in the following information from this dataset: Customer ID, Customer Name, City, Postal Code, and Sales. For demonstration purposes, let's assume that we are only interested in 5 records – rows 5-9. We can subset the DataFrame to extract only this much information using a single line of Python code.

Use the **loc** method to index the dataset by name of the columns and index of the rows:

```
df_subset = df.loc[
    [i for i in range(5,10)],
    ['Customer ID','Customer Name','City','Postal Code',
    'Sales']]
df_subset
```

The output is as follows:

	Customer ID	Customer Name	City	Postal Code	Sales
5	PG-18895	Noel Craig	Rochester	55901	19.990
6	RB-19465	Scott Hampton	Chicago	60610	95.976
7	LC-16870	Blythe Blake	Aurora	80013	238.896
8	JM-15250	Herrod Rodriguez	Charlotte	28205	74.112
9	PA-19060	Knox Summers	Orland Park	60462	339.960

Figure 4.2: DataFrame indexed by name of the columns

We need to pass on two arguments to the `loc` method – one for indicating the rows, and another for indicating the columns. These should be Python lists.

For the rows, we have to pass a list [5,6,7,8,9], but instead of writing that explicitly, we use a list comprehension, that is, `[i for i in range(5,10)]`.

Because the columns we are interested in are not contiguous, we cannot just put a continuous range and need to pass on a list containing the specific names. So, the second argument is just a simple list with specific column names.

The dataset shows the fundamental concepts of the process of subsetting a DataFrame based on business requirements.

An Example Use Case: Determining Statistics on Sales and Profit

This quick section shows a typical use case of subsetting. Suppose we want to calculate descriptive statistics (mean, median, standard deviation, and so on) of records 100-199 for sales and profit. This is how subsetting helps us to achieve that:

```
df_subset = df.loc[[i for i in range(100,200)],['Sales','Profit']]

df_subset.describe()
```

The output is as follows:

	Sales	Profit
count	100.00000	100.000000
mean	210.26862	46.104325
std	273.03642	85.869636
min	13.61600	-55.300000
25%	69.69000	10.329000
50%	115.37700	28.192650
75%	248.82750	52.953300
max	1619.91000	601.969900

Figure 4.3 Output of descriptive statistics of data

Furthermore, we can create boxplots of sales and profit figures from this final data.

We simply extract records 100-199 and run the **describe** function on it because we don't want to process all the data! For this particular business question, we are only interested in sales and profit numbers and therefore we should not take the easy route and run a describe function on all the data. For a real-life dataset, the number of rows and columns could often be in the millions, and we don't want to compute anything that is not asked for in the data wrangling task. We always aim to subset the exact data that is needed to be processed and run statistical or plotting functions on that partial data:

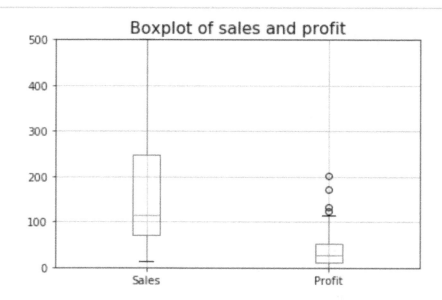

Figure 4.4: Boxplot of sales and profit

Exercise 49: The unique Function

Before continuing further with filtering methods, let's take a quick detour and explore a super useful function called **unique**. As the name suggests, this function is used to scan through the data quickly and extract only the unique values in a column or row.

After loading the superstore sales data, you will notice that there are columns like "Country", "State", and "City". A natural question will be to ask how many countries/states/cities are present in the dataset:

1. Extract the countries/states/cities for which the information is in the database, with one simple line of code, as follows:

```
df['State'].unique()
```

The output is as follows:

```
array(['California', 'Minnesota', 'Delaware', 'New York', 'Illinois',
       'Colorado', 'North Carolina', 'Pennsylvania', 'Louisiana', 'Texas',
       'Ohio', 'Florida', 'Oregon', 'Arizona', 'Michigan', 'Oklahoma',
       'Washington', 'Missouri', 'Wisconsin', 'Indiana', 'Mississippi',
       'Nebraska', 'New Jersey', 'New Hampshire', 'New Mexico', 'Georgia',
       'Maryland', 'Nevada', 'Virginia', 'Alabama', 'Vermont',
       'South Dakota', 'Massachusetts', 'Rhode Island', 'Arkansas',
       'Kentucky', 'Kansas', 'South Carolina', 'Utah', 'Maine',
       'Connecticut', 'Tennessee', 'Montana', 'Idaho', 'Iowa',
       'District of Columbia', 'North Dakota', 'West Virginia', 'Wyoming'],
      dtype=object)
```

Figure 4.5: Different states present in the dataset

You will see a list of all the states whose data is present in the dataset.

2. Use the **nunique** method to count the number of unique values, like so:

```
df['State'].nunique()
```

The output is as follows:

```
49
```

This returns 49 for this dataset. So, one out of 50 states in the US does not appear in this dataset.

Similarly, if we run this function on the Country column, we get an array with only one element, **United States**. Immediately, we can see that we don't need to keep the country column at all, because there is no useful information in that column except that all the entries are the same. This is how a simple function helped us to decide about dropping a column altogether – that is, removing 9,994 pieces of unnecessary data!

Conditional Selection and Boolean Filtering

Often, we don't want to process the whole dataset and would like to select only a partial dataset whose contents satisfy a particular condition. This is probably the most common use case of any data wrangling task.

In the context of our superstore sales dataset, think of these common questions that may arise from the daily activity of the business analytics team:

- What are the average sales and profit figures in California?

- Which states have the highest and lowest total sales?

- What consumer segment has the most variance in sales/profit?

- Among the top 5 states in sales, which shipping mode and product category are the most popular choices?

Countless examples can be given where the business analytics team or the executive management want to glean insight from a particular subset of data that meet certain criteria.

If you have any prior experience with SQL, you will know that these kinds of questions require fairly complex SQL query writing. Remember the WHERE clause?

We will show you how to use conditional subsetting and Boolean filtering to answer such questions.

First, we need to understand the critical concept of boolean indexing. This process essentially accepts a conditional expression as an argument and returns a dataset of booleans in which the **TRUE** value appears in places where the condition was satisfied. A simple example is shown in the following code. For demonstration purposes, we subset a small dataset of 10 records and 3 columns:

```
df_subset = df.loc[[i for i in range (10)],['Ship Mode','State','Sales']]

df_subset
```

The output is as follows:

	Ship Mode	State	Sales
0	Second Class	California	90.570
1	First Class	Minnesota	45.980
2	Standard Class	Delaware	45.000
3	First Class	New York	30.000
4	Standard Class	California	13.980
5	Standard Class	Minnesota	19.990
6	Standard Class	Illinois	95.976
7	Standard Class	Colorado	238.896
8	Standard Class	North Carolina	74.112
9	Standard Class	Illinois	339.960

Figure 4.6: Sample dataset

Now, if we just want to know the records with sales higher than $100, then we can write the following:

```
df_subset>100
```

This produces the following boolean DataFrame:

	Ship Mode	State	Sales
0	True	True	False
1	True	True	False
2	True	True	False
3	True	True	False
4	True	True	False
5	True	True	False
6	True	True	False
7	True	True	True
8	True	True	False
9	True	True	True

Figure 4.7: Records with sales higher than $100

Note the True and False entries in the **Sales** column. Values in the **Ship Mode** and **State** columns were not impacted by this code because the comparison was with a numerical quantity, and the only numeric column in the original DataFrame was **Sales**.

Now, let's see what happens if we pass this boolean DataFrame as an index to the original DataFrame:

```
df_subset[df_subset>100]
```

The output is as follows:

	Ship Mode	State	Sales
0	Second Class	California	NaN
1	First Class	Minnesota	NaN
2	Standard Class	Delaware	NaN
3	First Class	New York	NaN
4	Standard Class	California	NaN
5	Standard Class	Minnesota	NaN
6	Standard Class	Illinois	NaN
7	Standard Class	Colorado	238.896
8	Standard Class	North Carolina	NaN
9	Standard Class	Illinois	339.960

Figure 4.8: Results after passing the boolean DataFrame as an index to the original DataFrame

The NaN values came from the fact that the preceding code tried to create a DataFrame with TRUE indices (in the Boolean DataFrame) only.

The values which were TRUE in the boolen DataFrame were retained in the final output DataFrame.

The program inserted **NaN** values for the rows where data was not available (because they were discarded due to the Sales value being < $100).

Now, we probably don't want to work with this resulting DataFrame with **NaN** values. We wanted a smaller DataFrame with only the rows where **Sales > $100**. We can achieve that by simply passing only the **Sales** column:

```
df_subset[df_subset['Sales']>100]
```

This produces the expected result:

	Ship Mode	State	Sales
7	Standard Class	Colorado	238.896
9	Standard Class	Illinois	339.960

Figure 4.9: Results after removing the NaN values

We are not limited to conditional expressions involving numeric quantities only. Let's try to extract high sales values (> $100) for entries that do not involve Colorado.

We can write the following code to accomplish that:

```
df_subset[(df_subset['State']!='Colorado') & (df_subset['Sales']>100)]
```

Note the use of a conditional involving string. In this expression, we are joining two conditionals by an & operator. Both conditions must be wrapped inside parentheses.

The first conditional expression simply matches the entries in the **State** column to the string **Colorado** and assigns TRUE/FALSE accordingly. The second conditional is the same as before. Together, joined by the & operator, they extract only those rows for which **State** is not **Colorado** and **Sales** is > **$100**. We get the following result:

	Ship Mode	State	Sales
9	Standard Class	Illinois	339.96

Figure 4.10: Results where State is not California and Sales is higher than $100

Note

Although, in theory, there is no limit on how complex a conditional you can build using individual expressions and & (LOGICAL AND) and | (LOGICAL OR) operators, it is advisable to create intermediate boolean DataFrames with limited conditional expressions and build your final DataFrame step by step. This keeps the code legible and scalable.

Exercise 50: Setting and Resetting the Index

Sometimes, we may need to reset or eliminate the default index of a DataFrame and assign a new column as an index:

1. Create the **matrix_data**, **row_labels**, and **column_headings** functions using the following command:

```
matrix_data = np.matrix(
    '22,66,140;42,70,148;30,62,125;35,68,160;25,62,152')
row_labels = ['A','B','C','D','E']
column_headings = ['Age', 'Height', 'Weight']
```

2. Create a DataFrame using the **matrix_data**, **row_labels**, and **column_headings** functions:

```
df1 = pd.DataFrame(data=matrix_data,
                   index=row_labels,
                   columns=column_headings)
print("\nThe DataFrame\n", '-'*25, sep='')
print(df1)
```

The output is as follows:

```
The DataFrame
-------------------------
    Age  Height  Weight
A    22      66     140
B    42      70     148
C    30      62     125
D    35      68     160
E    25      62     152
```

Figure 4.11: The original DataFrame

3. Reset the index, as follows:

```
print("\nAfter resetting index\n",'-'*35, sep='')
print(df1.reset_index())
```

```
       After resetting index
       -----------------------------

         index  Age  Height  Weight
    0        A   22      66     140
    1        B   42      70     148
    2        C   30      62     125
    3        D   35      68     160
    4        E   25      62     152
```

Figure 4.12: DataFrame after resetting the index

4. Reset the index with **drop** set to **True**, as follows:

```
print("\nAfter resetting index with 'drop' option TRUE\n",'-'*45, sep='')
print(df1.reset_index(drop=True))
```

```
    After resetting index with 'drop' option TRUE
    ------------------------------------------------

       Age  Height  Weight
    0   22      66     140
    1   42      70     148
    2   30      62     125
    3   35      68     160
    4   25      62     152
```

Figure 4.13: DataFrame after resetting the index with the drop option set to true

5. Add a new column using the following command:

```
print("\nAdding a new column 'Profession'\n",'-'*45, sep='')
df1['Profession'] = "Student Teacher Engineer Doctor Nurse".split()
print(df1)
```

The output is as follows:

```
Adding a new column 'Profession'
-------------------------------
    Age  Height  Weight Profession
A    22      66     140    Student
B    42      70     148    Teacher
C    30      62     125   Engineer
D    35      68     160     Doctor
E    25      62     152      Nurse
```

Figure 4.14: DataFrame after adding a new column called Profession

6. Now, set the **Profession** column as an **index** using the following code:

```
print("\nSetting 'Profession' column as index\n",'-'*45, sep='')
print (df1.set_index('Profession'))
```

The output is as follows:

```
Setting 'Profession' column as index
------------------------------------
            Age  Height  Weight
Profession
Student      22      66     140
Teacher      42      70     148
Engineer     30      62     125
Doctor       35      68     160
Nurse        25      62     152
```

Figure 4.15: DataFrame after setting the Profession as an index

Exercise 51: The GroupBy Method

Group by refers to a process involving one or more of the following steps:

- Splitting the data into groups based on some criteria

- Applying a function to each group independently

- Combining the results into a data structure

In many situations, we can split the dataset into groups and do something with those groups. In the apply step, we might wish to do one of the following:

- **Aggregation**: Compute a summary statistic (or statistics) for each group – sum, mean, and so on

- **Transformation**: Perform a group-specific computation and return a like-indexed object – z-transformation or filling missing data with a value

- **Filtration**: Discard few groups, according to a group-wise computation that evaluates TRUE or FALSE

There is, of course, a describe method to this **GroupBy** object, which produces the summary statistics in the form of a DataFrame.

GroupBy is not limited to a single variable. If you pass on multiple variables (as a list), then you will get back a structure essentially similar to a Pivot Table (from Excel). The following is an example where we group together all the states and cities from the whole dataset (the snapshot is a partial view only).

> **Note**
>
> The name **GroupBy** should be quite familiar to those who have used a SQL-based tool before.

1. Create a 10-record subset using the following command:

    ```
    df_subset = df.loc[[i for i in range (10)],['Ship Mode','State','Sales']]
    ```

2. Create a pandas DataFrame using the **groupby** object, as follows:

    ```
    byState = df_subset.groupby('State')
    ```

3. Calculate the mean sales figure by state by using the following command:

```
print("\nGrouping by 'State' column and listing mean sales\n",'-'*50,
sep='')
print(byState.mean())
```

The output is as follows:

```
Grouping by 'State' column and listing mean sales
--------------------------------------------------
                    Sales
State
California         52.275
Colorado          238.896
Delaware           45.000
Illinois          217.968
Minnesota          32.985
New York           30.000
North Carolina     74.112
```

Figure 4.16: Output after grouping the state with the listing mean sales

4. Calculate the total sales figure by state by using the following command:

```
print("\nGrouping by 'State' column and listing total sum of sales\n",'-
'*50, sep='')
print(byState.sum())
```

The output is as follows:

```
Grouping by 'State' column and listing total sum of sales
--------------------------------------------------
                    Sales
State
California        104.550
Colorado          238.896
Delaware           45.000
Illinois          435.936
Minnesota          65.970
New York           30.000
North Carolina     74.112
```

Figure 4.17: The output after grouping the state with the listing sum of sales

5. Subset that DataFrame for a particular state and show the statistics:

```
pd.DataFrame(byState.describe().loc['California'])
```

The output is as follows:

		California
Sales	**count**	2.000000
	mean	52.275000
	std	54.157308
	min	13.980000
	25%	33.127500
	50%	52.275000
	75%	71.422500
	max	90.570000

Figure 4.18: Checking the statistics of a particular state

6. Perform a similar summarization by using the **Ship Mode** attribute:

```
df_subset.groupby('Ship Mode').describe().loc[['Second Class','Standard
Class']]
```

The output will be as follows:

	Sales							
	count	mean	std	min	25%	50%	75%	max
Ship Mode								
Second Class	1.0	90.570000	NaN	90.57	90.570	90.570	90.570	90.57
Standard Class	7.0	118.273429	123.860065	13.98	32.495	74.112	167.436	339.96

Figure 4.19: Checking the sales by summarizing the Ship Mode attribute

Note how pandas has grouped the data by **State** first and then by cities under each state.

7. Display the complete summary statistics of sales by every city in each state – all by two lines of code by using the following command:

```
byStateCity=df.groupby(['State','City'])
byStateCity.describe()['Sales']
```

The output is as follows:

State	City	count	mean	std	min	25%	50%	75%	max
Alabama	Auburn	6.0	294.471667	361.914543	3.760	8.8050	182.0300	456.40750	900.080
	Decatur	13.0	259.601538	385.660903	14.940	23.9200	44.9500	239.92000	1215.920
	Florence	5.0	399.470000	796.488863	4.980	7.2700	12.4800	152.76000	1819.860
	Hoover	4.0	131.462500	230.646923	7.160	13.3925	20.7250	138.79500	477.240
	Huntsville	10.0	248.437000	419.576667	3.620	26.8700	81.9200	171.80750	1319.960
	Mobile	11.0	496.635455	914.087425	8.960	46.8600	70.9800	505.96500	3040.000
	Montgomery	10.0	372.273000	475.397645	10.160	21.7075	187.2150	499.05500	1394.950
	Tuscaloosa	2.0	87.850000	76.523096	33.740	60.7950	87.8500	114.90500	141.960
Arizona	Avondale	6.0	157.801333	288.247527	14.576	18.1480	35.5960	88.67800	742.336
	Bullhead City	2.0	11.144000	4.559425	7.920	9.5320	11.1440	12.75600	14.368
	Chandler	7.0	153.821000	305.283748	8.544	9.1200	49.7920	78.89750	842.376
	Gilbert	15.0	278.158800	346.945589	5.904	36.1240	82.3680	375.80700	1113.024
	Glendale	23.0	126.863696	225.003236	2.368	14.8760	42.9760	109.13200	933.536
	Mesa	28.0	144.205000	155.275947	4.368	31.7640	81.6515	202.90250	552.000

Figure 4.20: Checking the summary statistics of sales

Detecting Outliers and Handling Missing Values

Outlier detection and handling missing values fall under the subtle art of data quality checking. A modeling or data mining process is fundamentally a complex series of computations whose output quality largely depends on the quality and consistency of the input data being fed. The responsibility of maintaining and gate keeping that quality often falls on the shoulders of a data wrangling team.

Apart from the obvious issue of poor quality data, missing data can sometimes wreak havoc with the machine learning (ML) model downstream. A few ML models, like Bayesian learning, are inherently robust to outliers and missing data, but commonly techniques like Decision Trees and Random Forest have an issue with missing data because the fundamental splitting strategy employed by these techniques depends on an individual piece of data and not a cluster. Therefore, it is almost always imperative to impute missing data before handing it over to such a ML model.

Outlier detection is a subtle art. Often, there is no universally agreed definition of an outlier. In a statistical sense, a data point that falls outside a certain range may often be classified as an outlier, but to apply that definition, you need to have a fairly high degree of certainty about the assumption of the nature and parameters of the inherent statistical distribution about the data. It takes a lot of data to build that statistical certainty and even after that, an outlier may not be just an unimportant noise but a clue to something deeper. Let's take an example with some fictitious sales data from an American fast food chain restaurant. If we want to model the daily sales data as a time series, we observe an unusual spike in the data somewhere around mid-April:

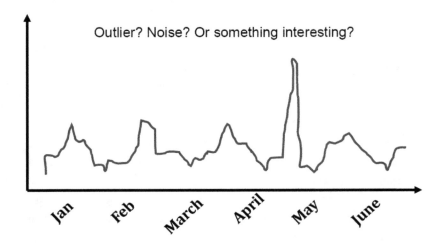

Figure 4.21: Fictitious sales data of an American fast food chain restaurant

A good data scientist or data wrangler should develop curiosity about this data point rather than just rejecting it just because it falls outside the statistical range. In the actual anecdote, the sales figure really spiked that day because of an unusual reason. So, the data was real. But just because it was real does not mean it is useful. In the final goal of building a smoothly varying time series model, this one point should not matter and should be rejected. But the chapter here is that we cannot reject outliers without paying some attention to them.

Therefore, the key to outliers is their systematic and timely detection in an incoming stream of millions of data or while reading data from a cloud-based storage. In this topic, we will quickly go over some basic statistical tests for detecting outliers and some basic imputation techniques for filling up missing data.

Missing Values in Pandas

One of the most useful functions to detect missing values is **isnull**. Here, we have a snapshot of a **DataFrame** called **df_missing** (sampled partially from the superstore DataFrame we are working with) with some missing values:

DataFrame with Missing values

	Customer	Product	Sales	Quantity	Discount	Profit
0	Leonard Middleton	NaN	1706.184	9.0	0.2	85.3092
1	Kean Nguyen	Phones	911.424	4.0	0.2	68.3568
2	Xylona Preis	Art	8.560	2.0	0.0	2.4824
3	NaN	Phones	NaN	3.0	0.2	16.0110
4	Jas O'Carroll	Binders	22.720	4.0	0.2	7.3840
5	Same Day	Binders	11.648	NaN	0.2	4.2224
6	Maris LaWare	Accessories	90.570	3.0	0.0	11.7741
7	Eileen Kiefer	NaN	77.880	2.0	0.0	NaN
8	NaN	Accessories	13.980	2.0	0.0	6.1512
9	Darrin Martin	Binders	25.824	6.0	0.2	9.3612
10	Chris Cortes	Paper	146.730	3.0	0.0	68.9631

Figure 4.22: DataFrame with missing values

Now, if we simply run the following code, we will get a DataFrame that's the same size as the original with boolean values as TRUE for the places where a **NaN** was encountered. Therefore, it is simple to test for the presence of any **NaN**/missing value for any row or column of the DataFrame. You just have to add the particular row and column of this boolean DataFrame. If the result is greater than zero, then you know there are some TRUE values (because FALSE here is denoted by 0 and TRUE here is denoted by 1) and correspondingly some missing values. Try the following snippet:

```
df_missing=pd.read_excel("Sample - Superstore.xls",sheet_name="Missing")
df_missing
```

The output is as follows:

	Customer	Product	Sales	Quantity	Discount	Profit
0	Leonard Middleton	NaN	1706.184	9.0	0.2	85.3092
1	Kean Nguyen	Phones	911.424	4.0	0.2	68.3568
2	Xylona Preis	Art	8.560	2.0	0.0	2.4824
3	NaN	Phones	NaN	3.0	0.2	16.0110
4	Jas O'Carroll	Binders	22.720	4.0	0.2	7.3840
5	Same Day	Binders	11.648	NaN	0.2	4.2224
6	Maris LaWare	Accessories	90.570	3.0	0.0	11.7741
7	Eileen Kiefer	NaN	77.880	2.0	0.0	NaN
8	NaN	Accessories	13.980	2.0	0.0	6.1512
9	Darrin Martin	Binders	25.824	6.0	0.2	9.3612
10	Chris Cortes	Paper	146.730	3.0	0.0	68.9631

Figure 4.23: DataFrame with the Excel values

Use the `isnull` function on the DataFrame and observe the results:

```
df_missing.isnull()
```

	Customer	Product	Sales	Quantity	Discount	Profit
0	False	True	False	False	False	False
1	False	False	False	False	False	False
2	False	False	False	False	False	False
3	False	False	True	False	False	False
4	False	False	False	False	False	False
5	False	False	False	True	False	False
6	False	False	False	False	False	False
7	False	True	False	False	False	True
8	True	False	False	False	False	False
9	False	False	False	False	False	False
10	False	False	False	False	False	False

Figure 4.24 Output highlighting the missing values

Here is an example of some very simple code to detect, count, and print out missing values in every column of a DataFrame:

```
for c in df_missing.columns:

    miss = df_missing[c].isnull().sum()

    if miss>0:

        print("{} has {} missing value(s)".format(c,miss))

    else:

        print("{} has NO missing value!".format(c))
```

This code scans every column of the DataFrame, calls the **isnull** function, and sums up the returned object (a pandas Series object, in this case) to count the number of missing values. If the missing value is greater than zero, it prints out the message accordingly. The output looks as follows:

```
Customer has 2 missing value(s)
Product has 2 missing value(s)
Sales has 1 missing value(s)
Quantity has 1 missing value(s)
Discount has NO missing value!
Profit has 1 missing value(s)
```

Figure 4.25: Output of counting the missing values

Exercise 52: Filling in the Missing Values with fillna

To handle missing values, you should first look for ways not to drop them altogether but to fill them somehow. The **fillna** method is a useful function for performing this task on pandas DataFrames. The **fillna** method may work for string data, but not for numerical columns like sales or profits. So, we should restrict ourselves in regards to this fixed string replacement to non-numeric text-based columns only. The **Pad** or **ffill** function is used to fill forward the data, that is, copy it from the preceding data of the series.

The **mean** function can be used to fill using the average of the two values:

1. Fill all missing values with the string **FILL** by using the following command:

    ```
    df_missing.fillna('FILL')
    ```

    The output is as follows:

	Customer	Product	Sales	Quantity	Discount	Profit
0	Leonard Middleton	FILL	1706.18	9	0.2	85.3092
1	Kean Nguyen	Phones	911.424	4	0.2	68.3568
2	Xylona Preis	Art	8.56	2	0.0	2.4824
3	FILL	Phones	FILL	3	0.2	16.011
4	Jas O'Carroll	Binders	22.72	4	0.2	7.384
5	Same Day	Binders	11.648	FILL	0.2	4.2224
6	Maris LaWare	Accessories	90.57	3	0.0	11.7741
7	Eileen Kiefer	FILL	77.88	2	0.0	FILL
8	FILL	Accessories	13.98	2	0.0	6.1512
9	Darrin Martin	Binders	25.824	6	0.2	9.3612
10	Chris Cortes	Paper	146.73	3	0.0	68.9631

Figure 4.26: Missing values replaced with FILL

2. Fill in the specified columns with the string **FILL** by using the following command:

```
df_missing[['Customer','Product']].fillna('FILL')
```

The output is as follows:

	Customer	Product
0	Leonard Middleton	FILL
1	Kean Nguyen	Phones
2	Xylona Preis	Art
3	FILL	Phones
4	Jas O'Carroll	Binders
5	Same Day	Binders
6	Maris LaWare	Accessories
7	Eileen Kiefer	FILL
8	FILL	Accessories
9	Darrin Martin	Binders
10	Chris Cortes	Paper

Figure 4.27: Specified columns replaced with FILL

> **Note**
>
> In all of these cases, the function works on a copy of the original DataFrame. So, if you want to make the changes permanent, you have to assign the DataFrames that are returned by these functions to the original DataFrame object.

3. Fill in the values using pad or backfill by using the following command:

```
df_missing['Sales'].fillna(method='ffill')
```

4. Use **backfill** or **bfill** to fill backward, that is, copy from the next data in the series:

```
df_missing['Sales'].fillna(method='bfill')
```

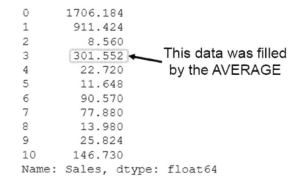

Figure 4.28: Using forward fill and backward fill to fill in missing data

5. You can also fill by using a function average of DataFrames. For example, we may want to fill the missing values in Sales by the average sales amount. Here is how we can do that:

```
df_missing['Sales'].fillna(df_missing.mean()['Sales'])
```

```
0       1706.184
1        911.424
2          8.560
3        301.552  ← This data was filled
4         22.720      by the AVERAGE
5         11.648
6         90.570
7         77.880
8         13.980
9         25.824
10       146.730
Name: Sales, dtype: float64
```

Figure 4.29: Using average to fill in missing data

Exercise 53: Dropping Missing Values with dropna

This function is used to simply drop the rows or columns that contain NaN/missing values. However, there is some choice involved.

If the axis parameter is set to zero, then rows containing missing values are dropped; if the axis parameter is set to one, then columns containing missing values are dropped. These are useful if we don't want to drop a particular row/column if the NaN values do not exceed a certain percentage.

Two arguments that are useful for the **dropna()** method are as follows:

- The **how** argument determines if a row or column is removed from a DataFrame, when we have at least one NaN or all NaNs

- The **thresh** argument requires that many non-NaN values to keep the row/column

1. To set the axis parameter to zero and drop all missing rows, use the following command:

```
df_missing.dropna(axis=0)
```

2. To set the axis parameter to one and drop all missing rows, use the following command:

```
df_missing.dropna(axis=1)
```

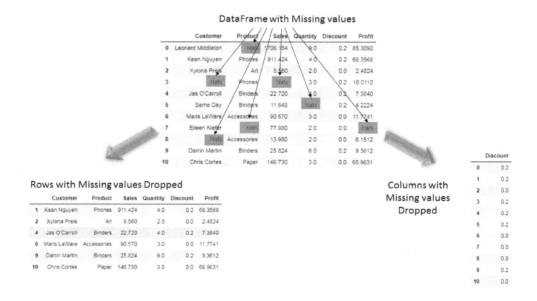

Figure 4.30: Dropping rows or columns to handle missing data

3. Drop the values with the axis set to one and thresh set to 10:

```
df_missing.dropna(axis=1,thresh=10)
```

The output is as follows:

	Sales	Quantity	Discount	Profit
0	1706.184	9.0	0.2	85.3092
1	911.424	4.0	0.2	68.3568
2	8.560	2.0	0.0	2.4824
3	NaN	3.0	0.2	16.0110
4	22.720	4.0	0.2	7.3840
5	11.648	NaN	0.2	4.2224
6	90.570	3.0	0.0	11.7741
7	77.880	2.0	0.0	NaN
8	13.980	2.0	0.0	6.1512
9	25.824	6.0	0.2	9.3612
10	146.730	3.0	0.0	68.9631

Figure 4.31: DataFrame with values dropped with axis=1 and thresh=10

All of these methods work on a temporary copy. To make a permanent change, you have to set **inplace=True** or assign the result to the original DataFrame, that is, overwrite it.

Outlier Detection Using a Simple Statistical Test

As we've already discussed, outliers in a dataset can occur due to many factors and in many ways:

- Data entry errors
- Experimental errors (data extraction related)
- Measurement errors due to noise or instrumental failure
- Data processing errors (data manipulation or mutations due to coding error)
- Sampling errors (extracting or mixing data from wrong or various sources)

It is impossible to pin-point one universal method for outlier detection. Here, we will show you some simple tricks for numeric data using standard statistical tests.

Boxplots may show unusual values. Corrupt two sales values by assigning negative, as follows:

```
df_sample = df[['Customer Name','State','Sales','Profit']].sample(n=50).copy()
df_sample['Sales'].iloc[5]=-1000.0
df_sample['Sales'].iloc[15]=-500.0
```

To plot the boxplot, use the following code:

```
df_sample.plot.box()
plt.title("Boxplot of sales and profit", fontsize=15)
plt.xticks(fontsize=15)
plt.yticks(fontsize=15)
plt.grid(True)
```

The output is as follows:

Figure 4.32: Boxplot of sales and profit

We can create simple boxplots to check for any unusual/nonsensical values. For example, in the preceding example, we intentionally corrupted two sales values to be negative and they were readily caught in a boxplot.

Note that profit may be negative, so those negative points are generally not suspicious. But sales cannot be negative in general, so they are detected as outliers.

We can create a distribution of a numerical quantity and check for values that lie at the extreme end to see if they are truly part of the data or outlier. For example, if a distribution is almost normal, then any value more than 4 or 5 standard deviations away may be a suspect:

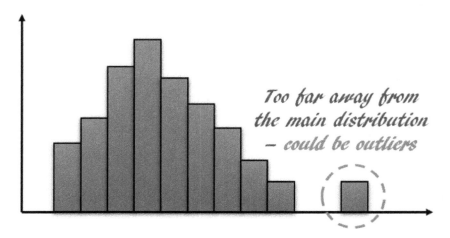

Figure 4.33: Value away from the main outliers

Concatenating, Merging, and Joining

Merging and joining tables or datasets are highly common operations in the day-to-day job of a data wrangling professional. These operations are akin to the JOIN query in SQL for relational database tables. Often, the key data is present in multiple tables, and those records need to be brought into one combined table that's matching on that common key. This is an extremely common operation in any type of sales or transactional data, and therefore must be mastered by a data wrangler. The pandas library offers nice and intuitive built-in methods to perform various types of JOIN queries involving multiple DataFrame objects.

Exercise 54: Concatenation

We will start by learning the concatenation of DataFrames along various axes (rows or columns). This is a very useful operation as it allows you to grow a DataFrame as the new data comes in or new feature columns need to be inserted in the table:

1. Sample 4 records each to create three DataFrames at random from the original sales dataset we are working with:

```
df_1 = df[['Customer Name','State','Sales','Profit']].sample(n=4)
df_2 = df[['Customer Name','State','Sales','Profit']].sample(n=4)
df_3 = df[['Customer Name','State','Sales','Profit']].sample(n=4)
```

2. Create a combined DataFrame with all the rows concatenated by using the following code:

```
df_cat1 = pd.concat([df_1,df_2,df_3], axis=0)
df_cat1
```

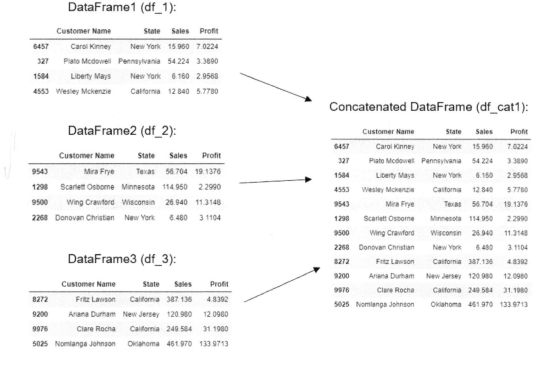

Figure 4.34: Concatenating DataFrames together

3. You can also try concatenating along the columns, although that does not make any practical sense for this particular example. However, pandas fills in the unavailable values with **NaN** for that operation:

```
df_cat2 = pd.concat([df_1,df_2,df_3], axis=1)
df_cat2
```

	Customer Name	State	Sales	Profit	Customer Name	State	Sales	Profit	Customer Name	State	Sales	Profit
1589	Maris Stevenson	Virginia	10.96	2.9592	NaN	NaN	NaN	NaN	NaN	NaN	NaN	NaN
3017	NaN	NaN	NaN	NaN	Shay Gallegos	Texas	22.608	-10.1736	NaN	NaN	NaN	NaN
3133	NaN	NaN	NaN	NaN	Eve Cortez	New York	12.672	4.4352	NaN	NaN	NaN	NaN
4249	Amir Hicks	Connecticut	751.92	150.3840	NaN	NaN	NaN	NaN	NaN	NaN	NaN	NaN
4261	NaN	NaN	NaN	NaN	NaN	NaN	NaN	NaN	Yuri Holmes	Minnesota	63.960	19.8276
4406	NaN	NaN	NaN	NaN	NaN	NaN	NaN	NaN	Leo Perkins	Indiana	9.080	4.0860
6541	Trevor Nash	Washington	139.92	23.7864	NaN	NaN	NaN	NaN	NaN	NaN	NaN	NaN
7187	NaN	NaN	NaN	NaN	NaN	NaN	NaN	NaN	Kimberley Fitzgerald	Texas	16.784	-22.2388
7491	Emi Holt	New York	119.94	5.9970	NaN	NaN	NaN	NaN	NaN	NaN	NaN	NaN
7532	NaN	NaN	NaN	NaN	NaN	NaN	NaN	NaN	Robin Duke	Colorado	483.136	54.3528
9343	NaN	NaN	NaN	NaN	Carter Walter	Ohio	455.970	-106.3930	NaN	NaN	NaN	NaN
9452	NaN	NaN	NaN	NaN	Regan Blanchard	California	81.792	26.5824	NaN	NaN	NaN	NaN

Figure 4.35: Output after concatenating the DataFrames

Exercise 55: Merging by a Common Key

Merging by a common key is an extremely common operation for data tables as it allows you to rationalize multiple sources of data in one master database – that is, if they have some common features/keys.

This is often the first step in building a large database for machine learning tasks where daily incoming data may be put into separate tables. However, at the end of the day, the most recent table needs to be merged with the master data table to be fed into the backend machine learning server, which will then update the model and its prediction capacity.

Here, we will show a simple example of an inner join with Customer Name as the key:

1. One DataFrame, **df_1**, had shipping information associated with the customer name, and another table, **df_2**, had the product information tabulated. Our goal is to merge these tables into one DataFrame on the common customer name:

```
df_1=df[['Ship Date','Ship Mode','Customer Name']][0:4]
df_1
```

The output is as follows:

	Customer Name	Ship Date	Ship Mode
0	Quinlan Graves	2016-01-20	Second Class
1	Joelle Swanson	2016-03-13	First Class
2	Gail Norton	2016-06-25	Standard Class
3	Paul Atkinson	2016-06-18	First Class

Figure 4.36: Entries in table df_1

The second DataFrame is as follows:

```
df_2=df[['Customer Name','Product Name','Quantity']][0:4]
df_2
```

The output is as follows:

	Customer Name	Product Name	Quantity
0	Quinlan Graves	Imation 8GB Mini TravelDrive USB 2.0 Flash Drive	3
1	Joelle Swanson	Verbatim 25 GB 6x Blu-ray Single Layer Recorda...	2
2	Gail Norton	Imation 8gb Micro Traveldrive Usb 2.0 Flash Drive	3
3	Paul Atkinson	Imation 8gb Micro Traveldrive Usb 2.0 Flash Drive	2

Figure 4.37: Entries in table df_2

2. Join these two tables by inner join by using the following command:

    ```
    pd.merge(df_1,df_2,on='Customer Name',how='inner')
    ```

    The output is as follows:

	Customer Name	Ship Date	Ship Mode	Product Name	Quantity
0	Quinlan Graves	2016-01-20	Second Class	Imation 8GB Mini TravelDrive USB 2.0 Flash Drive	3
1	Joelle Swanson	2016-03-13	First Class	Verbatim 25 GB 6x Blu-ray Single Layer Recorda...	2
2	Gail Norton	2016-06-25	Standard Class	Imation 8gb Micro Traveldrive Usb 2.0 Flash Drive	3
3	Paul Atkinson	2016-06-18	First Class	Imation 8gb Micro Traveldrive Usb 2.0 Flash Drive	2

Figure 4.38: Inner join on table df_1 and table df_2

3. Drop the duplicates by using the following command.

    ```
    pd.merge(df_1,df_2,on='Customer Name',how='inner').drop_duplicates()
    ```

    The output is as follows:

	Customer Name	Ship Date	Ship Mode	Product Name	Quantity
0	Quinlan Graves	2016-01-20	Second Class	Imation 8GB Mini TravelDrive USB 2.0 Flash Drive	3
1	Joelle Swanson	2016-03-13	First Class	Verbatim 25 GB 6x Blu-ray Single Layer Recorda...	2
2	Gail Norton	2016-06-25	Standard Class	Imation 8gb Micro Traveldrive Usb 2.0 Flash Drive	3
3	Paul Atkinson	2016-06-18	First Class	Imation 8gb Micro Traveldrive Usb 2.0 Flash Drive	2

Figure 4.39: Inner join on table df_1 and table df_2 after dropping the duplicates

4. Extract another small table called **df_3** to show the concept of an outer join:

```
df_3=df[['Customer Name','Product Name','Quantity']][2:6]
df_3
```

The output is as follows:

	Customer Name	Product Name	Quantity
2	Gail Norton	Imation 8gb Micro Traveldrive Usb 2.0 Flash Drive	3
3	Paul Atkinson	Imation 8gb Micro Traveldrive Usb 2.0 Flash Drive	2
4	Neve Weiss	Verbatim 25 GB 6x Blu-ray Single Layer Recorda...	2
5	Noel Craig	Logitech LS21 Speaker System - PC Multimedia -...	1

Figure 4.40: Creating table df_3

5. Perform an inner join on **df_1** and **df_3** by using the following command:

```
pd.merge(df_1,df_3,on='Customer Name',how='inner').drop_duplicates()
```

The output is as follows:

	Customer Name	Ship Date	Ship Mode	Product Name	Quantity
0	Gail Norton	2016-06-25	Standard Class	Imation 8gb Micro Traveldrive Usb 2.0 Flash Drive	3
1	Paul Atkinson	2016-06-18	First Class	Imation 8gb Micro Traveldrive Usb 2.0 Flash Drive	2

Figure 4.41: Merging table df_1 and table df_3 and dropping duplicates

6. Perform an outer join on **df_1** and **df_3** by using the following command:

```
pd.merge(df_1,df_3,on='Customer Name',how='outer').drop_duplicates()
```

The output is as follows:

	Customer Name	Ship Date	Ship Mode	Product Name	Quantity
0	Quinlan Graves	2016-01-20	Second Class	NaN	NaN
1	Joelle Swanson	2016-03-13	First Class	NaN	NaN
2	Gail Norton	2016-06-25	Standard Class	Imation 8gb Micro Traveldrive Usb 2.0 Flash Drive	3.0
3	Paul Atkinson	2016-06-18	First Class	Imation 8gb Micro Traveldrive Usb 2.0 Flash Drive	2.0
4	Neve Weiss	NaT	NaN	Verbatim 25 GB 6x Blu-ray Single Layer Recorda...	2.0
5	Noel Craig	NaT	NaN	Logitech LS21 Speaker System - PC Multimedia -...	1.0

Figure 4.42: Outer join on table df_1 and table df_2 and dropping the duplicates

Notice how some **NaN** and **NaT** values are inserted automatically because no corresponding entries could be found for those records, as those are the entries with unique customer names from their respective tables. **NaT** represents a Not a Time object, as the objects in the Ship Date column are of the nature of Timestamp objects.

Exercise 56: The join Method

Joining is performed based on **index keys** and is done by combining the columns of two potentially differently indexed DataFrames into a single one. It offers a faster way to accomplish merging by row indices. This is useful if the records in different tables are indexed differently but represent the same inherent data and you want to merge them into a single table:

1. Create the following tables with customer name as the index by using the following command:

```
df_1=df[['Customer Name','Ship Date','Ship Mode']][0:4]
df_1.set_index(['Customer Name'],inplace=True)
df_1
df_2=df[['Customer Name','Product Name','Quantity']][2:6]
df_2.set_index(['Customer Name'],inplace=True)
df_2
```

The outputs is as follows:

Customer Name	Ship Date	Ship Mode		Customer Name	Product Name	Quantity
Quinlan Graves	2016-01-20	Second Class		Gail Norton	Imation 8gb Micro Traveldrive Usb 2.0 Flash Drive	3
Joelle Swanson	2016-03-13	First Class		Paul Atkinson	Imation 8gb Micro Traveldrive Usb 2.0 Flash Drive	2
Gail Norton	2016-06-25	Standard Class		Neve Weiss	Verbatim 25 GB 6x Blu-ray Single Layer Recorda...	2
Paul Atkinson	2016-06-18	First Class		Noel Craig	Logitech LS21 Speaker System - PC Multimedia -...	1

Figure 4.43: DataFrames df_1 and df_2

2. Perform a left join on **df_1** and **df_2** by using the following command:

```
df_1.join(df_2,how='left').drop_duplicates()
```

The output is as follows:

Customer Name	Ship Date	Ship Mode	Product Name	Quantity
Quinlan Graves	2016-01-20	Second Class	NaN	NaN
Joelle Swanson	2016-03-13	First Class	NaN	NaN
Gail Norton	2016-06-25	Standard Class	Imation 8gb Micro Traveldrive Usb 2.0 Flash Drive	3.0
Paul Atkinson	2016-06-18	First Class	Imation 8gb Micro Traveldrive Usb 2.0 Flash Drive	2.0

Figure 4.44: Left join on table df_1 and table df_2 after dropping the duplicates

3. Perform a right join on **df_1** and **df_2** by using the following command:

```
df_1.join(df_2,how='right').drop_duplicates()
```

The output is as follows:

Customer Name	Ship Date	Ship Mode	Product Name	Quantity
Gail Norton	2016-06-25	Standard Class	Imation 8gb Micro Traveldrive Usb 2.0 Flash Drive	3
Paul Atkinson	2016-06-18	First Class	Imation 8gb Micro Traveldrive Usb 2.0 Flash Drive	2
Neve Weiss	NaT	NaN	Verbatim 25 GB 6x Blu-ray Single Layer Recorda...	2
Noel Craig	NaT	NaN	Logitech LS21 Speaker System - PC Multimedia -...	1

Figure 4.45: Right join on table df_1 and table df_2 after dropping the duplicates

4. Perform an inner join on **df_1** and **df_2** by using the following command:

```
df_1.join(df_2,how='inner').drop_duplicates()
```

The output is as follows:

Customer Name	Ship Date	Ship Mode	Product Name	Quantity
Gail Norton	2016-06-25	Standard Class	Imation 8gb Micro Traveldrive Usb 2.0 Flash Drive	3
Paul Atkinson	2016-06-18	First Class	Imation 8gb Micro Traveldrive Usb 2.0 Flash Drive	2

Figure 4.46: Inner join on table df_1 and table df_2 after dropping the duplicates

5. Perform an outer join on **df_1** and **df_2** by using the following command:

```
df_1.join(df_2,how='outer').drop_duplicates()
```

The output is as follows:

Customer Name	Ship Date	Ship Mode	Product Name	Quantity
Gail Norton	2016-06-25	Standard Class	Imation 8gb Micro Traveldrive Usb 2.0 Flash Drive	3.0
Joelle Swanson	2016-03-13	First Class	NaN	NaN
Neve Weiss	NaT	NaN	Verbatim 25 GB 6x Blu-ray Single Layer Recorda...	2.0
Noel Craig	NaT	NaN	Logitech LS21 Speaker System - PC Multimedia -...	1.0
Paul Atkinson	2016-06-18	First Class	Imation 8gb Micro Traveldrive Usb 2.0 Flash Drive	2.0
Quinlan Graves	2016-01-20	Second Class	NaN	NaN

Figure 4.47: Outer join on table df_1 and table df_2 after dropping the duplicates

Useful Methods of Pandas

In this topic, we will discuss some small utility functions that are offered by pandas so that we can work efficiently with DataFrames. They don't fall under any particular group of function, so they are mentioned here under the Miscellaneous category.

Exercise 57: Randomized Sampling

Sampling a random fraction of a big DataFrame is often very useful so that we can practice other methods on them and test our ideas. If you have a database table of 1 million records, then it is not computationally effective to run your test scripts on the full table.

However, you may also not want to extract only the first 100 elements as the data may have been sorted by a particular key and you may get an uninteresting table back, which may not represent the full statistical diversity of the parent database.

In these situations, the **sample** method comes in super handy so that we can randomly choose a controlled fraction of the DataFrame:

1. Specify the number of samples that you require from the DataFrame by using the following command:

```
df.sample(n=5)
```

The output is as follows:

	Order ID	Order Date	Ship Date	Ship Mode	Customer ID	Customer Name	Segment	City	State	Postal Code	Region	Product ID	Ca
7392	CA-2017-147844	2017-05-02	2017-05-06	Standard Class	DD-13570	Kyla Roman	Consumer	Los Angeles	California	90049	West	OFF-PA-10003016	S(
4876	US-2014-155817	2014-10-03	2014-10-09	Standard Class	SL-20155	Gretchen Galloway	Home Office	Durham	North Carolina	27707	South	OFF-ST-10000532	S(
850	CA-2016-152534	2016-06-20	2016-06-25	Second Class	DP-13105	Bo Watkins	Corporate	Salinas	California	93905	West	OFF-AR-10002335	S(
392	US-2014-135972	2014-09-21	2014-09-23	Second Class	JG-15115	Fleur Robles	Consumer	Des Moines	Washington	98198	West	TEC-CO-10002313	Tech
1072	CA-2017-106943	2017-11-14	2017-11-19	Standard Class	FO-14305	Ainsley Rodriquez	Consumer	New York City	New York	10035	East	OFF-BI-10003669	S(

Figure 4.48: DataFrame with 5 samples

2. Specify a definite fraction (percentage) of data to be sampled by using the following command:

```
df.sample(frac=0.1)
```

The output is as follows:

	Order ID	Order Date	Ship Date	Ship Mode	Customer ID	Customer Name	Segment	City	State	Postal Code	Region	Produ
5036	CA-2014-169803	2014-04-06	2014-04-12	Standard Class	SC-20260	McKenzie Day	Corporate	Seattle	Washington	98115	West	TEC-A 100034
4455	US-2015-146745	2015-09-03	2015-09-08	Standard Class	AS-10630	Iris Roach	Home Office	San Francisco	California	94110	West	FUR-CI 100023
7081	CA-2016-106950	2016-09-02	2016-09-06	Standard Class	JE-15715	Maris Barnes	Consumer	Charlotte	North Carolina	28205	South	TEC-A 100020
1782	CA-2015-	2015-07-09	2015-07-13	Standard Class	CB-12535	MacKenzie Branch	Corporate	Franklin	Massachusetts	2038	East	OFF-E 100015

Figure 4.49: DataFrame with 0.1% data sampled

You can also choose if sampling is done with replacement, that is, whether the same record can be chosen more than once. The default replace choice is FALSE, that is, no repetition, and sampling will try to choose new elements only.

3. Choose the sampling by using the following command:

```
df.sample(frac=0.1, replace=True)
```

The output is as follows:

	Order ID	Order Date	Ship Date	Ship Mode	Customer ID	Customer Name	Segment	City	State	Postal Code	Region	Product ID	Cate
5814	US-2015-106495	2015-06-15	2015-06-17	First Class	AC-10450	Fiona Holder	Consumer	Tampa	Florida	33614	South	TEC-AC-10002718	Techno
9650	CA-2016-107104	2016-11-26	2016-11-30	Standard Class	MS-17365	Colt Carson	Consumer	Los Angeles	California	90045	West	OFF-AR-10004269	C Sup
2488	CA-2015-104514	2015-01-02	2015-01-04	Second Class	CB-12535	Leandra Santiago	Corporate	Newark	Delaware	19711	East	OFF-PA-10004285	C Sup
6671	CA-2014-154837	2014-08-23	2014-08-27	Second Class	RB-19645	Ralph Carrillo	Corporate	Los Angeles	California	90032	West	OFF-BI-10001575	C Sup
2687	US-2016-128195	2016-08-04	2016-08-05	First Class	RA-19285	William Avila	Consumer	Peoria	Illinois	61604	Central	OFF-BI-10002003	C Sup
7542	US-2017-112347	2017-12-02	2017-12-06	Standard Class	BS-11380	Theodore Ferrell	Corporate	Denver	Colorado	80219	West	FUR-FU-10001488	Furn
6789	CA-2015-161445	2015-09-07	2015-09-09	Second Class	CC-12610	Kuame Yang	Corporate	Durham	North Carolina	27707	South	OFF-AR-10001953	C Sup
7942	CA-2017-134194	2017-12-25	2018-01-01	Standard Class	GA-14725	Cally Dorsey	Consumer	Dallas	Texas	75081	Central	OFF-BI-10003684	C Sup
4999	CA-2016-129238	2016-01-31	2016-02-04	Standard Class	SC-20050	Florence Page	Home Office	Los Angeles	California	90045	West	OFF-PA-10002764	C Sup
807	CA-2015-140921	2015-02-03	2015-02-05	First Class	AA-10375	Debra Roach	Consumer	Omaha	Nebraska	68104	Central	FUR-FU-10003347	Furn

Figure 4.50: DataFrame with 0.1% data sampled and repetition enabled

The value_counts Method

We discussed the **unique** method before, which finds and counts the unique records from a DataFrame. Another useful function in a similar vein is **value_counts**. This function returns an object containing counts of unique values. In the object that is returned, the first element is the most frequently used object. The elements are arranged in descending order.

Let's consider a practical application of this method to illustrate the utility. Suppose your manager asks you to list the top 10 customers from the big sales database that you have. So, the business question is: which 10 customers' names occur the most frequently in the sales table? You can achieve the same with an SQL query if the data is in a RDBMS, but in pandas, this can be done by using one simple function:

```
df['Customer Name'].value_counts()[:10]
```

The output is as follows:

```
Cyrus Justice        3
Thaddeus Potts       2
Phoebe Howe          2
Erin Goodman         2
Paul Manning         2
Jarrod Patrick       2
Lysandra Farmer      2
Dana Mendez          2
Arden Powers         2
Asher Jefferson      2
Name: Customer Name, dtype: int64
```

Figure 4.51: List of top 10 customers

The **value_counts** method returns a series of the counts of all unique customer names sorted by the frequency of the count. By asking for only the first 10 elements of that list, this code returns a series of the most frequently occurring top 10 customer names.

Pivot Table Functionality

Similar to group by, pandas also offer pivot table functionality, which works the same as a pivot table in spreadsheet programs like MS Excel. For example, in this sales database, you want to know the average sales, profit, and quantity sold, by Region and State (two levels of index).

We can extract this information by using one simple piece of code (we sample 100 records first for keeping the computation fast and then apply the code):

```
df_sample = df.sample(n=100)
```

```
df_sample.pivot_table(values=['Sales','Quantity','Profit'],
index=['Region','State'],aggfunc='mean')
```

The output is as follows (note that your specific output may be different due to random sampling):

Region	State	Profit	Quantity	Sales
Central	Illinois	-13.383540	3.200000	115.384000
	Indiana	39.889350	7.000000	167.595000
	Iowa	11.847700	3.000000	25.615000
	Michigan	23.808000	4.000000	79.360000
	Minnesota	160.623000	3.000000	535.410000
	Nebraska	8.017800	3.000000	17.430000
	Texas	-18.250420	3.700000	237.700280
East	Connecticut	117.106650	3.000000	573.240000
	Delaware	63.476600	2.000000	214.830000
	Massachusetts	19.149300	3.666667	92.990000
	New Jersey	4.950000	3.000000	45.000000
	New York	16.665840	3.800000	115.241200
	Ohio	-11.668240	5.800000	359.931600

Figure 4.52: Sample of 100 records

Exercise 58: Sorting by Column Values – the sort_values Method

Sorting a table by a particular column is one of the most frequently used operations in the daily work of an analyst. Not surprisingly, pandas provide a simple and intuitive method for sorting called the **sort_values** method:

1. Take a random sample of 15 records and then show how we can sort by the Sales column and then by both the Sales and State columns together:

   ```
   df_sample=df[['Customer Name','State','Sales','Quantity']].sample(n=15)
   df_sample
   ```

The output is as follows:

	Customer Name	State	Sales	Quantity
9664	Vincent Ferguson	California	12.960	2
6343	Trevor Keller	Delaware	30.440	2
2144	Kennedy Erickson	Pennsylvania	16.688	7
3919	Lisandra Harding	Virginia	61.680	4
6546	Oliver Daniels	Ohio	24.784	1
1866	Herman Macdonald	Nevada	196.450	5
462	Leo Cruz	Arizona	23.560	5
7615	Jamal Flores	Florida	6.642	9
3690	Serina Bush	Colorado	59.994	2
5511	Ahmed Stephenson	Oregon	32.896	4
2273	Karina Soto	California	1119.984	2
2642	Magee Cook	Illinois	186.048	6
3005	Regan Bryan	Wisconsin	91.680	3
8539	Jin Morgan	California	479.984	2
8684	Amir Michael	California	21.210	7

Figure 4.53: Sample of 15 records

2. Sort the values with respect to **Sales** by using the following command:

```
df_sample.sort_values(by='Sales')
```

The output is as follows:

	Customer Name	State	Sales	Quantity
7615	Jamal Flores	Florida	6.642	9
9664	Vincent Ferguson	California	12.960	2
2144	Kennedy Erickson	Pennsylvania	16.688	7
8684	Amir Michael	California	21.210	7
462	Leo Cruz	Arizona	23.560	5
6546	Oliver Daniels	Ohio	24.784	1
6343	Trevor Keller	Delaware	30.440	2
5511	Ahmed Stephenson	Oregon	32.896	4
3690	Serina Bush	Colorado	59.994	2
3919	Lisandra Harding	Virginia	61.680	4
3005	Regan Bryan	Wisconsin	91.680	3
2642	Magee Cook	Illinois	186.048	6
1866	Herman Macdonald	Nevada	196.450	5
8539	Jin Morgan	California	479.984	2
2273	Karina Soto	California	1119.984	2

Figure 4.54: DataFrame with the Sales value sorted

3. Sort the values with respect to Sales and State:

```
df_sample.sort_values(by=['State','Sales'])
```

The output is as follows:

	Customer Name	State	Sales	Quantity
462	Leo Cruz	Arizona	23.560	5
9664	Vincent Ferguson	California	12.960	2
8684	Amir Michael	California	21.210	7
8539	Jin Morgan	California	479.984	2
2273	Karina Soto	California	1119.984	2
3690	Serina Bush	Colorado	59.994	2
6343	Trevor Keller	Delaware	30.440	2
7615	Jamal Flores	Florida	6.642	9
2642	Magee Cook	Illinois	186.048	6
1866	Herman Macdonald	Nevada	196.450	5
6546	Oliver Daniels	Ohio	24.784	1
5511	Ahmed Stephenson	Oregon	32.896	4
2144	Kennedy Erickson	Pennsylvania	16.688	7
3919	Lisandra Harding	Virginia	61.680	4
3005	Regan Bryan	Wisconsin	91.680	3

Figure 4.55: DataFrame sorted with respect to Sales and State

Exercise 59: Flexibility for User-Defined Functions with the apply Method

The pandas library provides great flexibility to work with user-defined functions of arbitrary complexity through the **apply** method. Much like the native Python **apply** function, this method accepts a user-defined function and additional arguments and returns a new column after applying the function on a particular column element-wise.

As an example, suppose we want to create a column of categorical features like high/medium/low based on the sales price column. Note that it is a conversion from a numeric value to a categorical factor (string) based on certain conditions (threshold values of sales):

1. Create a user-defined function, as follows:

```
def categorize_sales(price):
    if price < 50:
        return "Low"
    elif price < 200:
        return "Medium"
    else:
        return "High"
```

2. Sample 100 records randomly from the database:

```
df_sample=df[['Customer Name','State','Sales']].sample(n=100)
df_sample.head(10)
```

The output is as follows:

	Customer Name	State	Sales
6566	Martina Sharp	Texas	243.992
3338	Margaret Everett	California	117.144
5734	Galena Payne	Connecticut	25.160
5951	Xander Giles	Mississippi	234.360
9444	Amir Mathis	Texas	95.840
7773	Brady Kirkland	Ohio	59.976
5520	Linda Howell	Pennsylvania	23.920
4025	Sierra Mosley	Texas	29.664
9511	Hamish Hurley	Illinois	9.264
6235	Russell Roach	Washington	79.960

Figure 4.56: 100 sample records from the database

3. Use the **apply** method to apply the categorization function onto the **Sales** column:

> **Note**
>
> We need to create a new column to store the category string values that are returned by the function.

```
df_sample['Sales Price Category']=df_sample['Sales'].apply(categorize_
sales)
df_sample.head(10)
```

The output is as follows:

	Customer Name	State	Sales	Sales Price Category
6566	Martina Sharp	Texas	243.992	High
3338	Margaret Everett	California	117.144	Medium
5734	Galena Payne	Connecticut	25.160	Low
5951	Xander Giles	Mississippi	234.360	High
9444	Amir Mathis	Texas	95.840	Medium
7773	Brady Kirkland	Ohio	59.976	Medium
5520	Linda Howell	Pennsylvania	23.920	Low
4025	Sierra Mosley	Texas	29.664	Low
9511	Hamish Hurley	Illinois	9.264	Low
6235	Russell Roach	Washington	79.960	Medium

Figure 4.57: DataFrame with 10 rows after using the apply function on the Sales column

4. The **apply** method also works with the built-in native Python functions. For practice, let's create another column for storing the length of the name of the customer. We can do that using the familiar **len** function:

```
df_sample['Customer Name Length']=df_sample['Customer Name'].apply(len)
df_sample.head(10)
```

The output is as follows:

	Customer Name	State	Sales	Sales Price Category	Customer Name Length
6566	Martina Sharp	Texas	243.992	High	13
3338	Margaret Everett	California	117.144	Medium	16
5734	Galena Payne	Connecticut	25.160	Low	12
5951	Xander Giles	Mississippi	234.360	High	12
9444	Amir Mathis	Texas	95.840	Medium	11
7773	Brady Kirkland	Ohio	59.976	Medium	14
5520	Linda Howell	Pennsylvania	23.920	Low	12
4025	Sierra Mosley	Texas	29.664	Low	13
9511	Hamish Hurley	Illinois	9.264	Low	13
6235	Russell Roach	Washington	79.960	Medium	13

Figure 4.58: DataFrame with a new column

5. Instead of writing out a separate function, we can even insert lambda expressions directly into the apply method for short functions. For example, let's say we are promoting our product and want to show the discounted sales price if the original price is > $200. We can do this using a **lambda** function and the **apply** method:

```
df_sample['Discounted Price']=df_sample['Sales'].apply(lambda x:0.85*x if
x>200 else x)
df_sample.head(10)
```

The output is as follows:

	Customer Name	State	Sales	Sales Price Category	Customer Name Length	Discounted Price
6566	Martina Sharp	Texas	243.992	High	13	207.3932
3338	Margaret Everett	California	117.144	Medium	16	117.1440
5734	Galena Payne	Connecticut	25.160	Low	12	25.1600
5951	Xander Giles	Mississippi	234.360	High	12	199.2060
9444	Amir Mathis	Texas	95.840	Medium	11	95.8400
7773	Brady Kirkland	Ohio	59.976	Medium	14	59.9760
5520	Linda Howell	Pennsylvania	23.920	Low	12	23.9200
4025	Sierra Mosley	Texas	29.664	Low	13	29.6640
9511	Hamish Hurley	Illinois	9.264	Low	13	9.2640
6235	Russell Roach	Washington	79.960	Medium	13	79.9600

Figure 4.59: Lambda function

Note

The lambda function contains a conditional, and a discount is applied to those records where the original sales price is > $200.

Activity 6: Working with the Adult Income Dataset (UCI)

In this activity, you will work with the Adult Income Dataset from the UCI machine learning portal. The Adult Income dataset has been used in many machine learning papers that address classification problems. You will read the data from a CSV file into a pandas DataFrame and do some practice on the advanced data wrangling you learned about in this chapter.

The aim of this activity is to practice various advanced pandas DataFrame operations, for example, for subsetting, applying user-defined functions, summary statistics, visualizations, boolean indexing, group by, and outlier detection on a real-life dataset. We have the data downloaded as a CSV file on the disk for your ease. However, it is recommended to practice data downloading on your own so that you are familiar with the process.

Here is the URL for the dataset: https://archive.ics.uci.edu/ml/machine-learning-databases/adult/.

Here is the URL for the description of the dataset and the variables: https://archive.ics.uci.edu/ml/machine-learning-databases/adult/adult.names.

These are the steps that will help you solve this activity:

1. Load the necessary libraries.

2. Read the adult income dataset from the following URL: https://github.com/TrainingByPackt/Data-Wrangling-with-Python/blob/master/Chapter04/Activity06/.

3. Create a script that will read a text file line by line.

4. Add a name of **Income** for the response variable to the dataset.

5. Find the missing values.

6. Create a DataFrame with only age, education, and occupation by using subsetting.

7. Plot a histogram of age with a bin size of 20.

8. Create a function to strip the whitespace characters.

9. Use the **apply** method to apply this function to all the columns with string values, create a new column, copy the values from this new column to the old column, and drop the new column.

10. Find the number of people who are aged between 30 and 50.

11. Group the records based on age and education to find how the mean age is distributed.

12. Group by occupation and show the summary statistics of age. Find which profession has the oldest workers on average and which profession has its largest share of the workforce above the 75th percentile.

13. Use subset and groupby to find outliers.

14. Plot the values on a bar chart.

15. Merge the data using common keys.

Note

The solution for this activity can be found on page 297.

Summary

In this chapter, we dived deep into the pandas library to learn advanced data wrangling techniques. We started with some advanced subsetting and filtering on DataFrames and round this up by learning about boolean indexing and conditional selection of a subset of data. We also covered how to set and reset the index of a DataFrame, especially while initializing.

Next, we learned about a particular topic that has a deep connection with traditional relational database systems – the group by method. Then, we dived deep into an important skill for data wrangling - checking for and handling missing data. We showed you how pandas help in handling missing data using various imputation techniques. We also discussed methods for dropping missing values. Furthermore, methods and usage examples of concatenation and merging of DataFrame objects were shown. We saw the join method and how it compares to a similar operation in SQL.

Lastly, miscellaneous useful methods on DataFrames, such as randomized sampling, `unique`, `value_count`, `sort_values`, and pivot table functionality were covered. We also showed an example of running an arbitrary user-defined function on a DataFrame using the `apply` method.

After learning about the basic and advanced data wrangling techniques with NumPy and pandas libraries, the natural question of data acquiring rises. In the next chapter, we will show you how to work with a wide variety of data sources, that is, you will learn how to read data in tabular format in pandas from different sources.

5

Getting Comfortable with Different Kinds of Data Sources

Learning Objectives

By the end of this chapter, you will be able to:

- Read CSV, Excel, and JSON files into pandas DataFrames

- Read PDF documents and HTML tables into pandas DataFrames

- Perform basic web scraping using powerful yet easy to use libraries such as Beautiful Soup

- Extract structured and textual information from portals

In this chapter, you will be exposed to real-life data wrangling techniques, as applied to web scraping.

Introduction

So far in this book, we have focused on learning pandas DataFrame objects as the main data structure for the application of wrangling techniques. Now, we will learn about various techniques by which we can read data into a DataFrame from external sources. Some of those sources could be text-based (CSV, HTML, JSON, and so on), whereas some others could be binary (Excel, PDF, and so on), that is, not in ASCII format. In this chapter, we will learn how to deal with data that is present in web pages or HTML documents. This holds very high importance in the work of a data practitioner.

> **Note**
>
> Since we have gone through a detailed example of basic operations with NumPy and pandas, in this chapter, we will often skip trivial code snippets such as viewing a table, selecting a column, and plotting. Instead, we will focus on showing code examples for the new topics we aim to learn about here.

Reading Data from Different Text-Based (and Non-Text-Based) Sources

One of the most valued and widely used skills of a data wrangling professional is the ability to extract and read data from a diverse array of sources into a structured format. Modern analytics pipelines depend on their ability to scan and absorb a variety of data sources to build and analyze a pattern-rich model. Such a feature-rich, multi-dimensional model will have high predictive and generalization accuracy. It will be valued by stakeholders and end users alike for any data-driven product.

In the first topic of this chapter, we will go through various data sources and how they can be imported into pandas DataFrames, thus imbuing wrangling professionals with extremely valuable data ingestion knowledge.

Data Files Provided with This Chapter

Because this topic is about reading from various data sources, we will use small files of various types in the following exercises. All of the data files are provided along with the Jupyter notebook in the code repository.

Libraries to Install for This Chapter

Because this chapter deals with reading various file formats, we need to have the support of additional libraries and software platforms to accomplish our goals.

Execute the following codes in your Jupyter notebook cells (don't forget the ! before each line of code) to install the necessary libraries:

```
!apt-get update
!apt-get install -y default-jdk

!pip install tabula-py xlrd lxml
```

Exercise 60: Reading Data from a CSV File Where Headers Are Missing

The pandas library provides a simple direct method called **read_csv** to read data in a tabular format from a comma-separated text file, or CSV. This is particularly useful because a CSV is a lightweight yet extremely handy data exchange format for many applications, including such domains as machine-generated data. It is not a proprietary format and therefore is universally used by a variety of data-generating sources.

At times, headers may be missing from a CSV file and you may have to add proper headers/column names of your own. Let's have a look at how this can be done:

1. Read the example CSV file (with a proper header) using the following code and examine the resulting DataFrame, as follows:

```
import numpy as np
import pandas as pd
df1 = pd.read_csv("CSV_EX_1.csv")
df1
```

The output is as follows:

	Bedroom	Sq. foot	Locality	Price ($)
0	2	1500	Good	300000
1	3	1300	Fair	240000
2	3	1900	Very good	450000
3	3	1850	Bad	280000
4	2	1640	Good	310000

Figure 5.1: Output of example CSV file

2. Read a .**csv** file with no header using a pandas DataFrame:

```
df2 = pd.read_csv("CSV_EX_2.csv")
df2
```

The output is as follows:

	2	1500	Good	300000
0	3	1300	Fair	240000
1	3	1900	Very good	450000
2	3	1850	Bad	280000
3	2	1640	Good	310000

Figure 5.2: Output of the .csv being read using a DataFrame

Certainly, the top data row has been mistakenly read as the column header. You can specify **header=None** to avoid this.

3. Read the .**csv** file by mentioning the header **None**, as follows:

```
df2 = pd.read_csv("CSV_EX_2.csv",header=None)
df2
```

However, without any header information, you will get back the following output. The default headers will be just some default numeric indices starting from 0:

	0	1	2	3
0	2	1500	Good	300000
1	3	1300	Fair	240000
2	3	1900	Very good	450000
3	3	1850	Bad	280000
4	2	1640	Good	310000

Figure 5.3: CSV file with a numeric column header

This may be fine for data analysis purposes, but if you want the DataFrame to truly reflect the proper headers, then you will have to add them using the **names** argument.

4. Add the **names** argument to get the correct headers:

```
df2 = pd.read_csv("CSV_EX_2.csv",header=None, names=['Bedroom','Sq.
ft','Locality','Price($)'])
df2
```

Finally, you will get a DataFrame that's as follows:

	Bedroom	Sq.ft	Locality	Price($)
0	2	1500	Good	300000
1	3	1300	Fair	240000
2	3	1900	Very good	450000
3	3	1850	Bad	280000
4	2	1640	Good	310000

Figure 5.4: CSV file with correct column header

Exercise 61: Reading from a CSV File where Delimiters are not Commas

Although CSV stands for comma-separated-values, it is fairly common to encounter raw data files where the separator/delimiter is a character other than a comma:

1. Read a **.csv** file using pandas DataFrames:

```
df3 = pd.read_csv("CSV_EX_3.csv")
df3
```

2. The output will be as follows:

	Bedroom; Sq. foot; Locality; Price ($)
0	2; 1500; Good; 300000
1	3; 1300; Fair; 240000
2	3; 1900; Very good; 450000
3	3; 1850; Bad; 280000
4	2; 1640; Good; 310000

Figure 5.5: A DataFrame that has a semi-colon as a separator

3. Clearly, the ; separator was not expected, and the reading is flawed. A simple work around is to specify the separator/delimiter explicitly in the read function:

```
df3 = pd.read_csv("CSV_EX_3.csv",sep=';')
df3
```

The output is as follows:

	Bedroom	Sq. foot	Locality	Price ($)
0	2	1500	Good	300000
1	3	1300	Fair	240000
2	3	1900	Very good	450000
3	3	1850	Bad	280000
4	2	1640	Good	310000

Figure 5.6: Semicolons removed from the DataFrame

Exercise 62: Bypassing the Headers of a CSV File

If your CSV file already comes with headers but you want to bypass them and put in your own, you have to specifically set **header = 0** to make it happen. If you try to set the names variable to your header list, unexpected things can happen:

1. Add names to a .csv file that has headers, as follows:

```
df4 = pd.read_csv("CSV_EX_1.csv",names=['A','B','C','D'])
df4
```

The output is as follows:

	A	B	C	D
0	Bedroom	Sq. foot	Locality	Price ($)
1	2	1500	Good	300000
2	3	1300	Fair	240000
3	3	1900	Very good	450000
4	3	1850	Bad	280000
5	2	1640	Good	310000

Figure 5.7: CSV file with headers overlapped

2. To avoid this, set **header** to zero and provide a names list:

```
df4 = pd.read_csv("CSV_EX_1.csv",header=0,names=['A','B','C','D'])
df4
```

The output is as follows:

	A	B	C	D
0	2	1500	Good	300000
1	3	1300	Fair	240000
2	3	1900	Very good	450000
3	3	1850	Bad	280000
4	2	1640	Good	310000

Figure 5.8: CSV file with defined headers

Exercise 63: Skipping Initial Rows and Footers when Reading a CSV File

Skipping initial rows is a widely useful method because, most of the time, the first few rows of a CSV data file are metadata about the data source or similar information, which is not read into the table:

Filetype: CSV			
	Info about some house		
Bedroom	Sq.foot	Locality	Price ($)
2	1500	Good	300000
3	1300	Fair	240000
3	1900	Very Good	450000
3	1850	Bad	280000
2	1640	Good	310000

Figure 5.9: Contents of the CSV file

Note

The first two lines in the CSV file are irrelevant data.

1. Read the CSV file and examine the results:

```
df5 = pd.read_csv("CSV_EX_skiprows.csv")
df5
```

The output is as follows:

	Filetype: CSV	Unnamed: 1	Unnamed: 2	Unnamed: 3
0	NaN	Info about some houses	NaN	NaN
1	Bedroom	Sq. foot	Locality	Price ($)
2	2	1500	Good	300000
3	3	1300	Fair	240000
4	3	1900	Very good	450000
5	3	1850	Bad	280000
6	2	1640	Good	310000

Figure 5.10: DataFrame with an unexpected error

2. Skip the first two rows and read the file:

```
df5 = pd.read_csv("CSV_EX_skiprows.csv",skiprows=2)
df5
```

The output is as follows:

	Bedroom	Sq. foot	Locality	Price ($)
0	2	1500	Good	300000
1	3	1300	Fair	240000
2	3	1900	Very good	450000
3	3	1850	Bad	280000
4	2	1640	Good	310000

Figure 5.11: Expected DataFrame after skipping two rows

3. Similar to skipping the initial rows, it may be necessary to skip the footer of a file. For example, we do not want to read the data at the end of the following file:

Filetype: CSV			
	Info about some houses		
Bedroom	Sq. foot	Locality	Price ($)
2	1500	Good	300000
3	1300	Fair	240000
3	1900	Very good	450000
3	1850	Bad	280000
2	1640	Good	310000
	This is the end of file		

Figure 5.12: Contents of the CSV file

We have to use **skipfooter** and the **engine='python'** option to enable this. There are two engines for these CSV reader functions – based on C or Python, of which only the Python engine supports the **skipfooter** option.

4. Use the **skipfooter** option in Python:

```
df6 = pd.read_csv("CSV_EX_skipfooter.csv",skiprows=2,
skipfooter=1,engine='python')
df6
```

The output is as follows:

	Bedroom	Sq. foot	Locality	Price ($)
0	2	1500	Good	300000
1	3	1300	Fair	240000
2	3	1900	Very good	450000
3	3	1850	Bad	280000
4	2	1640	Good	310000

Figure 5.13: DataFrame without a footer

Reading Only the First N Rows (Especially Useful for Large Files)

In many situations, we may not want to read a whole data file but only the first few rows. This is particularly useful for extremely large data files, where we may just want to read the first couple of hundred rows to check an initial pattern and then decide to read the whole data later on. Reading the entire file can take a long time and slow down the entire data wrangling pipeline.

A simple option, called **nrows**, in the **read_csv** function enables us to do just that:

```
df7 = pd.read_csv("CSV_EX_1.csv",nrows=2)
df7
```

The output is as follows:

	Bedroom	Sq. foot	Locality	Price ($)
0	2	1500	Good	300000
1	3	1300	Fair	240000

Figure 5.14: DataFrame with the first few rows of the CSV file

Exercise 64: Combining Skiprows and Nrows to Read Data in Small Chunks

Continuing our discussion about reading a very large data file, we can cleverly combine **skiprows** and **nrows** to read in such a large file in smaller chunks of pre-determined sizes. The following code demonstrates just that:

1. Create a list where DataFrames will be stored:

    ```
    list_of_dataframe = []
    ```

2. Store the number of rows to be read into a variable:

    ```
    rows_in_a_chunk = 10
    ```

3. Create a variable to store the number of chunks to be read:

    ```
    num_chunks = 5
    ```

4. Create a dummy DataFrame to get the column names:

    ```
    df_dummy = pd.read_csv("Boston_housing.csv",nrows=2)
    colnames = df_dummy.columns
    ```

5. Loop over the CSV file to read only a fixed number of rows at a time:

    ```
    for i in range(0,num_chunks*rows_in_a_chunk,rows_in_a_chunk):
        df = pd.read_csv("Boston_housing.csv",header=0,skiprows=i,nrows=rows_
    in_a_chunk,names=colnames)
        list_of_dataframe.append(df)
    ```

Note how the **iterator** variable is set up inside the **range** function to break it into chunks. Say the number of chunks is 5 and the rows per chunk is 10. Then, the iterator will have a range of (0,5*10,10), where the final 10 is step-size, that is, it will iterate with indices of (0,9,19,29,39,49).

Setting the skip_blank_lines Option

By default, **read_csv** ignores blank lines. But sometimes, you may want to read them in as NaN so that you can count how many such blank entries were present in the raw data file. In some situations, this is an indicator of the default data streaming quality and consistency. For this, you have to disable the **skip_blank_lines** option:

```
df9 = pd.read_csv("CSV_EX_blankline.csv",skip_blank_lines=False)
df9
```

The output is as follows:

	Bedroom	Sq. foot	Locality	Price ($)
0	2.0	1500.0	Good	300000.0
1	3.0	1300.0	Fair	240000.0
2	NaN	NaN	NaN	NaN
3	3.0	1900.0	Very good	450000.0
4	3.0	1850.0	Bad	280000.0
5	NaN	NaN	NaN	NaN
6	2.0	1640.0	Good	310000.0

Figure 5.15: DataFrame that has blank rows of a .csv file

Read CSV from a Zip file

This is an awesome feature of pandas, in that it allows you to read directly from a compressed file such as .zip, .gz, .bz2, or .xz. The only requirement is that the intended data file (CSV) should be the only file inside the compressed file.

In this example, we compressed the example CSV file with a 7-Zip program and read from it directly using the **read_csv** method:

```
df10 = pd.read_csv('CSV_EX_1.zip')

df10
```

The output is as follows:

	Bedroom	Sq. foot	Locality	Price ($)
0	2	1500	Good	300000
1	3	1300	Fair	240000
2	3	1900	Very good	450000
3	3	1850	Bad	280000
4	2	1640	Good	310000

Figure 5.16: DataFrame of a compressed CSV

Reading from an Excel File Using sheet_name and Handling a Distinct sheet_name

Next, we will turn our attention to a Microsoft Excel file. It turns out that most of the options and methods we learned about in the previous exercises with the CSV file apply directly to the reading of Excel files too. Therefore, we will not repeat them here. Instead, we will focus on their differences. An Excel file can consist of multiple worksheets and we can read a specific sheet by passing in a particular argument, that is, **sheet_name**.

For example, in the associated data file, **Housing_data.xlsx**, we have three tabs, and the following code reads them one by one in three separate DataFrames:

```
df11_1 = pd.read_excel("Housing_data.xlsx",sheet_name='Data_Tab_1')

df11_2 = pd.read_excel("Housing_data.xlsx",sheet_name='Data_Tab_2')

df11_3 = pd.read_excel("Housing_data.xlsx",sheet_name='Data_Tab_3')
```

If the Excel file has multiple distinct sheets but the **sheet_name** argument is set to **None**, then an ordered dictionary will be returned by the **read_excel** function. Thereafter, we can simply iterate over that dictionary or its keys to retrieve individual DataFrames.

Let's consider the following example:

```
dict_df = pd.read_excel("Housing_data.xlsx",sheet_name=None)

dict_df.keys()
```

The output is as follows:

```
odict_keys(['Data_Tab_1', 'Data_Tab_2', 'Data_Tab_3'])
```

Exercise 65: Reading a General Delimited Text File

General text files can be read as easily as we read CSV files. However, you have to pass on the proper separator if it is anything other than a whitespace or a tab:

1. A comma-separated file, saved with the **.txt** extension, will result in the following DataFrame if read without explicitly setting the separator:

   ```
   df13 = pd.read_table("Table_EX_1.txt")
   df13
   ```

The output is as follows:

	Bedroom, Sq. foot, Locality, Price ($)
0	2, 1500, Good, 300000
1	3, 1300, Fair, 240000
2	3, 1900, Very good, 450000
3	3, 1850, Bad, 280000
4	2, 1640, Good, 310000

Figure 5.17: DataFrame that has a comma-separated CSV file

2. In this case, we have to set the separator explicitly, as follows:

```
df13 = pd.read_table("Table_EX_1.txt",sep=',')
df13
```

The output is follows:

	Bedroom	Sq. foot	Locality	Price ($)
0	2	1500	Good	300000
1	3	1300	Fair	240000
2	3	1900	Very good	450000
3	3	1850	Bad	280000
4	2	1640	Good	310000

Figure 5.18: DataFrame read using a comma separator

Reading HTML Tables Directly from a URL

The pandas library allows us to read HTML tables directly from a URL. This means that they already have some kind of built-in HTML parser that processes the HTML content of a given page and tries to extract various tables in the page.

> **Note**
>
> The **read_html** method returns a list of DataFrames (even if the page has a single DataFrame) and you have to extract the relevant tables from the list.

Consider the following example:

```
url = 'https://www.fdic.gov/resources/resolutions/bank-failures/failed-bank-list/'

list_of_df = pd.read_html(url)

df14 = list_of_df[0]

df14.head()
```

These results are shown in the following DataFrame:

	Bank Name	City	ST	CERT	Acquiring Institution	Closing Date	Updated Date
0	Washington Federal Bank for Savings	Chicago	IL	30570	Royal Savings Bank	December 15, 2017	February 21, 2018
1	The Farmers and Merchants State Bank of Argonia	Argonia	KS	17719	Conway Bank	October 13, 2017	February 21, 2018
2	Fayette County Bank	Saint Elmo	IL	1802	United Fidelity Bank, fsb	May 26, 2017	July 26, 2017
3	Guaranty Bank, (d/b/a BestBank in Georgia & Mi...	Milwaukee	WI	30003	First-Citizens Bank & Trust Company	May 5, 2017	March 22, 2018
4	First NBC Bank	New Orleans	LA	58302	Whitney Bank	April 28, 2017	December 5, 2017

Figure 5.19: Results of reading HTML tables

Exercise 66: Further Wrangling to Get the Desired Data

As discussed in the preceding exercise, this HTML-reading function almost always returns more than one table for a given HTML page and we have to further parse through the list to extract the particular table we are interested in:

1. For example, if we want to get the table of the 2016 summer Olympics medal tally (by nation), we can easily search to get a page on Wikipedia that we can pass on to pandas. We can do this by using the following command:

```
list_of_df = pd.read_html("https://en.wikipedia.org/wiki/2016_Summer_
Olympics_medal_table",header=0)
```

2. If we check the length of the list returned, we will see it is 6:

```
len(list_of_df)
```

The output is as follows:

```
6
```

3. To look for the table, we can run a simple loop:

```
for t in list_of_df:
    print(t.shape)
```

The output is as follows:

```
(1, 1)
(87, 6)
(10, 8)
(0, 2)
(1, 1)
(4, 2)
```

Figure 5.20: Shape of the tables

4. It looks like the second element in this list is the table we are looking for:

```
df15=list_of_df[1]
df15.head()
```

5. The output is as follows:

	Rank	NOC	Gold	Silver	Bronze	Total
0	1	United States (USA)	46	37	38	121.0
1	2	Great Britain (GBR)	27	23	17	67.0
2	3	China (CHN)	26	18	26	70.0
3	4	Russia (RUS)	19	17	20	56.0
4	5	Germany (GER)	17	10	15	42.0

Figure 5.21: Output of the data in the second table

Exercise 67: Reading from a JSON File

Over the last 15 years, JSON has become a ubiquitous choice for data exchange on the web. Today, it is the format of choice for almost every publicly available web API, and it is frequently used for private web APIs as well. It is a schema-less, text-based representation of structured data that is based on key-value pairs and ordered lists.

The pandas library provides excellent support for reading data from a JSON file directly into a DataFrame. To practice with this chapter, we have included a file called **movies. json**. This file contains the cast, genre, title, and year (of release) information for almost all major movies since 1900:

1. Extract the cast list for the 2012 Avengers movie (from Marvel comics):

```
df16 = pd.read_json("movies.json")
df16.head()
```

The output is as follows:

	cast	genres	title	year
0	[]	[]	After Dark in Central Park	1900
1	[]	[]	Boarding School Girls' Pajama Parade	1900
2	[]	[]	Buffalo Bill's Wild West Parad	1900
3	[]	[]	Caught	1900
4	[]	[]	Clowns Spinning Hats	1900

Figure 5.22: DataFrame displaying the Avengers movie cast

2. To look for the cast where the title is "Avengers", we can use filtering:

```
cast_of_avengers=df16[(df16['title']=="The Avengers") &
(df16['year']==2012)]['cast']
print(list(cast_of_avengers))
```

The output will be as follows:

```
[['Robert Downey, Jr.', 'Chris Evans', 'Mark Ruffalo', 'Chris Hemsworth',
'Scarlett Johansson', 'Jeremy Renner', 'Tom Hiddleston', 'Clark Gregg',
'Cobie Smulders', 'Stellan SkarsgÃyrd', 'Samuel L. Jackson']]
```

Reading a Stata File

The pandas library provides a direct reading function for Stata files, too. Stata is a popular statistical modeling platform that's used in many governmental and research organizations, especially by economists and social scientists.

The simple code to read in a Stata file (**.dta** format) is as follows:

```
df17 = pd.read_stata("wu-data.dta")
```

Exercise 68: Reading Tabular Data from a PDF File

Among the various types of data sources, the PDF format is probably the most difficult to parse in general. While there are some popular packages in Python for working with PDF files for general page formatting, the best library to use for table extraction from PDF files is **tabula-py**.

From the GitHub page of this package, **tabula-py** is a simple Python wrapper of **tabula-java**, which can read a table from a PDF. You can read tables from PDFs and convert them into pandas DataFrames. The **tabula-py** library also enables you to convert a PDF file into a CSV/TSV/JSON file.

You will need the following packages installed on your system before you can run this, but they are free and easy to install:

- urllib3
- pandas
- pytest
- flake8
- distro
- pathlib

1. Find the PDF file in the following link: https://github.com/TrainingByPackt/Data-Wrangling-with-Python/blob/master/Chapter05/Exercise60-68/Housing_data.xlsx. The following code retrieves the tables from two pages and joins them to make one table:

```
from tabula import read_pdf
df18_1 = read_pdf('Housing_data.pdf',pages=[1],pandas_
options={'header':None})
df18_1
```

The output is as follows:

	0	1	2	3	4	5	6	7	8	9
0	0.17004	12.5	7.87	0	0.524	6.004	85.9	6.5921	5	311
1	0.22489	12.5	7.87	0	0.524	6.377	94.3	6.3467	5	311
2	0.11747	12.5	7.87	0	0.524	6.009	82.9	6.2267	5	311
3	0.09378	12.5	7.87	0	0.524	5.889	39.0	5.4509	5	311

Figure 5.23: DataFrame with a table derived by merging a table flowing over two pages in a PDF

2. Retrieve the table from another page of the same PDF by using the following command:

```
df18_2 = read_pdf('Housing_data.pdf',pages=[2],pandas_
options={'header':None})
df18_2
```

The output is as follows:

	0	1	2	3
0	15.2	386.71	17.10	18.9
1	15.2	392.52	20.45	15.0
2	15.2	396.90	13.27	18.9
3	15.2	390.50	15.71	21.7

Figure 5.24: DataFrame displaying a table from another page

3. To concatenate the tables that were derived from the first two steps, execute the following code:

```
df18=pd.concat([df18_1,df18_2],axis=1)
df18
```

The output is as follows:

	0	1	2	3	4	5	6	7	8	9	0	1	2	3
0	0.17004	12.5	7.87	0	0.524	6.004	85.9	6.5921	5	311	15.2	386.71	17.10	18.9
1	0.22489	12.5	7.87	0	0.524	6.377	94.3	6.3467	5	311	15.2	392.52	20.45	15.0
2	0.11747	12.5	7.87	0	0.524	6.009	82.9	6.2267	5	311	15.2	396.90	13.27	18.9
3	0.09378	12.5	7.87	0	0.524	5.889	39.0	5.4509	5	311	15.2	390.50	15.71	21.7

Figure 5.25: DataFrame derived by concatenating two tables

4. With PDF extraction, most of the time, headers will be difficult to extract automatically. You have to pass on the list of headers with the **names** argument in the **read-pdf** function as **pandas_option**, as follows:

```
names=['CRIM','ZN','INDUS','CHAS','NOX','RM',
'AGE','DIS','RAD','TAX','PTRATIO','B','LSTAT','PRICE']
df18_1 = read_pdf('Housing_data.pdf',pages=[1],pandas_
options={'header':None,'names':names[:10]})
df18_2 = read_pdf('Housing_data.pdf',pages=[2],pandas_
options={'header':None,'names':names[10:]})
df18=pd.concat([df18_1,df18_2],axis=1)
df18
```

The output is as follows:

	CRIM	ZN	INDUS	CHAS	NOX	RM	AGE	DIS	RAD	TAX	PTRATIO	B	LSTAT	PRICE
0	0.17004	12.5	7.87	0	0.524	6.004	85.9	6.5921	5	311	15.2	386.71	17.10	18.9
1	0.22489	12.5	7.87	0	0.524	6.377	94.3	6.3467	5	311	15.2	392.52	20.45	15.0
2	0.11747	12.5	7.87	0	0.524	6.009	82.9	6.2267	5	311	15.2	396.90	13.27	18.9
3	0.09378	12.5	7.87	0	0.524	5.889	39.0	5.4509	5	311	15.2	390.50	15.71	21.7

Figure 5.26: DataFrame with correct column headers for PDF data

We will have a full activity on reading tables from a PDF report and processing them at the end of this chapter.

Introduction to Beautiful Soup 4 and Web Page Parsing

The ability to read and understand web pages is one of paramount interest for a person collecting and formatting data. For example, consider the task of gathering data about movies and then formatting it for a downstream system. Data for the movies is best obtained by the websites such as IMDB and that data does not come pre-packaged in nice forms(CSV, JSON< and so on), so you need to know how to download and read web page.

Furthermore, you also need to be equipped with the knowledge of the structure of a web page so that you can design a system that can search for (query) a particular piece of information from a whole web page and get the value of it. This involves understanding the grammar of markup languages and being able to write something that can parse them. Doing this, and keeping all the edge cases in mind, for something like HTML is already incredibly complex, and if you extend the scope of the bespoke markup language to include XML as well, then it becomes full-time work for a team of people.

Thankfully, we are using Python, and Python has a very mature and stable library to do all of the complicated jobs for us. This library is called **BeautifulSoup** (it is, at present, in version 4 and thus we will call it **bs4** in short from now on). **bs4** is a library for getting data from HTML or XML documents, and it gives you a nice, normalized, idiomatic way of navigating and querying a document. It does not include a parser but it supports different ones.

Structure of HTML

Before we jump into **bs4** and start working with it, we need to examine the structure of a HTML document. **H**yper **T**ext **M**arkup **L**anguage is a structured way of telling web browsers about the organization of a web page, meaning which kind of elements (text, image, video, and so on) come from where, in which place inside the page they should appear, what they look like, what they contain, and how they will behave with user input. HTML5 is the latest version of HTML. An HTML document can be viewed as a tree, as we can see from the following diagram:

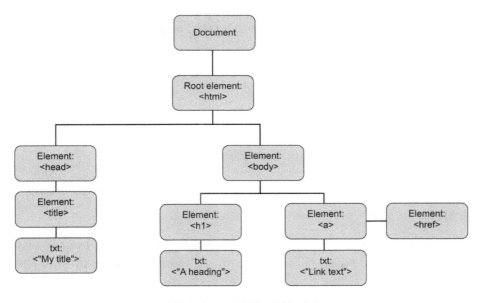

Document Object Model

Figure 5.27: HTML structure

Each node of the tree represents one element in the document. An element is anything that starts with **<** and ends with **>**. For example, **<html>**, **<head>**, **<p>**, **
, **<img>, and so on are various HTML elements. Some elements have a start and end element, where the end element begins with "**</**" and has the same name as the start element, such as **<p>** and **</p>**, and they can contain an arbitrary number of elements of other types in them. Some elements do not have an ending part, such as the **
** element, and they cannot contain anything within them.

The only other thing that we need to know about an element at this point is the fact that elements can have attributes, which are there to modify the default behavior of an element. An **<a>** element requires a **href** attribute to tell the browser which website it should navigate to when that particular **<a>** is clicked, like this: **<a href="http://cnn. com">**. The CNN news channel, **</a>**, will take you to cnn.com when clicked:

The CNN news channel

Figure 5.28: CNN news channel hyperlink

So, when you are at a particular element of the tree, you can visit all the children of that element to get the contents and attributes of them.

Equipped with this knowledge, let's see how we can read and query data from a HTML document.

In this topic, we will cover the reading and parsing of web pages, but we do not request them from a live website. Instead, we read them from disk. A section on reading them from the internet will follow in a future chapter.

Exercise 69: Reading an HTML file and Extracting its Contents Using BeautifulSoup

In this exercise, we will do the simplest thing possible. We will import the **BeautifulSoup** library and then use it to read an HTML document. Then, we will examine the different kinds of objects it returns. While doing the exercises for this topic, you should have the example HTML file open in a text editor all the time so that you can check for the different tags and their attributes and contents:

1. Import the **bs4** library:

```
from bs4 import BeautifulSoup
```

2. Please download the following test HTML file and save it on your disk and the use bs4 to read it from the disk:

```
with open("test.html", "r") as fd:
    soup = BeautifulSoup(fd)
    print(type(soup))
```

The output is as follows:

```
<class 'bs4.BeautifulSoup'>
```

You can pass a file handler directly to the constructor of the **BeautifulSoup** object and it will read the contents from the file that the handler is attached to. We will see that return-type is an instance of **bs4.BeautifulSoup**. This class holds all the methods we need to navigate through the DOM tree that the document represents.

3. Print the contents of the file in a nice way by using the **prettify** method from the class like this:

```
print(soup.prettify())
```

The output is as follows:

```
<html>
 <body>
  <h1>
   Lorem ipsum dolor sit amet consectetuer adipiscing
elit
  </h1>
  <p>
   Lorem ipsum dolor sit amet, consectetuer adipiscing
elit. Aenean commodo ligula eget dolor. Aenean massa
   <strong>
    strong
   </strong>
   . Cum sociis natoque penatibus
et magnis dis parturient montes, nascetur ridiculus
mus. Donec quam felis, ultricies nec, pellentesque
eu, pretium quis, sem. Nulla consequat massa quis
enim. Donec pede justo, fringilla vel, aliquet nec,
vulputate eget, arcu. In enim justo, rhoncus ut,
imperdiet a, venenatis vitae, justo. Nullam dictum
```

Figure 5.29: Contents of the HTML file

The same information can also be obtained by using the **soup.contents** member variable. The differences are: first, it won't print anything pretty and, second, it is essentially a list.

If we look carefully at the contents of the HTML file in a separate text editor, we will see that there are many paragraph tags, or **<p>** tags. Let's read content from one such **<p>** tag. We can do that using the simple . access modifier as we would have done for a normal member variable of a class.

4. The magic of **bs4** is the fact that it gives us this excellent way to dereference tags as member variables of the **BeautifulSoup** class instance:

```
with open("test.html", "r") as fd:
    soup = BeautifulSoup(fd)
    print(soup.p)
```

The output is as follows:

```
<p>Lorem ipsum dolor sit amet, consectetuer adipiscing
elit. Aenean commodo ligula eget dolor. Aenean massa
<strong>strong</strong>. Cum sociis natoque penatibus
et magnis dis parturient montes, nascetur ridiculus
mus. Donec quam felis, ultricies nec, pellentesque
eu, pretium quis, sem. Nulla consequat massa quis
enim. Donec pede justo, fringilla vel, aliquet nec,
vulputate eget, arcu. In enim justo, rhoncus ut,
imperdiet a, venenatis vitae, justo. Nullam dictum
felis eu pede <a class="external ext" href="#">link</a>
mollis pretium. Integer tincidunt. Cras dapibus.
Vivamus elementum semper nisi. Aenean vulputate
eleifend tellus. Aenean leo ligula, porttitor eu,
consequat vitae, eleifend ac, enim. Aliquam lorem ante,
dapibus in, viverra quis, feugiat a, tellus. Phasellus
viverra nulla ut metus varius laoreet. Quisque rutrum.
Aenean imperdiet. Etiam ultricies nisi vel augue.
Curabitur ullamcorper ultricies nisi.</p>
```

Figure 5.30: Text from the <p> tag

As we can see, this is the content of a **<p>** tag.

We saw how to read a tag in the last exercise, but we can easily see the problem with this approach. When we look into our HTML document, we can see that we have more than one **<p>** tag there. How can we access all the **<p>** tags? It turns out that this is easy.

5. Use the **findall** method to extract the content from the tag:

```
with open("test.html", "r") as fd:
    soup = BeautifulSoup(fd)
    all_ps = soup.find_all('p')
    print("Total number of <p>  --- {}".format(len(all_ps)))
```

The output is as follows:

```
Total number of <p>   --- 6
```

This will print 6, which is exactly the number of **<p>**tags in the document.

We have seen how to access all the tags of the same type. We have also seen how to get the content of the entire HTML document.

6. Now, we will see how to get the contents under a particular HTML tag, as follows:

```
with open("test.html", "r") as fd:
    soup = BeautifulSoup(fd)
    table = soup.table
    print(table.contents)
```

The output is as follows:

```
['\n   ', <tbody><tr>
    <th>Entry Header 1</th>
    <th>Entry Header 2</th>
    <th>Entry Header 3</th>
    <th>Entry Header 4</th>
  </tr>
  <tr>
    <td>Entry First Line 1</td>
    <td>Entry First Line 2</td>
    <td>Entry First Line 3</td>
    <td>Entry First Line 4</td>
  </tr>
  <tr>
    <td>Entry Line 1</td>
    <td>Entry Line 2</td>
    <td>Entry Line 3</td>
    <td>Entry Line 4</td>
  </tr>
  <tr>
    <td>Entry Last Line 1</td>
    <td>Entry Last Line 2</td>
    <td>Entry Last Line 3</td>
    <td>Entry Last Line 4</td>
  </tr>
</tbody>]
```

Figure 5.31: Content under the <table> tag

Here, we are getting the (first) table from the document and then using the same "." notation, to get the contents under that tag.

We saw in the previous exercise that we can access the entire content under a particular tag. However, HTML is represented as a tree and we are able to traverse the children of a particular node. There are a few ways to do this.

7. The first way is by using the **children** generator from any **bs4** instance, as follows:

```
with open("test.html", "r") as fd:
    soup = BeautifulSoup(fd)
    table = soup.table
    for child in table.children:
        print(child)
        print("*****")
```

When we execute the code, we will see something like the following:

```
*****
<tbody><tr>
    <th>Entry Header 1</th>
    <th>Entry Header 2</th>
    <th>Entry Header 3</th>
    <th>Entry Header 4</th>
  </tr>
  <tr>
    <td>Entry First Line 1</td>
    <td>Entry First Line 2</td>
    <td>Entry First Line 3</td>
    <td>Entry First Line 4</td>
  </tr>
  <tr>
    <td>Entry Line 1</td>
    <td>Entry Line 2</td>
    <td>Entry Line 3</td>
    <td>Entry Line 4</td>
  </tr>
  <tr>
    <td>Entry Last Line 1</td>
    <td>Entry Last Line 2</td>
    <td>Entry Last Line 3</td>
    <td>Entry Last Line 4</td>
  </tr>
</tbody>
*****
```

Figure 5.32: Traversing the children of a table node

It seems that the loop has only been executed twice! Well, the problem with the "**children**" generator is that it only takes into account the immediate children of the tag. We have **<tbody>** under the **<table>** and our whole table structure is wrapped in it. That's why it was considered a single child of the **<table>** tag.

We looked into how to browse the immediate children of a tag. We will see how we can browse all the possible children of a tag and not only the immediate one.

8. To do that, we use the **descendants** generator from the **bs4** instance, as follows:

```
with open("test.html", "r") as fd:
    soup = BeautifulSoup(fd)
    table = soup.table
    children = table.children
    des = table.descendants
    print(len(list(children)), len(list(des)))
```

The output is as follows:

```
9 61
```

The comparison print at the end of the code block will show us the difference between **children** and **descendants**. The length of the list we got from **children** is only 9, whereas the length of the list we got from **descendants** is 61.

Exercise 70: DataFrames and BeautifulSoup

So far, we have seen some basic ways to navigate the tags inside a HTML document using **bs4**. Now, we are going to go one step further and use the power of **bs4** combined with the power of pandas to generate a DataFrame out of a plain HTML table. This particular knowledge is very useful for us. With the knowledge we will acquire now, it will be fairly easy for us to prepare a pandas DataFrame to perform EDA (exploratory data analysis) or modeling. We are going to show this process on a simple small table from the test HTML file, but the exact same concept applies to any arbitrarily large table as well:

1. Import **pandas** and read the document, as follows:

```
import pandas as pd
fd = open("test.html", "r")
soup = BeautifulSoup(fd)
data = soup.findAll('tr')
print("Data is a {} and {} items long".format(type(data), len(data)))
```

The output is as follows:

```
Data is a <class 'bs4.element.ResultSet'> and 4 items long
```

2. Check the original table structure in the HTML source. You will see that the first row is the column headings and all of the following rows are the data. We assign two different variables for the two sections, as follows:

```
data_without_header = data[1:]
headers = data[0]
header
```

The output is as follows:

```
<tr>
<th>Entry Header 1</th>
<th>Entry Header 2</th>
<th>Entry Header 3</th>
<th>Entry Header 4</th>
</tr>
```

> **Note**
>
> Keep in mind that the art of scraping a HTML page goes hand in hand with an understanding of the source HTML structure. So, whenever you want to scrape a page, the first thing you need to do is right-click on it and then use "View Source" from the browser to see the source HTML.

3. Once we have separated the two sections, we need two list comprehensions to make them ready to go in a DataFrame. For the header, this is easy:

```
col_headers = [th.getText() for th in headers.findAll('th')]
col_headers
```

The output is as follows:

```
['Entry Header 1', 'Entry Header 2', 'Entry Header 3', 'Entry Header 4']
```

4. Data preparation is a bit tricky for a pandas DataFrame. You need to have a two-dimensional list, which is a list of lists. We accomplish that in the following way:

```
df_data = [[td.getText() for td in tr.findAll('td')] for tr in data_without_
header]
df_data
```

The output is as follows:

```
[['Entry First Line 1',
  'Entry First Line 2',
  'Entry First Line 3',
  'Entry First Line 4'],
 ['Entry Line 1', 'Entry Line 2', 'Entry Line 3', 'Entry Line 4'],
 ['Entry Last Line 1',
  'Entry Last Line 2',
  'Entry Last Line 3',
  'Entry Last Line 4']]
```

Figure 5.33: Output as a two-dimensional list

5. Invoke the **pd.DataFrame** method and supply the right arguments by using the following code:

```
df = pd.DataFrame(df_data, columns=col_headers)
df.head()
```

	Entry Header 1	Entry Header 2	Entry Header 3	Entry Header 4
0	Entry First Line 1	Entry First Line 2	Entry First Line 3	Entry First Line 4
1	Entry Line 1	Entry Line 2	Entry Line 3	Entry Line 4
2	Entry Last Line 1	Entry Last Line 2	Entry Last Line 3	Entry Last Line 4

Figure 5.34: Output in tabular format with column headers

Exercise 71: Exporting a DataFrame as an Excel File

In this exercise, we will see how we can save a DataFrame as an Excel file. Pandas can natively do this, but it needs the help of the **openpyxl** library to achieve this goal:

1. Install the **openpyxl** library by using the following command:

```
!pip install openpyxl
```

2. To save the DataFrame as an Excel file, use the following command from inside of the Jupyter notebook:

```
writer = pd.ExcelWriter('test_output.xlsx')
df.to_excel(writer, "Sheet1")
writer.save()
writer
```

The output is as follows:

```
<pandas.io.excel._XlsxWriter at 0x24feb2939b0>
```

Exercise 72: Stacking URLs from a Document using bs4

Previously (while discussing stack), we explained how important it is to have a stack that we can push the URLs from a web page to so that we can pop them at a later time to follow each of them. Here, in this exercise, we will see how that works.

In the given test, HTML file links or **<a>** tags are under a **<ul>** tag, and each of them is contained inside a **</li>** tag:

1. Find all the **<a>** tags by using the following command:

```
d = open("test.html", "r")
soup = BeautifulSoup(fd)
lis = soup.find('ul').findAll('li')
stack = []
for li in lis:
    a = li.find('a', href=True)
```

2. Define a stack before you start the loop. Then, inside the loop, use the **append** method to push the links in the stack:

```
stack.append(a['href'])
```

3. Print the stack:

```
['https://en.wikipedia.org/wiki/Entropy_(information_theory)', 'http://www.gutenberg.org/browse/sc
ores/top', 'https://www.imdb.com/chart/top']
```

Figure 5.35: Output of the stack

Activity 7: Reading Tabular Data from a Web Page and Creating DataFrames

In this activity, you have been given a Wikipedia page where you have the GDP of all countries listed. You have been asked to create three **DataFrames** from the three sources mentioned in the page (https://en.wikipedia.org/wiki/List_of_countries_by_GDP_(nominal)):

You will have to do the following:

1. Open the page in a separate Chrome/Firefox tab and use something like an **Inspect Element** tool to view the source HTML and understand its structure

2. Read the page using bs4

3. Find the table structure you will need to deal with (how many tables there are?)

4. Find the right table using bs4

5. Separate the source names and their corresponding data

6. Get the source names from the list of sources you have created

7. Separate the header and data from the data that you separated before for the first source only, and then create a DataFrame using that

8. Repeat the last task for the other two data sources

> **Note**
>
> The solution for this activity can be found on page 308.

Summary

In this topic, we looked at the structure of an HTML document. HTML documents are the cornerstone of the World Wide Web and, given the amount of data that's contained on it, we can easily infer the importance of HTML as a data source.

We learned about bs4 (BeautifulSoup4), a Python library that gives us Pythonic ways to read and query HTML documents. We used bs4 to load an HTML document and also explored several different ways to navigate the loaded document. We also got necessary information about the difference between all of these methods.

We looked at how we can create a pandas DataFrame from an HTML document (which contains a table). Although there are some built-in ways to do this job in pandas, they fail as soon as the target table is encoded inside a complex hierarchy of elements. So, the knowledge we gathered in this topic by transforming an HTML table into a pandas DataFrame in a step-by-step manner is invaluable.

Finally, we looked at how we can create a stack in our code, where we push all the URLs that we encounter while reading the HTML file and then use them at a later time. In the next chapter, we will discuss list comprehensions, zip, format and outlier detection and cleaning.

Learning the Hidden Secrets of Data Wrangling

Learning Objectives

By the end of this chapter, you will be able to:

- Clean and handle real-life messy data

- Prepare data for data analysis by formatting data in the format required by downstream systems

- Identify and remove outliers from data

In this chapter, you will learn about data issues that happen in real-life. You will also learn how to solve these issues.

Introduction

In this chapter, we will learn about the secret sauce behind creating a successful data wrangling pipeline. In the previous chapters, we were introduced to the basic data structures and building blocks of Data Wrangling, such as pandas and NumPy. In this chapter, we will look at the data handling section of data wrangling.

Imagine that you have a database of patients who have heart diseases, and like any survey, the data is either missing, incorrect, or has outliers. Outliers are values that are abnormal and tend to be far away from the central tendency, and thus including it into your fancy machine learning model may introduce a terrible bias that we need to avoid. Often, these problems can cause a huge difference in terms of money, man-hours, and other organizational resources. It is undeniable that someone with the skills to solve these problems will prove to be an asset to an organization.

Additional Software Required for This Section

The code for this exercise depends on two additional libraries. We need to install **SciPy** and **python-Levenshtein**, and we are going to install them in the running Docker container. Be wary of this, as we are not in the container.

To install the libraries, type the following command in the running Jupyter notebook:

```
!pip install scipy python-Levenshtein
```

Advanced List Comprehension and the zip Function

In this topic, we will deep dive into the heart of list comprehension. We have already seen a basic form of it, including something as simple as `a = [i for i in range(0, 30)]` to something a bit more complex that involves one conditional statement. However, as we already mentioned, list comprehension is a very powerful tool and, in this topic, we will explore the power of this amazing tool further. We will investigate another close relative of list comprehension called **generators**, and also work with **zip** and its related functions and methods. By the end of this topic, you will be confident in handling complicated logical problems.

Introduction to Generator Expressions

Previously, while discussing advanced data structures, we witnessed functions such as **repeat**. We said that they represent a special type of function known as iterators. We also showed you how the lazy evaluation of an iterator can lead to an enormous amount of space saving and time efficiency.

Iterators are one brick in the functional programming construct that Python has to offer. Functional programming is indeed a very efficient and safe way to approach a problem. It offers various advantages over other methods, such as modularity, ease of debugging and testing, composability, formal provability (a theoretical computer science concept), and so on.

Exercise 73: Generator Expressions

In this exercise, we will be introduced to generator expressions, which are considered another brick of functional programming (as a matter of fact, they are inspired by the pure functional language known as Haskell). Since we have seen some amount of list comprehension already, generator expressions will look familiar to us. However, they also offer some advantages over list comprehension:

1. Write the following code using list comprehension to generate a list of all the odd numbers between 0 and 100,000:

    ```
    odd_numbers2 = [x for x in range(100000) if x % 2 != 0]
    ```

2. Use **getsizeof** from **sys** by using the following code:

    ```
    from sys import getsizeof
    getsizeof(odd_numbers2)
    ```

    The output is as follows:

    ```
    406496
    ```

    We will see that it takes a good amount of memory to do this. It is also not very time efficient. How can we change that? Using something like **repeat** is not applicable here because we need to have the logic of the list comprehension. Fortunately, we can turn any list comprehension into a generator expression.

3. Write the equivalent generator expression for the aforementioned list comprehension:

```
odd_numbers = (x for x in range(100000) if x % 2 != 0)
```

Notice that the only change we made is to surround the list comprehension statement with round brackets instead of square ones. That makes it shrink to only around 100 bytes! This makes it become a lazy evaluation, and thus is more efficient.

4. Print the first 10 odd numbers, as follows:

```
for i, number in enumerate(odd_numbers):
    print(number)
    if i > 10:
        break
```

The output is as follows:

```
1
3
5
7
9
11
13
15
17
19
21
23
```

Exercise 74: One-Liner Generator Expression

In this exercise, we will use our knowledge of generator expressions to generate an expression that will read one word at a time from a list of words and will remove newline characters at the end of them and make them lowercase. This can certainly be done using a **for** loop explicitly:

1. Create a words string, as follows:

```
words = ["Hello\n", "My name", "is\n", "Bob", "How are you", "doing\n"]
```

2. Write the following generator expression to achieve the task, as follows:

```
modified_words = (word.strip().lower() for word in words)
```

3. Create a list comprehension to get words one by one from the generator expression and finally print the list, as follows:

```
final_list_of_word = [word for word in modified_words]
final_list_of_word
```

The output is as follows:

```
In [13]:  final_list_of_word = [word for word in modified_words]
          final_list_of_word

Out[13]:  ['hello', 'my name', 'is', 'bob', 'how are you', 'doing']
```

Figure 6.1: List comprehension of words

Exercise 75: Extracting a List with Single Words

If we look at the output of the previous exercise, we will notice that due to the messy nature of the source data (which is normal in the real world), we ended up with a list where, in some cases, we have more than one word together, separated by a space. To improve this, and to get a list of single words, we will have to modify the generator expressions:

1. Write the generator expression and then write the equivalent nested for loops so that we can compare the results:

```
words = ["Hello\n", "My name", "is\n", "Bob", "How are you", "doing\n"]
modified_words2 = (w.strip().lower() for word in words for w in word.split("
"))
final_list_of_word = [word for word in modified_words2]
final_list_of_word
```

The output is as follows:

```
In [21]:  final_list_of_word = [word for word in modified_words2]
          final_list_of_word
Out[21]:  ['hello', 'my', 'name', 'is', 'bob', 'how', 'are', 'you', 'doing']
```

Figure 6.2: List of words from the string

2. Write an equivalent to this by following a nested **for** loop, as follows:

```
modified_words3 = []
for word in words:
    for w in word.split(" "):
        modified_words3.append(w.strip().lower())
modified_words3
```

The output is as follows:

```
['hello', 'my', 'name', 'is', 'bob', 'how', 'are', 'you', 'doing']
```

Figure 6.3: List of words from the string using a nested loop

We must admit that the generator expression was not only space and time saving but also a more elegant way to write the same logic.

To remember how the nested loop in generator expressions works, keep in mind that the loops are evaluated from left to right and the final loop variable (in our example, which is denoted by the single letter "w") is given back (thus we could call **strip** and **lower** on it).

The following diagram will help you remember the trick about nested **for** loops in list comprehension or generator expression:

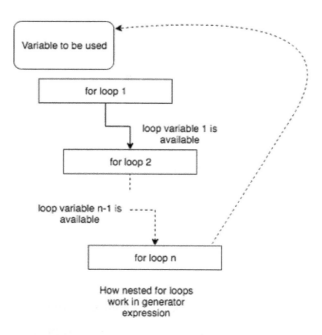

Figure 6.4: Nested loops illustration

We have learned about nested **for** loops in generator expressions previously, but now we are going to learn about independent **for** loops in a generator expression. We will have two output variables from two **for** loops and they must be treated as a tuple so that they don't have ambiguous grammar in Python.

Create the following two lists:

```
marbles = ["RED", "BLUE", "GREEN"]
counts = [1, 5, 13]
```

You are asked to generate all possible combinations of marbles and counts after being given the preceding two lists. How will you do that? Surely using a nested **for** loop and with list's **append** method you can accomplish the task. How about a generator expression? A more elegant and easy solution is as follows:

```
marble_with_count = ((m, c) for m in marbles for c in counts)
```

This generator expression creates a tuple in each iteration of the simultaneous **for** loops. This code is equivalent to the following explicit code:

```
marble_with_count_as_list_2 = []

for m in marbles:

    for c in counts:

        marble_with_count_as_list_2.append((m, c))

marble_with_count_as_list_2
```

The output is as follows:

```
In [24]:  marble_with_count_as_list = list(marble_with_count)
          marble_with_count_as_list

Out[24]:  [('RED', 1),
           ('RED', 5),
           ('RED', 13),
           ('BLUE', 1),
           ('BLUE', 5),
           ('BLUE', 13),
           ('GREEN', 1),
           ('GREEN', 5),
           ('GREEN', 13)]
```

Figure 6.5: Appending the marbles and counts

This generator expression creates a tuple in each iteration of the simultaneous for loops. Once again, the generator expression is easy, elegant, and efficient.

Exercise 76: The zip Function

In this exercise, we will examine the **zip** function and compare it with the generator expression we wrote in the previous exercise. The problem with the previous generator expression is the fact that, it produced all possible combinations. For instance, if we need to relate countries with its capitals, doing so using generator expression will be difficult. Fortunately, Python gives us a built-in function called **zip** for just this purpose:

1. Create the following two lists:

```
countries = ["India", "USA", "France", "UK"]
capitals = ["Delhi", "Washington", "Paris", "London"]
```

2. Generate a list of tuples where the first element is the name of the country and the second element is the name of the capital by using the following commands:

```
countries_and_capitals = [t for t in zip(countries, capitals)]
```

3. This is not very well represented. We can use **dict** where keys are the names of the countries, whereas the values are the names of the capitals by using the following command:

```
countries_and_capitals_as_dict = dict(zip(countries, capitals))
```

The output is as follows:

```
In [32]: countries_and_capitals_as_dict = dict(zip(countries, capitals))
         countries_and_capitals_as_dict

Out[32]: {'India': 'Delhi', 'USA': 'Washington', 'France': 'Paris', 'UK': 'London'}
```

Figure 6.6: Dictionary with countries and capitals

Exercise 77: Handling Messy Data

As always, in real life, data is messy. So, the nice equal length lists of countries and capitals that we just saw are not available.

The **zip** function cannot be used with unequal length lists, because **zip** will stop working as soon as one of the lists comes to an end. To save us in such a situation, we have **ziplongest** in the **itertools** module:

1. Create two lists of unequal length, as follows:

```
countries = ["India", "USA", "France", "UK", "Brasil", "Japan"]
capitals = ["Delhi", "Washington", "Paris", "London"]
```

2. Create the final **dict** and put **None** as the value to the countries who do not have a capital in the capital's list:

```
from itertools import zip_longest
countries_and_capitals_as_dict_2 = dict(zip_longest(countries, capitals))
countries_and_capitals_as_dict_2
```

The output is as follows:

```
In [36]: countries = ["India", "USA", "France", "UK", "Brasil", "Japan"]
         capitals = ["Delhi", "Washington", "Paris", "London"]
         from itertools import zip_longest
         countries_and_capitals_as_dict_2 = dict(zip_longest(countries, capitals))
         countries_and_capitals_as_dict_2

Out[36]: {'India': 'Delhi',
          'USA': 'Washington',
          'France': 'Paris',
          'UK': 'London',
          'Brasil': None,
          'Japan': None}
```

Figure 6.7: Output using ziplongest

We should pause here for a second and think about how many lines of explicit code and difficult-to-understand **if-else** conditional logic we just saved by calling a single function and just giving it the two source data lists. It is indeed amazing!

With these exercises, we are ending the first topic of this chapter. Advanced list comprehension, generator expressions, and functions such as **zip** and **ziplongest** are some very important tricks that we need to master if we want to write clean, efficient, and maintainable code. Code that does not have these three qualities are considered sub-par in the industry, and we certainly don't want to write such code.

However, we did not cover one important object here, that is, **generators**. Generators are a special type of function that shares the behavioral traits with generator expressions. However, being a function, they have a broader scope and they are much more flexible. We strongly encourage you to learn about them.

Data Formatting

In this topic, we will format a given dataset. The main motivations behind formatting data properly are as follows:

- It helps all the downstream systems to have a single and pre-agreed form of data for each data point, thus avoiding surprises and, in effect, breaking it.

- To produce a human-readable report from lower-level data that is, most of the time, created for machine consumption.

- To find errors in data.

There are a few ways to do data formatting in Python. We will begin with the modulus operator.

The % operator

Python gives us the % operator to apply basic formatting on data. To demonstrate this, we will load the data first by reading the CSV file, and then we will apply some basic formatting on it.

Load the data from the CSV file by using the following command:

```
from csv import DictReader

raw_data = []

with open("combinded_data.csv", "rt") as fd:
    data_rows = DictReader(fd)
    for data in data_rows:
        raw_data.append(dict(data))
```

Now, we have a list called **raw_data** that contains all the rows of the CSV file. Feel free to print it to check out what it looks like.

The output is as follows:

```
In [19]:  raw_data

Out[19]:  [{'Name': 'Bob',
            'Age': '23.0',
            'Height': '1.7',
            'Weight': '70',
            'Disease_history': 'N',
            'Heart_problem': 'N'},
           {'Name': 'Alex',
            'Age': '45',
            'Height': '1.61',
            'Weight': '61',
            'Disease_history': 'Y',
            'Heart_problem': 'N'},
           {'Name': 'George',
            'Age': '12.5',
            'Height': '1.4',
            'Weight': '40',
            'Disease_history': 'N',
            'Heart_problem': ''},
           {'Name': 'Alice',
            'Age': '34',
            'Height': '1.56',
            'Weight': '51',
            'Disease_history': 'N',
            'Heart_problem': 'Y'}]
```

Figure 6.8: Raw data

We will be producing a report on this data. This report will contain one section for each data point and will report the name, age, weight, height, history of family disease, and finally the present heart condition of the person. These points must be clear and easily understandable English sentences.

We do this in the following way:

```
for data in raw_data:

    report_str = """%s is %s years old and is %s meter tall weighing about %s
kg.\n

    Has a history of family illness: %s.\n

    Presently suffering from a heart disease: %s

    """ % (data["Name"], data["Age"], data["Height"], data["Weight"],
data["Disease_history"], data["Heart_problem"])

    print(report_str)
```

The output is as follows:

```
Bob is 23.0 years old and is 1.7 meter tall weiging about 70 kg.

    Has a hsitory of family illness: N.

    Presently suffering from a heart disease: N

Alex is 45 years old and is 1.61 meter tall weiging about 61 kg.

    Has a hsitory of family illness: Y.

    Presently suffering from a heart disease: N

George is 12.5 years old and is 1.4 meter tall weiging about 40 kg.

    Has a hsitory of family illness: N.

    Presently suffering from a heart disease:

Alice is 34 years old and is 1.56 meter tall weiging about 51 kg.

    Has a hsitory of family illness: N.

    Presently suffering from a heart disease: Y
```

Figure 6.9: Raw data in a presentable format

The % operator is used in two different ways:

- When used inside a quote, it signifies what kind of data to expect here. **%s** stands for string, whereas **%d** stands for integer. If we indicate a wrong data type, it will throw an error. Thus, we can effectively use this kind of formatting as an error filter in the incoming data.

- When we use the % operator outside the quote, it basically tells Python to start the replacement of all the data inside with the values provided for them outside.

Using the format Function

In this section, we will be looking at the exact same formatting problem, but this time we will use a more advanced approach. We will use Python's **format** function.

To use the **format** function, we do the following:

```
for data in raw_data:
    report_str = """{} is {} years old and is {} meter tall weighing about {}
kg.\n
    Has a history of family illness: {}.\n
    Presently suffering from a heart disease: {}
    """.format(data["Name"], data["Age"], data["Height"], data["Weight"],
data["Disease_history"], data["Heart_problem"])
    print(report_str)
```

The output is as follows:

```
Bob is 23.0 years old and is 1.7 meter tall weiging about 70 kg.

    Has a hsitory of family illness: N.

    Presently suffering from a heart disease: N

Alex is 45 years old and is 1.61 meter tall weiging about 61 kg.

    Has a hsitory of family illness: Y.

    Presently suffering from a heart disease: N

George is 12.5 years old and is 1.4 meter tall weiging about 40 kg.

    Has a hsitory of family illness: N.

    Presently suffering from a heart disease:

Alice is 34 years old and is 1.56 meter tall weiging about 51 kg.

    Has a hsitory of family illness: N.

    Presently suffering from a heart disease: Y
```

Figure 6.10: Data formatted using the format function of the string

Notice that we have replaced the **%s** with {} and instead of the % outside the quote, we have called the **format** function.

We will see how the powerful **format** function can make the previous code a lot more readable and understandable. Instead of simple and blank {}, we mention the key names inside and then use the special Python ****** operation on a **dict** to unpack it and give that to the format function. It is smart enough to figure out how to replace the key names inside the quote with the values from the actual **dict** by using the following command:

```
for data in raw_data:
    report_str = """{Name} is {Age} years old and is {Height} meter tall
weighing about {Weight} kg.\n
    Has a history of family illness: {Disease_history}.\n
    Presently suffering from a heart disease: {Heart_problem}
    """.format(**data)
    print(report_str)
```

The output is as follows:

```
Bob is 23.0 years old and is 1.7 meter tall weighing about 70 kg.

    Has a history of family illness: N.

    Presently suffering from a heart disease: N

Alex is 45 years old and is 1.61 meter tall weighing about 61 kg.

    Has a history of family illness: Y.

    Presently suffering from a heart disease: N

George is 12.5 years old and is 1.4 meter tall weighing about 40 kg.

    Has a history of family illness: N.

    Presently suffering from a heart disease:

Alice is 34 years old and is 1.56 meter tall weighing about 51 kg.

    Has a history of family illness: N.

    Presently suffering from a heart disease: Y
```

Figure 6.11: Readable file using the ** operation

This approach is indeed much more concise and maintainable.

Exercise 78: Data Representation Using {}

The {} notation inside the quote is powerful and we can change our data representation significantly by using it:

1. Change a decimal number to its binary form by using the following command:

```
original_number = 42
print("The binary representation of 42 is - {0:b}".format(original_number))
```

The output is as follows:

```
In [30]: original_number = 42
         print("The binary representation of 42 is - {0:b}".format(original_number))

         The binary representation of 42 is - 101010
```

Figure 6.12: A number in its binary representation

2. Printing a string that's center oriented:

```
print("{:^42}".format("I am at the center"))
```

The output is as follows:

```
In [31]: print("{:^42}".format("I am at the center"))
                      I am at the center
```

Figure 6.13: A string that's been center formatted

3. Printing a string that's center oriented, but this time with padding on both sides:

```
print("{:=^42}".format("I am at the center"))
```

The output is as follows:

```
In [33]: print("{:=^42}".format("I am at the center"))
         ============I am at the center============
```

Figure 6.14: A string that's been center formatted with padding

As we've already mentioned, the format statement is a powerful one.

It is important to format date as date has various formats depending on what the source of the data is, and it may need several transformations inside the data wrangling pipeline.

We can use the familiar date formatting notations with format as follows:

```
from datetime import datetime

print("The present datetime is {:%Y-%m-%d %H:%M:%S}".format(datetime.
utcnow()))
```

The output is as follows:

```
The present datetime is 2018-10-14 09:57:15
```

Figure 6.15: Data after being formatted

Compare it with the actual output of **datetime.utcnow** and you will see the power of this expression easily.

Identify and Clean Outliers

When confronted with real-world data, we often see a specific thing in a set of records: there are some data points that do not fit with the rest of the records. They have some values that are too big, or too small, or completely missing. These kinds of records are called **outliers**.

Statistically, there is a proper definition and idea about what an outlier means. And often, you need deep domain expertise to understand when to call a particular record an outlier. However, in this present exercise, we will look into some basic techniques that are commonplace to flag and filter outliers in real-world data for day-to-day work.

Exercise 79: Outliers in Numerical Data

In this exercise, we will first construct a notion of an outlier based on numerical data. Imagine a cosine curve. If you remember the math for this from high school, then a cosine curve is a very smooth curve within the limit of [1, -1]:

1. To construct a cosine curve, execute the following command:

```
from math import cos, pi
ys = [cos(i*(pi/4)) for i in range(50)]
```

2. Plot the data by using the following code:

```
import matplotlib.pyplot as plt
plt.plot(ys)
```

The output is as follows:

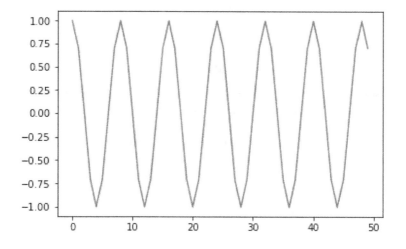

Figure 6.16: Cosine wave

As we can see, it is a very smooth curve, and there is no outlier. We are going to introduce some now.

3. Introduce some outliers by using the following command:

```
ys[4]  = ys[4]  + 5.0
ys[20] = ys[20] + 8.0
```

4. Plot the curve:

```
plt.plot(ys)
```

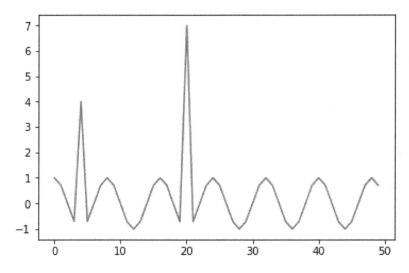

Figure 6.17: Wave with outliers

We can see that we have successfully introduced two values in the curve, which broke the smoothness and hence can be considered as outliers.

A good way to detect if our dataset has an outlier is to create a box plot. A boxplot is a way of plotting numerical data based on their central tendency and some **buckets** (in reality, we call them **quartiles**). In a box plot, the outliers are usually drawn as separate points. The **matplotlib** library helps draw boxplots out of a series of numerical data, which isn't hard at all. This is how we do it:

```
plt.boxplot(ys)
```

Once you execute the preceding code, you will be able to see that there is a nice boxplot where the two outliers that we had created are clearly shown, just like in the following diagram:

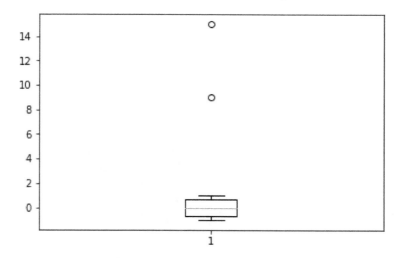

Figure 6.18: Boxplot with outliers

Z-score

A z-score is a measure on a set of data that gives you a value for each data point regarding how much that data point is spread out with respect to the standard deviation and mean of the dataset. We can use z-score to numerically detect outliers in a set of data. Normally, any data point with a z-score greater than +3 or less then –3 is considered an outlier. We can use this concept with a bit of help from the excellent SciPy and **pandas** libraries to filter out the outliers.

Use SciPy and calculate the z-score by using the following command:

```
from scipy import stats

cos_arr_z_score = stats.zscore(ys)

Cos_arr_z_score
```

The output is as follows:

```
In [57]:  from scipy import stats
          cos_arr_z_score = stats.zscore(ys)

In [58]:  cos_arr_z_score

Out[58]:  array([  0.17787522,   0.06102532,  -0.22107528,  -0.50317588,   3.36947919,
                  -0.50317588,  -0.22107528,   0.06102532,   0.17787522,   0.06102532,
                  -0.22107528,  -0.50317588,  -0.62002578,  -0.50317588,  -0.22107528,
                   0.06102532,   0.17787522,   0.06102532,  -0.22107528,  -0.50317588,
                   5.76318218,  -0.50317588,  -0.22107528,   0.06102532,   0.17787522,
                   0.06102532,  -0.22107528,  -0.50317588,  -0.62002578,  -0.50317588,
                  -0.22107528,   0.06102532,   0.17787522,   0.06102532,  -0.22107528,
                  -0.50317588,  -0.62002578,  -0.50317588,  -0.22107528,   0.06102532,
                   0.17787522,   0.06102532,  -0.22107528,  -0.50317588,  -0.62002578,
                  -0.50317588,  -0.22107528,   0.06102532,   0.17787522,   0.06102532])
```

Figure 6.19: The z-score values

Exercise 80: The Z-Score Value to Remove Outliers

In this exercise, we will discuss how to get rid of outliers in a set of data. In the last exercise, we calculated the z-score of each data point. In this exercise, we will use that to remove outliers from our data:

1. Import **pandas** and create a DataFrame:

   ```
   import pandas as pd
   df_original = pd.DataFrame(ys)
   ```

2. Assign outliers with a z-score less than 3:

   ```
   cos_arr_without_outliers = df_original[(cos_arr_z_score < 3)]
   ```

3. Use the **print** function to print the new and old shape:

   ```
   print(cos_arr_without_outliers.shape)
   print(df_original.shape)
   ```

From the two prints (48, 1 and 50, 1), it is clear that the derived DataFrame has two rows less. These are our outliers. If we plot the **cos_arr_without_outliers** DataFrame, then we will see the following output:

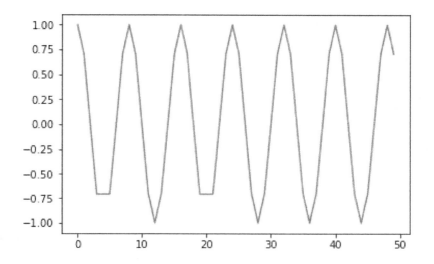

Figure 6.20: Cosine wave without outliers

As expected, we got back the smooth curve and got rid of the outliers.

Detecting and getting rid of outliers is an involving and critical process in any data wrangling pipeline. They need deep domain knowledge, expertise in descriptive statistics, mastery over the programming language (and all the useful libraries), and a lot of caution. We recommend being very careful when doing this operation on a dataset.

Exercise 81: Fuzzy Matching of Strings

In this exercise, we will look into a slightly different problem which, at the first glance, may look like an outlier. However, upon careful examination, we will see that it is indeed not, and we will learn about a useful concept that is sometimes referred to as fuzzy matching of strings.

Levenshtein distance is an advanced concept. We can think of it as the minimum number of single-character edits that are needed to convert one string into another. When two strings are identical, the distance between them is 0 – the more the difference, the higher the number. We can consider a threshold of distance under which we will consider two strings as the same. Thus, we can not only rectify human error but also spread a safety net so that we don't pass all the candidates.

Levenshtein distance calculation is an involving process, and we are not going to implement it from scratch here. Thankfully, like a lot of other things, there is a library available for us to do this. It is called python-Levenshtein:

1. Create the load data of a ship on three different dates:

```
In [72]:  ship_data = {"Sea Princess": {"date": "12/08/18", "load": 40000},
                       "Sea Pincess": {"date": "10/06/18", "load": 30000},
                       "Sea Princes": {"date": "12/04/18", "load": 30000},
                      }

In [74]:  from Levenshtein import distance
          name_of_ship = "Sea Princess"
          for k, v in ship_data.items():
              print("{} {} {}".format(k, name_of_ship, distance(name_of_ship, k)))

          Sea Princess Sea Princess 0
          Sea Pincess Sea Princess 1
          Sea Princes Sea Princess 1

In [ ]:
```

Figure 6.21: Initialized ship_data variable

If you look carefully, you will notice that the name of the ship is spelled differently in all three different cases. Let's assume that the actual name of the ship is "Sea Princess". From a normal perspective, it does look like there had been a human error and the data points do describe a single ship. Removing two of them on a strict basis of outliers may not be the best thing to do.

2. Then, we simply need to import the distance function from it and pass two strings to it to calculate the distance between them:

```
from Levenshtein import distance
name_of_ship = "Sea Princess"
for k, v in ship_data.items():
    print("{} {} {}".format(k, name_of_ship, distance(name_of_ship, k)))
```

The output is as follows:

```
In [72]: ship_data = {"Sea Princess": {"date": "12/08/18", "load": 40000},
                       "Sea Pincess": {"date": "10/06/18", "load": 30000},
                       "Sea Princes": {"date": "12/04/18", "load": 30000},
                      }

In [74]: from Levenshtein import distance
         name_of_ship = "Sea Princess"
         for k, v in ship_data.items():
             print("{} {} {}".format(k, name_of_ship, distance(name_of_ship, k)))

         Sea Princess Sea Princess 0
         Sea Pincess Sea Princess 1
         Sea Princes Sea Princess 1

In [ ]:
```

Figure 6.22: Distance between the strings

We will notice that the distance between the strings are different. It is 0 when they are identical, and it is a positive integer when they are not. We can use this concept in our data wrangling jobs and say that strings with distance less than or equal to a certain number is the same string.

Here, again, we need to be cautious about when and how to use this kind of fuzzy string matching. Sometimes, they are needed, and other times they will result in a very bad bug.

Activity 8: Handling Outliers and Missing Data

In this activity, we will identify and get rid of outliers. Here, we have a CSV file. The goal here is to clean the data by using the knowledge that we have learned about so far and come up with a nicely formatted DataFrame. Identify the type of outliers and their effect on the data and clean the messy data.

The steps that will help you solve this activity are as follows:

1. Read the **visit_data.csv** file.
2. Check for duplicates.
3. Check if any essential column contains NaN.
4. Get rid of the outliers.
5. Report the size difference.

6. Create a box plot to check for outliers.

7. Get rid of any outliers.

> **Note**
>
> The solution for this activity can be found on page 312.

Summary

In this chapter, we learned about interesting ways to deal with list data by using a **generator** expression. They are easy and elegant and once mastered, they give us a powerful trick that we can use repeatedly to simplify several common data wrangling tasks. We also examined different ways to format data. Formatting of data is not only useful for preparing beautiful reports – it is often very important to guarantee data integrity for the downstream system.

We ended the chapter by checking out some methods to identify and remove outliers. This is important for us because we want our data to be properly prepared and ready for all our fancy downstream analysis jobs. We also observed how important it is to take time and use domain expertise to set up rules for identifying outliers, as doing this incorrectly can do more harm than good.

In the next chapter, we will cover the how to read web pages, XML files, and APIs.

Advanced Web Scraping and Data Gathering

Learning Objectives

By the end of this chapter, you will be able to:

- Make use of **requests** and **BeautifulSoup** to read various web pages and gather data from them

- Perform read operations on XML files and the web using an Application Program Interface (API)

- Make use of regex techniques to scrape useful information from a large and messy text corpus

In this chapter, you will learn how to gather data from web pages, XML files, and APIs.

Introduction

The previous chapter covered how to create a successful data wrangling pipeline. In this chapter, we will build a real-life web scraper using all of the techniques that we have learned so far. This chapter builds on the foundation of **BeautifulSoup** and introduces various methods for scraping a web page and using an API to gather data.

The Basics of Web Scraping and the Beautiful Soup Library

In today's connected world, one of the most valued and widely used skill for a data wrangling professional is the ability to extract and read data from web pages and databases hosted on the web. Most organizations host data on the cloud (public or private), and the majority of web microservices these days provide some kind of API for the external users to access data:

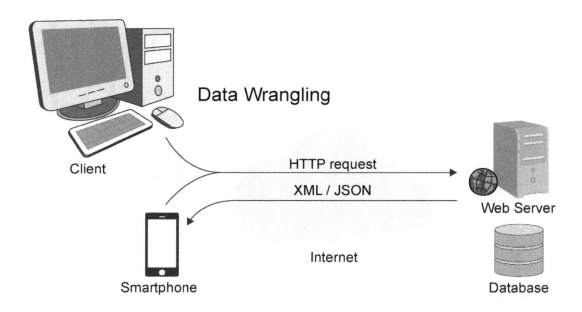

Figure 7.1: Data wrangling HTTP request and an XML/JSON reply

It is necessary that, as a data wrangling engineer, you know about the structure of web pages and Python libraries so that you are able to extract data from a web page. The World Wide Web is an ever-growing, ever-changing universe, in which different data exchange protocols and formats are used. A few of these are widely used and have become standard.

Libraries in Python

Python comes equipped with built-in modules, such as **urllib 3**, which that can place HTTP requests over the internet and receive data from the cloud. However, these modules operate at a lower level and require deeper knowledge of HTTP protocols, encoding, and requests.

We will take advantage of two Python libraries in this chapter: **Requests** and **BeautifulSoup**. To avoid dealing with HTTP methods on a lower level, we will use the **Requests** library. It is an API built on top of pure Python web utility libraries, which makes placing HTTP requests easy and intuitive.

BeautifulSoup is one of the most popular HTML parser packages. It parses the HTML content you pass on and builds a detailed tree of all tags and markups within the page for easy and intuitive traversal. This tree can be used by a programmer to look for certain markup elements (for example, a table, a hyperlink, or a blob of text within a particular div ID) to scrape useful data.

Exercise 81: Using the Requests Library to Get a Response from the Wikipedia Home Page

The Wikipedia home page consists of many elements and scripts, all of which are a mix of HTML, CSS, and JavaScript code blocks. To read the home page of Wikipedia and extract some useful textual information, we need to move step by step, as we are not interested in all of the code or markup tags; only some selected portions of text.

In this exercise, we will peel off the layers of HTML/CSS/JavaScript to pry away the information we are interested in.

1. Import the **requests** library:

    ```
    import requests
    ```

2. Assign the home page URL to a variable, **wiki_home**:

    ```
    # First assign the URL of Wikipedia home page to a strings
    wiki_home = "https://en.wikipedia.org/wiki/Main_Page"
    ```

3. Use the **get** method from the **requests** library to get a response from this page:

    ```
    response = requests.get(wiki_home)
    ```

4. To get information about the response object, enter the following code:

```
type(response)
```

The output is as follows:

```
requests.models.Response
```

It is a model data structure that's defined in the **requests** library.

The web is an extremely dynamic place. It is possible that the home page of Wikipedia will have changed by the time somebody uses your code, or that a particular web server will be down and your request will essentially fail. If you proceed to write more complex and elaborate code without checking the status of your request, then all that subsequent work will be fruitless.

A web page request generally comes back with various codes. Here are some of the common codes you may encounter:

Code	Description	Code	Description
200	OK	400	Bad Request
201	Created	401	Unauthorized
202	Accepted	403	Forbidden
301	Moved Permanently	404	Not Found
303	See Other	410	Gone
304	Not Modified	500	Internal Server Error
307	Temporary Redirect	503	Service Unavailable

Figure 7.2: Web requests and their description

So, we write a function to check the code and print out messages as needed. These kinds of small helper/utility functions are incredibly useful for complex projects.

Exercise 82: Checking the Status of the Web Request

Next, we will write a small utility function to check the status of the response.

We will start by getting into the a habit of writing small functions to accomplish small modular tasks, instead of writing long scripts, which are hard to debug and track:

1. Create a **status_check** function by using the following command:

```
def status_check(r):
    if r.status_code==200:
        print("Success!")
        return 1
    else:
        print("Failed!")
        return -1
```

Note that, along with printing the appropriate message, we are returning either 1 or -1 from this function. This is important.

2. Check the response using the **status_check** command:

```
status_check(response)
```

The output is as follows:

```
status_check(response)

    Success!

1
```

Figure 7.3 : The output of status_check

In this chapter, we will not use these returned values, but later, for more complex programming activity, you will proceed only if you get one as the return value for this function, that is, you will write a conditional statement to check the return value and then execute the subsequent code based on that.

Checking the Encoding of the Web Page

We can also write a utility function to check the encoding of the web page. Various encodings are possible with any HTML document, although the most popular is UTF-8. Some of the most popular encodings are ASCII, Unicode, and UTF-8. ASCII is the simplest, but it cannot capture the complex symbols used in various spoken and written languages all over the world, so UTF-8 has become the almost universal standard in web development these days.

When we run this function on the Wikipedia home page, we get back the particular encoding type that's used for that page. This function, like the previous one, takes the **requests** response object as an argument and returns a value:

```
def encoding_check(r):
    return (r.encoding)
```

Check the response:

```
encoding_check(response)
```

The output is as follows:

```
'UTF-8'
```

Here, UTF-8 denotes the most popular character encoding scheme that's used in the digital medium and on the web today. It employs variable-length encoding with 1-4 bytes, thereby representing all Unicode characters in various languages around the world.

Exercise 83: Creating a Function to Decode the Contents of the Response and Check its Length

The final aim of this series of steps is to get a page's contents as a blob of text or as a string object that Python can process afterward. Over the internet, data streams move in an encoded format. Therefore, we need to decode the content of the response object. For this purpose, we need to perform the following steps:

1. Write a utility function to decode the contents of the response:

```
def decode_content(r,encoding):
    return (r.content.decode(encoding))

contents = decode_content(response,encoding_check(response))
```

2. Check the type of the decoded object:

```
type(contents)
```

The output is as follows:

```
str
```

We finally got a string object by reading the HTML page!

> **Note**
>
> Note that the answer in this chapter and in the exercise in Jupyter notebook may vary because of updates that have been made to the Wikipedia page.

3. Check the length of the object and try printing some of it:

```
len(contents)
```

The output is as follows:

```
74182
```

If you print the first 10,000 characters of this string, it will look some similar to this:

```
<!DOCTYPE html>
<html class="client-nojs" lang="en" dir="ltr">
<head>
<meta charset="UTF-8"/>
<title>Wikipedia, the free encyclopedia</title>
<script>document.documentElement.className = document.documentElement.className.replace( /(^|\s)client-nojs(\s|$)/, "
$1client-js$2" );</script>
<script>(window.RLQ=window.RLQ||[]).push(function(){mw.config.set({"wgCanonicalNamespace":"","wgCanonicalSpecialPageN
ame":false,"wgNamespaceNumber":0,"wgPageName":"Main_Page","wgTitle":"Main Page","wgCurRevisionId":865422981,"wgRevisi
onId":865422981,"wgArticleId":15580374,"wgIsArticle":true,"wgIsRedirect":false,"wgAction":"view","wgUserName":null,"w
gUserGroups":["*"],"wgCategories":[],"wgBreakFrames":false,"wgPageContentLanguage":"en","wgPageContentModel":"wikitex
t","wgSeparatorTransformTable":["",""],"wgDigitTransformTable":["",""],"wgDefaultDateFormat":"dmy","wgMonthNames":[""
,"January","February","March","April","May","June","July","August","September","October","November","December"],"wgMo
nthNamesShor
```

Figure 7.4: Output showing a mixed blob of HTML markup tags, text and element names, and properties

Obviously, this is a mixed blob of various HTML markup tags, text, and elements names/properties. We cannot hope to extract meaningful information from this without using sophisticated functions or methods. Fortunately, the **BeautifulSoup** library provides such methods, and we will see how to use them next.

Exercise 84: Extracting Human-Readable Text From a BeautifulSoup Object

It turns out that a **BeautifulSoup** object has a **text** method, which can be used just to extract text:

1. Import the package and then pass on the whole string (HTML content) to a method for parsing:

    ```
    from bs4 import BeautifulSoup
    soup = BeautifulSoup(contents, 'html.parser')
    ```

2. Execute the following code in your notebook:

    ```
    txt_dump=soup.text
    ```

3. Find the type of the **txt_dmp**:

    ```
    type(txt_dump)
    ```

    The output is as follows:

    ```
    str
    ```

4. Find the length of the **txt_dmp**:

    ```
    len(txt_dump)
    ```

    The output is as follows:

    ```
    15326
    ```

5. Now, the length of the text dump is much smaller than the raw HTML's string length. This is because **bs4** has parsed through the HTML and extracted only human-readable text for further processing.

6. Print the initial portion of this text.

    ```
    print(txt_dump[10000:11000])
    ```

You will see something similar to the following:

```
or Wikipedia-related communication in languages other than English.
Reference desk - Serving as virtual librarians, Wikipedia volunteers tackle
s.
Site news - Announcements, updates, articles and press releases on Wikipedi
Village pump - For discussions about Wikipedia itself, including areas for

Wikipedia's sister projects
.mw-parser-output #sister-projects-list{text-align:left;background:transpar
rojects-list>div{width:32%;min-width:20em;white-space:nowrap;margin:0 1px;d
ter-projects-list>div>div{display:inline-block;vertical-align:middle;margin
er-projects-list>div>div:first-child{min-width:50px;text-align:center}
Wikipedia is hosted by the Wikimedia Foundation, a non-profit organization
```

Figure 7.5: Output showing the initial portion of text

Extracting Text from a Section

Now, let's move on to a more exciting data wrangling task. If you open the Wikipedia home page, you are likely to see a section called **From today's featured article**. This is an excerpt from the day's prominent article, which is randomly selected and promoted on the home page. In fact, this article can also change throughout the day:

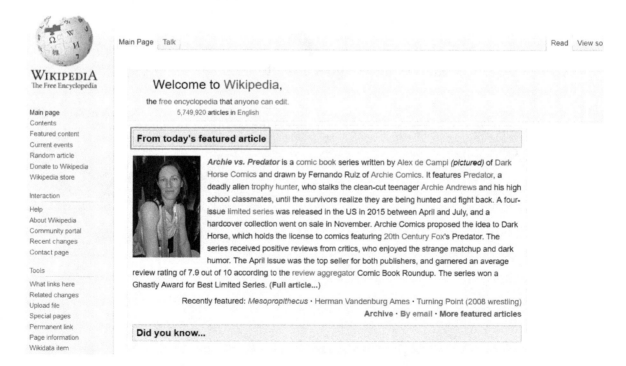

Figure 7.6: Sample Wikipedia page highlighting the "From today's featured article" section

You need to extract the text from this section. There are number of ways to accomplish this task. We will go through a simple and intuitive method for doing so here.

First, we try to identify two indices – the start index and end index of the string, which demarcate the start and end of the text we are interested in. In the next screenshot, the indices are shown:

Figure 7.7: Wikipedia page highlighting the text to be extracted

The following code accomplishes the extraction:

```
idx1=txt_dump.find("From today's featured article")

idx2=txt_dump.find("Recently featured")


print(txt_dump[idx1+len("From today's featured article"):idx2])
```

Note, that we have to add the length of the **From today's featured article** string to **idx1** and then pass that as the starting index. This is because idx1 finds where the *From today's featured article* string starts, not ends.

It prints out something like this (this is a sample output):

> *Archie vs. Predator is a comic book series written by Alex de Campi (pictured) of Dark Horse Comics and drawn by Fernando Ruiz of Archie Comics. It features Predator, a deadly alien trophy hunter, who stalks the clean-cut teenager Archie Andrews and his high school classmates, until the survivors realize they are being hunted and fight back. A four-issue limited series was released in the US in 2015 between April and July, and a hardcover collection went on sale in November. Archie Comics proposed the idea to Dark Horse,*

Figure 7.8: The extracted text

Extracting Important Historical Events that Happened on Today's Date

Next, we will try to extract the text corresponding to the important historical events that happened on today's date. This can generally be found at the bottom-right corner as shown in the following screenshot:

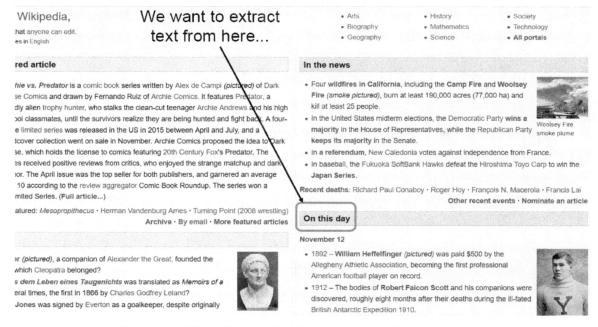

Figure 7.9: Wikipedia page highlighting the "On this day" section

So, can we apply the same technique as we did for "**From today's featured article**"? Apparently not, because there is text just below where we want our extraction to end, which is not fixed, unlike in the previous case. Note that, in the previous exercise, the fixed string "**Recently featured**" occurs at the exact place where we want the extraction to stop. So, we could use it in our code. However, we cannot do that in this case, and the reason for this is illustrated in the following screenshot:

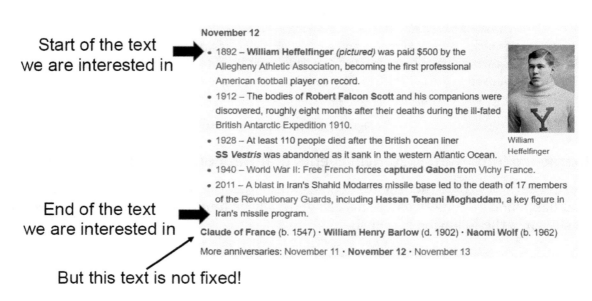

Figure 7.10: Wikipedia page highlighting the text to be extracted

So, in this section, we just want to find out what the text looks like around the main content we are interested in. For that, we must find out the start of the string "On this day" and print out the next 1,000 characters, using the following command:

```
idx3=txt_dump.find("On this day")
```

```
print(txt_dump[idx3+len("On this day"):idx3+len("On this day")+1000])
```

This looks as follows:

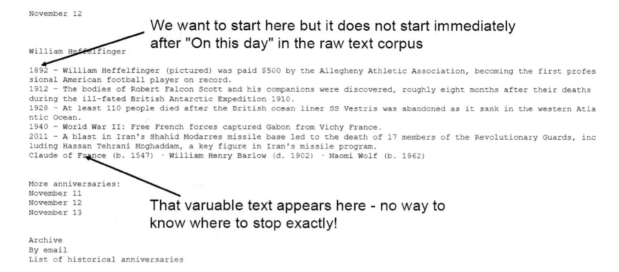

Figure 7.11: Output of the "On this day" section from Wikipedia

To address this issue, we need to think differently and use some other methods from BeautifulSoup (and write another utility function).

Exercise 85: Using Advanced BS4 Techniques to Extract Relevant Text

HTML pages are made of many markup tags, such as <div>, which denotes a division of text/images, or <ul>, which denotes lists. We can take advantage of this structure and look at the element that contains the text we are interested in. In the Mozilla Firefox browser, we can easily do this by right-clicking and selecting the "**Inspect Element**" option:

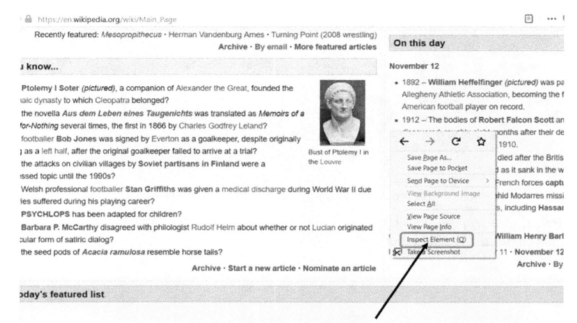

Figure 7.12: Inspecting elements on Wikipedia

As you hover over this with the mouse, you will see different portions of the page being highlighted. By doing this, it is easy to discover the precise block of markup text, that is responsible for the textual information we are interested in. Here, we can see that a certain **<ul>** block contains the text:

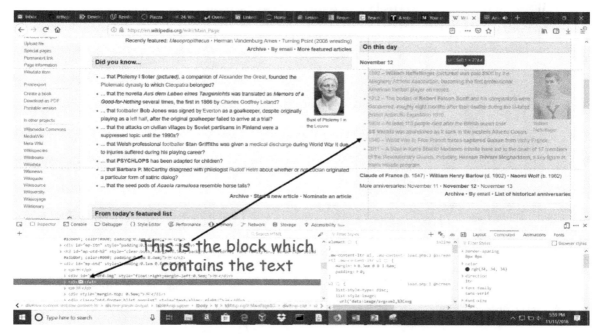

Figure 7.13: Identifying the HTML block that contains text

Now, it is prudent to find the **<div>** tag that contains this **<ul>** block within it. By looking around the same screen as before, we find the **<div>** and also its ID:

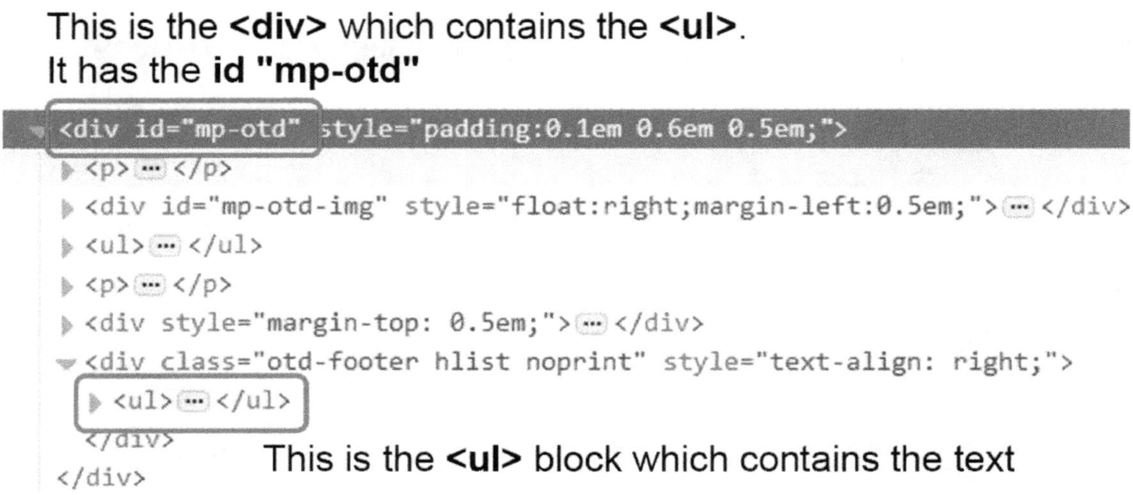

This is the **<div>** which contains the **<ul>**.
It has the **id "mp-otd"**

```
<div id="mp-otd" style="padding:0.1em 0.6em 0.5em;">
  <p>⋯</p>
  <div id="mp-otd-img" style="float:right;margin-left:0.5em;">⋯</div>
  <ul>⋯</ul>
  <p>⋯</p>
  <div style="margin-top: 0.5em;">⋯</div>
  <div class="otd-footer hlist noprint" style="text-align: right;">
    <ul>⋯</ul>
  </div>
</div>
```

This is the **<ul>** block which contains the text

Figure 7.14: The <ul> tag containing the text

1. Use the **find_all** method from BeautifulSoup, which scans all the tags of the HTML page (and their sub-elements) to find and extract the text associated with this particular **<div>** element.

> **Note**
>
> Note how we are utilizing the 'mp-otd' ID of the <div> to identify it among tens of other <div> elements.

The **find_all** method returns a **NavigableString** class, which has a useful **text** method associated with it for extraction.

2. To put these ideas together, we will create an empty list and append the text from the **NavigableString** class to this list as we traverse the page:

```
text_list=[] #Empty list


for d in soup.find_all('div'):
        if (d.get('id')=='mp-otd'):
            for i in d.find_all('ul'):
                text_list.append(i.text)
```

3. Now, if we examine the **text_list** list, we will see that it has three elements. If we print the elements, separated by a marker, we will see that the text we are interested in appears as the first element!

```
for i in text_list:
    print(i)
    print('-'*100)
```

> **Note**
>
> In this example, it is the first element of the list that we are interested in. However, the exact position will depend on the web page.

The output is as follows:

This is the text, we are interested in!

```
1892 - William Heffelfinger (pictured) was paid $500 by the Allegheny Athletic Association, becoming the first profes
sional American football player on record.
1912 - The bodies of Robert Falcon Scott and his companions were discovered, roughly eight months after their deaths
during the ill-fated British Antarctic Expedition 1910.
1928 - At least 110 people died after the British ocean liner SS Vestris was abandoned as it sank in the western Atla
ntic Ocean.
1940 - World War II: Free French forces captured Gabon from Vichy France.
2011 - A blast in Iran's Shahid Modarres missile base led to the death of 17 members of the Revolutionary Guards, inc
luding Hassan Tehrani Moghaddam, a key figure in Iran's missile program.
```

```
November 11
November 12
November 13
----------------------------------------------------------------------------------------------------------
Archive
By email
List of historical anniversaries
----------------------------------------------------------------------------------------------------------
```

Figure 7.15: The text highlighted

Exercise 86: Creating a Compact Function to Extract the "On this Day" Text from the Wikipedia Home Page

As we discussed before, it is always good to try to functionalize specific tasks, particularly in a web scraping application:

1. Create a function, whose only job is to take the URL (as a string) and to return the text corresponding to the **On this day** section. The benefit of such a functional approach is that you can call this function from any Python script and use it anywhere in another program as a standalone module:

```
def wiki_on_this_day(url="https://en.wikipedia.org/wiki/Main_Page"):
    """
```

2. Extract the text from the "On this day" section on the Wikipedia home page. Accept the Wikipedia home page URL as a string. A default URL is provided:

```
    """
    import requests
    from bs4 import BeautifulSoup

    wiki_home = str(url)
    response = requests.get(wiki_home)

    def status_check(r):
        if r.status_code==200:
            return 1
        else:
            return -1

    status = status_check(response)
    if status==1:
        contents = decode_content(response,encoding_check(response))
    else:
        print("Sorry could not reach the web page!")
        return -1

    soup = BeautifulSoup(contents, 'html.parser')
    text_list=[]
```

```
for d in soup.find_all('div'):
        if (d.get('id')=='mp-otd'):
            for i in d.find_all('ul'):
                text_list.append(i.text)


    return (text_list[0])
```

3. Note how this function utilizes the status check and prints out an error message if the request failed. When we test this function with an intentionally incorrect URL, it behaves as expected:

```
print(wiki_on_this_day("https://en.wikipedia.org/wiki/Main_Page1"))
 Sorry could not reach the web page!
```

Reading Data from XML

XML, or Extensible Markup Language, is a web markup language that's similar to HTML but with significant flexibility (on the part of the user) built in, such as the ability to define your own tags. It was one of the most hyped technologies in the 1990s and early 2000s. It is a meta-language, that is, a language that allows us to define other languages using its mechanics, such as RSS, MathML (a mathematical markup language widely used for web publication and the display of math-heavy technical information), and so on. XML is also heavily used in regular data exchanges over the web, and as a data wrangling professional, you should have enough familiarity with its basic features to tap into the data flow pipeline whenever you need to extract data for your project.

Exercise 87: Creating an XML File and Reading XML Element Objects

Let's create some random data to understand the XML data format better. Type in the following code snippets:

1. Create an XML file using the following command:

```
data = '''
<person>
  <name>Dave</name>
  <surname>Piccardo</surname>
  <phone type="intl">
     +1 742 101 4456
  </phone>
  <email hide="yes">
  dave.p@gmail.com</email>
</person>'''
```

2. This is a triple-quoted string or multiline string. If you print this object, you will get the following output. This is an XML-formatted data string in a tree structure, as we will see soon, when we parse the structure and tease apart the individual parts:

```
<person>
  <name>Dave</name>
  <surname>Piccardo</surname>
  <phone type="intl">
     +1 742 101 4456
  </phone>
  <email hide="yes">
  dave.p@gmail.com</email>
</person>
```

Figure 7.16: The XML file output

3. To process and wrangle with the data, we have to read it as an **Element** object using the Python XML parser engine:

```
import xml.etree.ElementTree as ET
tree = ET.fromstring(data)

type (tree)
```

The output is as follows:

```
xml.etree.ElementTree.Element
```

Exercise 88: Finding Various Elements of Data within a Tree (Element)

We can use the **find** method to search for various pieces of useful data within an XML element object and print them (or use them in whatever processing code we want) using the **text** method. We can also use the **get** method to extract the specific attribute we want:

1. Use the **find** method to find **Name**:

   ```
   # Print the name of the person
   print('Name:', tree.find('name').text)
     Dave
   ```

2. Use the **find** method to find **Surname**:

   ```
   # Print the surname
   print('Surname:', tree.find('surname').text)
     Piccardo
   ```

3. Use the **find** method to find **Phone**. Note the use of the **strip** method to strip away any trailing spaces/blanks:

   ```
   # Print the phone number
   print('Phone:', tree.find('phone').text.strip())
   ```

   The output will be as follows:

   ```
   +1 742 101 4456
   ```

4. Use the **find** method to find **email status** and **actual email**. Note the use of the **get** method to extract the status:

   ```
   # Print email status and the actual email
   print('Email hidden:', tree.find('email').get('hide'))
   print('Email:', tree.find('email').text.strip())
   ```

   The output will be as follows:

   ```
   Email hidden: yes
   Email: dave.p@gmail.com
   ```

Reading from a Local XML File into an ElementTree Object

We can also read from an XML file (saved locally on disk).

This is a fairly common situation where a frontend web scraping module has already downloaded a lot of XML files by reading a table of data on the web and now the data wrangler needs to parse through this XML file to extract meaningful pieces of numerical and textual data.

We have a file associated with this chapter, called "**xml1.xml**". Please make sure you have the file in the same directory that you are running your Jupyter Notebook from:

```
tree2=ET.parse('xml1.xml')

type(tree2)

The output will be as follows: xml.etree.ElementTree.ElementTree
```

Note how we use the **parse** method to read this XML file. This is slightly different than using the **fromstring** method used in the previous exercise, where we were directly reading from a string object. This produces an **ElementTree** object instead of a simple **Element**.

The idea of building a tree-like object is the same as in the domains of computer science and programming:

- There is a root
- There are children objects attached to the root
- There could be multiple levels, that is, children of children recursively going down
- All of the nodes of the tree (root and children alike) have attributes attached to them that contain data
- Tree traversal algorithms can be used to search for a particular attribute
- If provided, special methods can be used to probe a node deeper

Exercise 89: Traversing the Tree, Finding the Root, and Exploring all Child Nodes and their Tags and Attributes

Every node in the XML tree has tags and attributes. The idea is as follows:

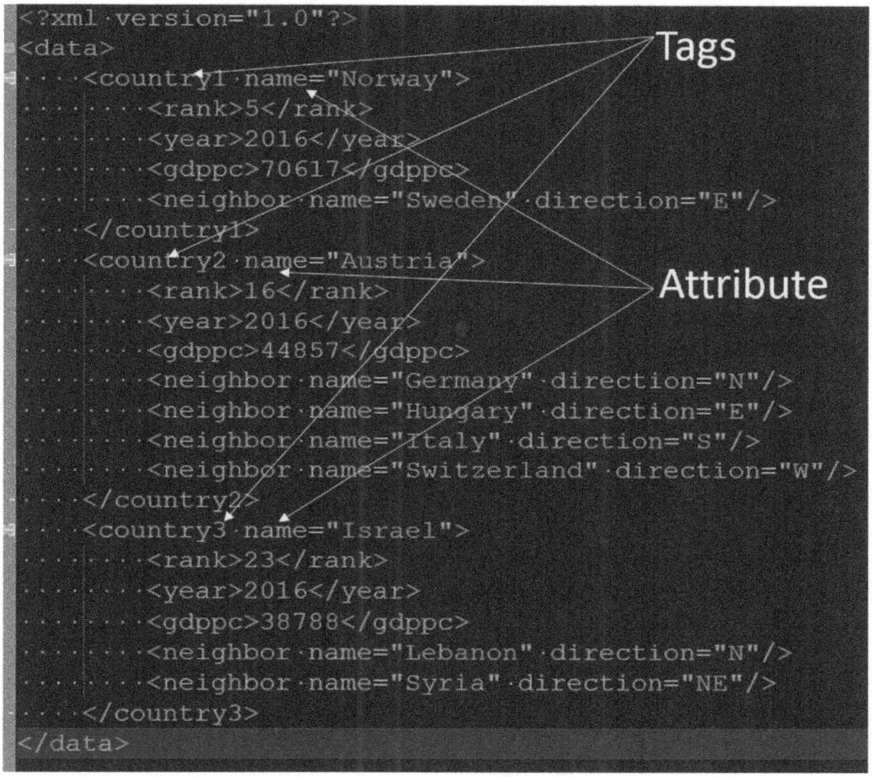

Figure 7.17: Finding the root and child nodes of an XML tag

1. Explore these tags and attributes using the following code:

```
root=tree2.getroot()

for child in root:
    print ("Child:",child.tag, "| Child attribute:",child.attrib)
```

The output will be as follows:

```
Child tag: country1 | Child attribute: {'name': 'Norway'}
Child tag: country2 | Child attribute: {'name': 'Austria'}
Child tag: country3 | Child attribute: {'name': 'Israel'}
```

Figure 7.18: The output showing the extracted XML tags

> **Note**
>
> Remember that every XML data file could follow a different naming or structural format, but using an element tree approach puts the data into a somewhat structured flow that can be explored systematically. Still, it is best to examine the raw XML file structure once and understand (even if at a high level) the data format before attempting automatic extractions.

Exercise 90: Using the `text` Method to Extract Meaningful Data

We can almost think of the XML tree as a **list of lists** and index it accordingly:

1. Access the element **root[0][2]** by using the following code:

   ```
   root[0][2]
   ```

   The output will be as follows:

   ```
   <Element 'gdppc' at 0x00000000051FF278>
   ```

   So, this points to the **'gdppc'** piece of data. Here, **'gdppc'** is the tag and the actual GDP/per capita data is attached to this tag.

2. Use the **text** method to access the data:

   ```
   root[0][2].text
   ```

   The output will be as follows:

   ```
   '70617'
   ```

3. Use the **tag** method to access **gdppc**:

   ```
   root[0][2].tag
   ```

   The output will be as follows:

   ```
   'gdppc'
   ```

4. Check **root[0]**:

```
root[0]
```

The output will be as follows:

```
<Element 'country1' at 0x00000000050298B8>
```

5. Check the tag:

```
root[0].tag
```

The output will be as follows:

```
'country1'
```

We can use the **attrib** method to access it:

```
root[0].attrib
```

The output will be as follows:

```
{'name': 'Norway'}
```

So, **root[0]** is again an element, but it has different a set of tags and attributes than **root[0][2]**. This is expected because they are all part of the tree as nodes, but each is associated with a different level of data.

This last piece of code output is interesting because it returns a dictionary object. Therefore, we can just index it by its keys. We will do that in the next exercise.

Extracting and Printing the GDP/Per Capita Information Using a Loop

Now that we know how to read the GDP/per capita data and how to get a dictionary back from the tree, we can easily construct a simple dataset by running a loop over the tree:

```
for c in root:
    country_name=c.attrib['name']
    gdppc = int(c[2].text)
    print("{}: {}".format(country_name,gdppc))
```

The output is as follows:

```
Norway: 70617
Austria: 44857
Israel: 38788
```

We can put these in a DataFrame or CSV file for saving to a local disk or further processing, such as a simple plot!

Exercise 91: Finding All the Neighboring Countries for each Country and Printing Them

As we mentioned before, there are efficient search algorithms for tree structures, and one such method for XML trees is **findall**. We can use this, for this example, to find all the neighbors a country has and print them out.

Why do we need to use **findall** over find? Well, because not all the countries have an equal number of neighbors and **findall** searches for all the data with that tag that is associated with a particular node, and we want to traverse all of them:

```
for c in root:
    ne=c.findall('neighbor') # Find all the neighbors
    print("Neighbors\n"+"-"*25)
    for i in ne: # Iterate over the neighbors and print their 'name' attribute
        print(i.attrib['name'])
    print('\n')
```

The output looks something like this:

Figure 7.19: The output that's generated by using findall

Exercise 92: A Simple Demo of Using XML Data Obtained by Web Scraping

In the last topic of this chapter, we learned about simple web scraping using the `requests` library. So far, we have worked with static XML data (i.e., data from a local file or a string object that we've scripted). Now, it is time to read XML data directly over the internet (as you are expected to do most of the time).

We are going to read data from an API at **https://exchangerate.host/**. This API provides a currency conversion service. The aim of the exercise is to code the functionality to convert an amount into three different currencies.

Documentation for the API can be found here: https://exchangerate.host/#/#docs. The code for the exercise can be found at the following link: https://github.com/TrainingByPackt/Data-Wrangling-with-Python/blob/master/Chapter07/Exercise87-92/Exercise_92_update.ipynb.

Perform the following steps to complete the exercise:

1. Import the required libraries to make the API call, then set up the base URL. The documentation linked above gives info on the URL format needed. In this case, we'll use the URL to set the base currency as USD, and the currencies we want to convert to as EUR, GBP, and INR:

```
import requests, urllib.parse
serviceurl = 'https://api.exchangerate.host/
latest?base=USD&symbols=EUR,GBP,INR&format=xml&amount='
```

2. Ask the user to enter the USD amount that they want to convert. Read their input and append it to the URL, then send the request to the API and store the response as text. Print the number of characters returned by the API call.

```
value = str(input('Enter the amount to convert: '))
url = serviceurl + value
uh = requests.get(url)
data = uh.text
print('Retrieved', len(data), 'characters')
```

3. Run the code and enter a search value when prompted. Note that the input text should be a number only. The currency is not needed (it's already specified in the URL above). In this case, we'll ask it to convert an amount of 2000 USD:

```
Enter the amount to convert: 2000
```

Figure 7.20: Inputting a search value when prompted

The output will be as follows.

```
Enter the amount to convert: 2000
Retrieved 344 characters
```

Note that the currency conversion rates will vary over time, so your outputs throughout this exercise may be slightly different to those stated here.

4. Let's look at the raw string data returned. Type and run the following code to print the output:

```
print(data)
```

The output is shown in the image below. In the text, you can see the XML structure. There is a separate **<data>** element for each currency, and then a **<code>** element that states the currency code, a **<rate>** element that gives the converted amount in the specified currency (based on the current exchange rate), a **<base>** element that states USD as the currency for the input value, and a **<date>** element with the date of the query.

```
<?xml version="1.0" encoding="UTF-8"?>
<document>
<data>
<code>EUR</code><rate>1726,139816</rate><base>USD</base><date>2021-11-03</date></data>
<data>
<code>GBP</code><rate>1468,429356</rate><base>USD</base><date>2021-11-03</date></data>
<data>
<code>INR</code><rate>149156,92974</rate><base>USD</base><date>2021-11-03</date></data>
</document>
```

Figure 7.21: Text output showing the API response

> **Note**
>
> The values you get in *Figure 7.21* will depend on the value you input in *step 2* of this exercise. They will also depend on the current exchange rate at the time you run the code.

5. Now we can turn the raw string data into XML, read and decode it, and use it to create an XML tree:

```
import xml.etree.ElementTree as ET
tree3 = ET.fromstring(data)
```

6. Let's now use another useful method, called **iter**, which iterates over the nodes under an element and lets us print the text:

```
for elem in tree3.iter():
    print(elem.text)
```

Running this code gives the output shown in the image below. You can see that only the descriptive text of the elements is printed, with each one on a new line. The tags (which start with < and end with >) have been stripped out.

```
EUR
1726,139816
USD
2021-11-03


GBP
1468,429356
USD
2021-11-03


INR
149156,92974
USD
2021-11-03
```

Figure 7.22: Output generated using the iter method

7. We can use the **find** method to search for specific elements and extract the required content. This is why it is important to scan through the XML data manually and check which attributes are used. Remember, this means scanning the raw string data, not the tree structure.

Let's search for just the currency code and the converted amount in that currency using the **find** method. We'll then output some descriptive text to provide that information. We'll also include the original user input (which we called **value**) to make the message clearer:

```
for elem in tree3.iter():
    curr=elem.find('code')
    amount=elem.find('rate')
    if curr!=None and amount!=None:
        print(value + " USD = " + amount.text + " " + curr.text)
```

Note the use of **!=None** in this code. This can be difficult to anticipate when you first run code like this. You may get an error because some of the tags return a **None** object, that is, they were empty for some reason in this XML data stream. This kind of situation is fairly common and cannot be anticipated beforehand. You have to use your Python knowledge and programming intuition to get around it if you receive such an error. Here, we check for the type of the object; if it is not **None**, then we extract the text associated with it.

The output is as follows:

```
2000 USD = 1726,139816 EUR
2000 USD = 1468,429356 GBP
2000 USD = 149156,92974 INR
```

Figure 7.23: Final output showing neatly formatted exchange rates

As you can see in the output of this exercise, we get a neat and tidy readable output with the converted amount for each currency. You can try running the code again from the start and inputting different values to see what is returned. Remember that the output will vary daily according to the latest exchange rates. You could also edit the base URL in the code to test out some other currencies. As an extension to this exercise, you could try removing the hardcoding of the currencies and adding functionality for the user to specify the currencies they want to search for, in addition to the conversion amount.

This concludes the exercise. You have used your knowledge of making HTTP requests and getting data from the internet and mixed it with your newly acquired knowledge of parsing and traversing XML documents to accomplish a small but functional data pipeline.

Reading Data from an API

Fundamentally, an API or Application Programming Interface is some kind of interface to a computing resource (for example, an operating system or database table), which has a set of exposed methods (function calls) that allow a programmer to access particular data or internal features of that resource.

A web API is, as the name suggests, an API over the web. Note that it is not a specific technology or programming framework, but an architectural concept. Think of an API like a fast food restaurant's customer service center. Internally, there are many food items, raw materials, cooking resources, and recipe management systems, but all you see are fixed menu items on the board and you can only interact through those items. It is like a port that can be accessed using an HTTP protocol and is able to deliver data and services if used properly.

Web APIs are extremely popular these days for all kinds of data services. In the very first chapter, we talked about how UC San Diego's data science team pulls data from Twitter feeds to analyze occurrence of forest fires. For this, they do not go to twitter.com and scrape the data by looking at HTML pages and text. Instead, they use the Twitter API, which sends this data continuously in a streaming format.

Therefore, it is very important for a data wrangling professional to understand the basics of data extraction from a web API as you are extremely likely to find yourself in a situation where large quantities of data must be read through an API interface for processing and wrangling. These days, most APIs stream data out in JSON format. In this chapter, we will use a free API to read some information about various countries around the world in JSON format and process it.

We will use Python's built-in **urllib** module for this topic, along with pandas to make a DataFrame. So, we can import them now. We will also import Python's **JSON** module:

```
import urllib.request, urllib.parse

from urllib.error import HTTPError,URLError

import json

import pandas as pd
```

Defining the Base URL (or API Endpoint)

First, we need to set the base URL. When we are dealing with API microservices, this is often called the **API endpoint**. Therefore, look for such a phrase in the web service portal you are interested in and use the endpoint URL they give you:

```
serviceurl = 'https://restcountries.eu/rest/v2/name/'
```

API-based microservices are extremely dynamic in nature in terms of what and how they offer their service and data. It can change at any time. At the time of this chapter planning, we found this particular API to be a nice choice for extracting data easily and without using authorization keys (login or special API keys).

For most APIs, however, you need to have your own API key. You get that by registering with their service. A basic usage (up to a fixed number of requests or a data flow limit) is often free, but after that you will be charged. To register for an API key, you often need to enter credit card information.

We wanted to avoid all that hassle to teach you the basics and that's why we chose this example, which does not require such authorization. But, depending on what kind of data you will encounter in your work, please be prepared to learn about using an API key.

Exercise 93: Defining and Testing a Function to Pull Country Data from an API

This particular API serves basic information about countries around the world:

1. Define a function to pull out data when we pass the name of a country as an argument. The crux of the operation is contained in the following two lines of code:

```
url = serviceurl + country_name
uh = urllib.request.urlopen(url)
```

2. The first line of code appends the country name as a string to the base URL and the second line sends a **get** request to the API endpoint. If all goes well, we get back the data, decode it, and read it as a JSON file. This whole exercise is coded in the following function, along with some error-handling code wrapped around the basic actions we talked about previously:

```
def get_country_data(country):
    """
    Function to get data about country from "https://restcountries.eu" API
    """
    country_name=str(country)
    url = serviceurl + country_name

    try:
        uh = urllib.request.urlopen(url)
    except HTTPError as e:
        print("Sorry! Could not retrieve anything on {}".format(country_
name))
        return None
    except URLError as e:
        print('Failed to reach a server.')
        print('Reason: ', e.reason)
        return None
    else:
        data = uh.read().decode()
        print("Retrieved data on {}. Total {} characters
read.".format(country_name,len(data)))
        return data
```

3. Test this function by passing some arguments. We pass a correct name and an erroneous name. The response is as follows:

> **Note**
>
> This is an example of rudimentary error handling. You have to think about various possibilities and put in such code to catch and gracefully respond to user input when you are building a real-life web or enterprise application.

```
country_name = 'Switzerland'

data=get_country_data(country_name)

Retrieved data on Switzerland. Total 1090 characters read.

country_name1 = 'Switzerland1'   An erroneous input

data1=get_country_data(country_name1)

Sorry! Could not retrive anything on Switzerland1
```

Figure 7.24: Input arguments

Using the Built-In JSON Library to Read and Examine Data

As we have already mentioned, JSON looks a lot like a Python dictionary.

In this exercise, we will use Python's **json** module to read raw data in that format and see what we can process further:

```
x=json.loads(data)

y=x[0]

type(y)
```

The output will be as follows:

```
dict
```

So, we get a list back when we use the **loads** method from the **json** module. It reads a string datatype into a list of dictionaries. In this case, we get only one element in the list, so we extract that and check its type to make sure it is a dictionary.

We can quickly check the keys of the dictionary, that is the JSON data (note that a full screenshot is not shown here). We can see the relevant country data, such as calling codes, population, area, time zones, borders, and so on:

```
dict_keys(['name', 'topLevelDomain', 'alpha2Code', 'alpha3Code', 'callingCodes',
n', 'population', 'latlng', 'demonym', 'area', 'gini', 'timezones', 'borders', '
uages', 'translations', 'flag', 'regionalBlocs', 'cioc'])
```

Figure 7.25: The output of dict_keys

Printing All the Data Elements

This task is extremely simple given that we have a dictionary at our disposal! All we have to do is iterate over the dictionary and print the keys/items pair one by one:

```
for k,v in y.items():

    print("{}: {}".format(k,v))
```

The output is as follows:

```
name: Switzerland
topLevelDomain: ['.ch']
alpha2Code: CH
alpha3Code: CHE
callingCodes: ['41']
capital: Bern
altSpellings: ['CH', 'Swiss Confederation', 'Schweiz', 'Suisse', 'Svizzera', 'Svizra']
region: Europe
subregion: Western Europe
population: 8341600
latlng: [47.0, 8.0]
demonym: Swiss
area: 41284.0
gini: 33.7
timezones: ['UTC+01:00']
borders: ['AUT', 'FRA', 'ITA', 'LIE', 'DEU']
nativeName: Schweiz
numericCode: 756
currencies: [{'code': 'CHF', 'name': 'Swiss franc', 'symbol': 'Fr'}]
languages: [{'iso639_1': 'de', 'iso639_2': 'deu', 'name': 'German', 'nativeName': 'Deutsch'},
ra', 'name': 'French', 'nativeName': 'français'}, {'iso639_1': 'it', 'iso639_2': 'ita', 'name
ano'}]
translations: {'de': 'Schweiz', 'es': 'Suiza', 'fr': 'Suisse', 'ja': 'スイス', 'it': 'Svizzera
'nl': 'Zwitserland', 'hr': 'Švicarska', 'fa': 'سوئیس'}
flag: https://restcountries.eu/data/che.svg
```

Figure 7.26: The output using dict

Note that the items in the dictionary are not of the same type, that is, they are not similar objects. Some are floating-point numbers, such as the area, many are simple strings, but some are lists or even lists of dictionaries!

This is fairly common with JSON data. The internal data structure of JSON can be arbitrarily complex and multilevel, that is, you can have a dictionary of lists of dictionaries of dictionaries of lists of lists.... and so on.

> **Note**
>
> It is clear, therefore, that there is no universal method or processing function for JSON data format, and you have to write custom loops and functions to extract data from such a dictionary object based on your particular needs.

Now, we will write a small loop to extract the languages spoken in Switzerland. First, let's examine the dictionary closely and see where the language data is:

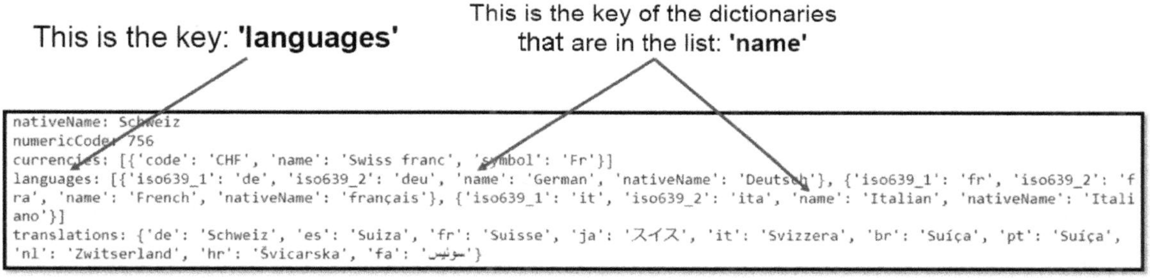

Figure 7.27: The tags

So, the data is embedded inside a list of dictionaries, which is accessed by a particular key of the main dictionary.

We can write simple two-line code to extract this data:

```
for lang in y['languages']:
    print(lang['name'])
```

The output is as follows:

```
for lang in y['languages']:
    print(lang['name'])

German
French
Italian
```

Figure 7.28: The output showing the languages

Using a Function that Extracts a DataFrame Containing Key Information

Here, we are interested in writing a function that can take a list of countries and return a pandas DataFrame with some key information:

- Capital
- Region
- Sub-region
- Population
- Latitude/longitude
- Area
- Gini index
- Time zones
- Currencies
- Languages

> **Note**
>
> This is the kind of wrapper function you are generally expected to write in real-life data wrangling tasks, that is, a utility function that can take a user argument and output a useful data structure (or a mini database type object) with key information extracted over the internet about the item the user is interested in.

We will show you the whole function first and then discuss some key points about it. It is a slightly complex and long piece of code. However, based on your Python- based data wrangling knowledge, you should be able to examine this function closely and understand what it is doing:

```python
import pandas as pd

import json

def build_country_database(list_country):
    """
    Takes a list of country names.
    Output a DataFrame with key information about those countries.
    """
    # Define an empty dictionary with keys
    country_dict={'Country':[],'Capital':[],'Region':[],'Sub-
region':[],'Population':[],

'Lattitude':[],'Longitude':[],'Area':[],'Gini':[],'Timezones':[],
                'Currencies':[],'Languages':[]}
```

> **Note**
>
> The code has been truncated here. Please find the entire code at the following GitHub link and code bundle folder link https://github.com/TrainingByPackt/ Data-Wrangling-with-Python/blob/master/Chapter07/Exercise93-94/Reading%20 Data%20From%20API.ipynb.

Here are some of the key points about this function:

- It starts by building an empty dictionary of lists. This is the chosen format for finally passing to the pandas **DataFrame** method, which can accept such a format and returns a nice DataFrame with column names set to the dictionary keys' names.

- We use the previously defined **get_country_data** function to extract data for each country in the user-defined list. For this, we simply iterate over the list and call this function.

- We check the output of the **get_country_data** function. If, for some reason, it returns a **None** object, we will know that the API reading was not successful, and we will print out a suitable message. Again, this is an example of an error-handling mechanism and you must have them in your code. Without such small error checking code, your application won't be robust enough for the occasional incorrect input or API malfunction!

- For many data types, we simply extract the data from the main JSON dictionary and append it to the corresponding list in our data dictionary.

- However, for special data types, such as time zones, currencies, and languages, we write a special loop to extract the data without error.

- We also take care of the fact that these special data types can have a variable length, that is, some countries may have multiple spoken languages, but most will have only one entry. So, we check whether the length of the list is greater than one and handle the data accordingly.

Exercise 94: Testing the Function by Building a Small Database of Countries' Information

Finally, we test this function by passing a list of country names:

1. To test its robustness, we pass in an erroneous name – such as 'Turmeric' in this case!

See the output... it detected that it did not get any data back for the incorrect entry and printed out a suitable message. The key is that, if you do not have the error checking and handling code in your function, then it will stop execution on that entry and will not return the expected mini database. To avoid this behavior, such error handling code is invaluable:

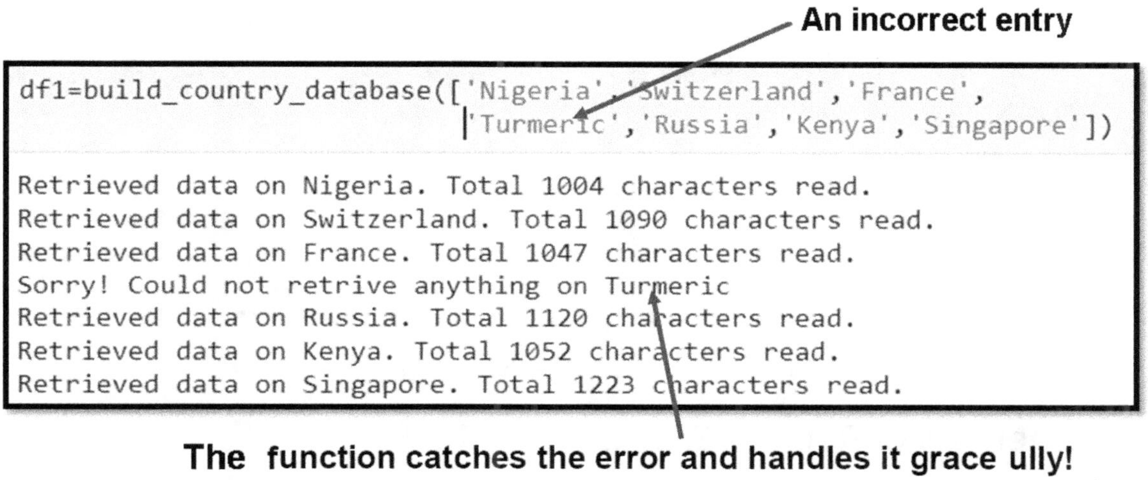

An incorrect entry

```
df1=build_country_database(['Nigeria','Switzerland','France',
                            'Turmeric','Russia','Kenya','Singapore'])

Retrieved data on Nigeria. Total 1004 characters read.
Retrieved data on Switzerland. Total 1090 characters read.
Retrieved data on France. Total 1047 characters read.
Sorry! Could not retrive anything on Turmeric
Retrieved data on Russia. Total 1120 characters read.
Retrieved data on Kenya. Total 1052 characters read.
Retrieved data on Singapore. Total 1223 characters read.
```

The function catches the error and handles it grace ully!

Figure 7.29: The incorrect entry highlighted

2. Finally, the output is a pandas DataFrame, which is as follows:

Single or multiple pieces of data do not matter. They are extracted correctly.

	Area	Capital	Country	Currencies	Gini	Languages	Lattitude	Longitude	Population	Region	Sub-region
0	923768.0	Abuja	Nigeria	Nigerian naira	48.8	English	10.000000	8.0	186988000	Africa	Western Africa
1	41284.0	Bern	Switzerland	Swiss franc	33.7	German,French,Italian	47.000000	8.0	8341600	Europe	Western Europe
2	640679.0	Paris	France	Euro	32.7	French	46.000000	2.0	66710000	Europe	Western Europe
3	17124442.0	Moscow	Russian Federation	Russian ruble	40.1	Russian	60.000000	100.0	146599183	Europe	Eastern Europe
4	580367.0	Nairobi	Kenya	Kenyan shilling	47.7	English,Swahili	1.000000	38.0	47251000	Africa	Eastern Africa
5	710.0	Singapore	Singapore	Brunei dollar,Singapore dollar	48.1	English,Malay,Tamil,Chinese	1.366667	103.8	5535000	Asia	South-Eastern Asia

Figure 7.30: The data extracted correctly

Fundamentals of Regular Expressions (RegEx)

Regular **ex**pressions or **regex** are used to identify whether a pattern exists in a given sequence of characters a (string) or not. They help in manipulating textual data, which is often a prerequisite for data science projects that involve text mining.

Regex in the Context of Web Scraping

Web pages are often full of text and while there are some methods in `BeautifulSoup` or XML parser to extract raw text, there is no method for the intelligent analysis of that text. If, as a data wrangler, you are looking for a particular piece of data (for example, email IDs or phone numbers in a special format), you have to do a lot of string manipulation on a large corpus to extract email IDs or phone numbers. RegEx are very powerful and save data wrangling professional a lot of time and effort with string manipulation because they can search for complex textual patterns with wildcards of an arbitrary length.

RegEx is like a mini-programming language in itself and common ideas are used not only Python, but in all widely used web app languages like JavaScript, PHP, Perl, and so on. The RegEx module is in-built in Python, and you can import it by using the following code:

```
import re
```

Exercise 95: Using the match Method to Check Whether a Pattern matches a String/Sequence

One of the most common regex methods is **match**. This is used to check for an exact or partial match at a beginning of the string (by default):

1. Import the RegEx module:

   ```
   import re
   ```

2. Define a string and a pattern:

   ```
   string1 = 'Python'
   pattern = r"Python"
   ```

3. Write a conditional expression to check for a match:

   ```
   if re.match(pattern,string1):
       print("Matches!")
   else:
       print("Doesn't match.")
   ```

   The preceding code should give an affirmative answer, that is, "Matches!".

4. Test this with a string that only differs in the first letter by making it lowercase:

   ```
   string2 = 'python'
   if re.match(pattern,string2):
       print("Matches!")
   else:
       print("Doesn't match.")
   ```

   The output is as follows:

   ```
   Doesn't match.
   ```

Using the Compile Method to Create a Regex Program

In a program or module, if we are making heavy use of a particular pattern, then it is better to use the **compile** method and create a regex program and then call methods on this program.

Here is how you compile a regex program:

```
prog = re.compile(pattern)
prog.match(string1)
```

The output is as follows:

```
<_sre.SRE_Match object; span=(0, 6), match='Python'>
```

This code produced an **SRE.Match** object that has a **span** of (0,6) and the matched string of 'Python'. The span here simply denotes the start and end indices of the pattern that was matched. These indices may come in handy in a text mining program where the subsequent code uses the indices for further search or decision-making purposes. We will see some examples of that later.

Exercise 96: Compiling Programs to Match Objects

Compiled objects act like functions in that they return **None** if the pattern does not match. Here, we are going to check that by writing a simple conditional. This concept will come in handy later when we write a small utility function to check for the type of the returned object from regex-compiled programs and act accordingly. We cannot be sure whether a pattern will match a given string or whether it will appear in a corpus of the text (if we are searching for the pattern anywhere within the text). Depending on the situation, we may encounter **Match** objects or **None** as the returned value, and we have to handle this gracefully:

```
#string1 = 'Python'

#string2 = 'python'

#pattern = r"Python"
```

1. Use the **compile** function in RegEx:

    ```
    prog = re.compile(pattern)
    ```

2. Match it with the first string:

    ```
    if prog.match(string1)!=None:
        print("Matches!")
    else:
        print("Doesn't match.")
    ```

    The output is as follows:

    ```
    Matches!
    ```

3. Match it with the second string:

```
if prog.match(string2)!=None:
    print("Matches!")
else:
    print("Doesn't match.")
```

The output is as follows:

```
Doesn't match.
```

Exercise 97: Using Additional Parameters in Match to Check for Positional Matching

By default, **match** looks for pattern matching at the beginning of the given string. But sometimes, we need to check matching at a specific location in the string:

1. Match **y** for the second position:

```
prog = re.compile(r'y')
prog.match('Python',pos=1)
```

The output is as follows:

```
<_sre.SRE_Match object; span=(1, 2), match='y'>
```

2. Check for a pattern called **thon** starting from **pos=2**, that is, the third character:

```
prog = re.compile(r'thon')
prog.match('Python',pos=2)
```

The output is as follows:

```
<_sre.SRE_Match object; span=(2, 6), match='thon'>
```

3. Find a match in a different string by using the following command:

```
prog.match('Marathon',pos=4)
```

The output is as follows:

```
<_sre.SRE_Match object; span=(4, 8), match='thon'>
```

Finding the Number of Words in a List That End with "ing"

Suppose we want to find out if a given string has the last three letters: 'ing'. This kind of query may come up in a text analytics/text mining program where somebody is interested in finding instances of present continuous tense words, which are highly likely to end with 'ing'. However, other nouns may also end with 'ing' (as we will see in this example):

```
prog = re.compile(r'ing')

words = ['Spring','Cycling','Ringtone']
```

Create a **for** loop to find words ending with 'ing':

```
for w in words:

    if prog.match(w,pos=len(w)-3)!=None:

        print("{} has last three letters 'ing'".format(w))

    else:

        print("{} does not have last three letter as 'ing'".format(w))
```

The output is as follows:

```
Spring has last three letters 'ing'

Cycling has last three letters 'ing'

Ringtone does not have last three letter as 'ing'
```

> **Note**
>
> It looks plain and simple, and you may well wonder what the purpose of using a special regex module for this is. A simple string method should have been sufficient. Yes, it would have been OK for this particular example, but the whole point of using regex is to be able to use very complex string patterns that are not at all obvious when it comes to how they are written using simple string methods. We will see the real power of regex compared to string methods shortly. But before that, let's explore another of the most commonly used methods, called **search**.

Exercise 98: The search Method in Regex

Search and **match** are related concepts and they both return the same Match object. The real difference between them is that **match works for only the first match** (either at the beginning of the string or at a specified position, as we saw in the previous exercises), whereas **search looks for the pattern anywhere in the string** and returns the appropriate position if it finds a match:

1. Use the **compile** method to find matching strings:

   ```
   prog = re.compile('ing')
   if prog.match('Spring')==None:
       print("None")
   ```

2. The output is as follows:

   ```
   None
   ```

3. Search the string by using the following command:

   ```
   prog.search('Spring')
   <_sre.SRE_Match object; span=(3, 6), match='ing'>


   prog.search('Ringtone')
   <_sre.SRE_Match object; span=(1, 4), match='ing'>
   ```

   As you can see, the **match** method returns **None** for the input **spring**, and we had to write code to print that out explicitly (because in Jupyter notebook, nothing will show up for a None object). But **search** returns a **Match** object with **span=(3,6)** as it finds the **ing** pattern spanning those positions.

Similarly, for the **Ringtone** string, it finds the correct position of the match and returns **span=(1,4)**.

Exercise 99: Using the span Method of the Match Object to Locate the Position of the Matched Pattern

As you will understand by now, the **span** contained in the **Match** object is useful for locating the exact position of the pattern as it appears in the string.

1. Intitialize **prog** with pattern ing.

   ```
   prog = re.compile(r'ing')
   words = ['Spring','Cycling','Ringtone']
   ```

2. Create a function to return a tuple of start and end positions of match.

```
for w in words:
    mt = prog.search(w)
    # Span returns a tuple of start and end positions of the match
    start_pos = mt.span()[0] # Starting position of the match
    end_pos = mt.span()[1] # Ending position of the match
```

3. Print the words ending with ing in the start or end position.

```
print("The word '{}' contains 'ing' in the position {}-{}".
format(w,start_pos,end_pos))
```

The output is as follows:

```
The word 'Spring' contains 'ing' in the position 3-6

The word 'Cycling' contains 'ing' in the position 4-7

The word 'Ringtone' contains 'ing' in the position 1-4
```

Exercise 100: Examples of Single Character Pattern Matching with search

Now, we will start getting into the real usage of regex with examples of various useful pattern matching. First, we will explore single-character matching. We will also use the **group** method, which essentially returns the matched pattern in a string format so that we can print and process it easily:

1. Dot (.) matches any single character except a newline character:

```
prog = re.compile(r'py.')
print(prog.search('pygmy').group())
print(prog.search('Jupyter').group())
```

The output is as follows:

```
pyg
pyt
```

2. \w (lowercase w) matches any single letter, digit, or underscore:

```
prog = re.compile(r'c\wm')
print(prog.search('comedy').group())
print(prog.search('camera').group())
print(prog.search('pac_man').group())
print(prog.search('pac2man').group())
```

The output is as follows:

```
com
cam
c_m
c2m
```

3. **\W** (uppercase W) matches anything not covered with **\w**:

```
prog = re.compile(r'4\W1')
print(prog.search('4/1 was a wonderful day!').group())
print(prog.search('4-1 was a wonderful day!').group())
print(prog.search('4.1 was a wonderful day!').group())
print(prog.search('Remember the wonderful day 04/1?').group())
```

The output is as follows:

```
4/1
4-1
4.1
4/1
```

4. **\s** (lowercase s) matches a single whitespace character, such as a space, newline, tab, or return:

```
prog = re.compile(r'Data\swrangling')

print(prog.search("Data wrangling is cool").group())
print("-"*80)
print("Data\twrangling is the full string")
print(prog.search("Data\twrangling is the full string").group())
print("-"*80)

print("Data\nwrangling is the full string")
print(prog.search("Data\nwrangling").group())
```

The output is as follows:

```
Data wrangling
-----------------------------------------------------------------
Data  wrangling is the full string
Data  wrangling
-----------------------------------------------------------------
Data
wrangling is the full string
Data
wrangling
```

5. **\d** matches numerical digits 0 – 9:

```
prog = re.compile(r"score was \d\d")

print(prog.search("My score was 67").group())
print(prog.search("Your score was 73").group())
```

The output is as follows:

```
score was 67
score was 73
```

Exercise 101: Examples of Pattern Matching at the Start or End of a String

In this exercise, we will match patterns with strings. The focus is to find out whether the pattern is present at the start or the end of the string:

1. Write a function to handle cases where match is not found, that is, to handle **None** objects as returns:

```
def print_match(s):
    if prog.search(s)==None:
        print("No match")
    else:
        print(prog.search(s).group())
```

2. Use **^** (Caret) to match a pattern at the start of the string:

```
prog = re.compile(r'^India')
```

```
print_match("Russia implemented this law")
print_match("India implemented that law")
print_match("This law was implemented by India")
The output is as follows: No match
 India
 No match
```

3. Use **$** (dollar sign) to match a pattern at the end of the string:

```
prog = re.compile(r'Apple$')
```

```
print_match("Patent no 123456 belongs to Apple")
print_match("Patent no 345672 belongs to Samsung")
print_match("Patent no 987654 belongs to Apple")
```

The output is as follows:

```
Apple
No match
Apple
```

Exercise 102: Examples of Pattern Matching with Multiple Characters

Now, we will turn to more exciting and useful pattern matching with examples of multiple characters matching. You should start seeing and appreciating the real power of regex by now.

> **Note:**
>
> For these examples and exercises, also try to think how you would implement them without regex, that is, by using simple string methods and any other logic that you can think of. Then, compare that solution to the ones implemented with regex for brevity and efficiency.

1. Use * to match 0 or more repetitions of the preceding **RE**:

```
prog = re.compile(r'ab*')

print_match("a")
print_match("ab")
print_match("abbb")
print_match("b")
print_match("bbab")
print_match("something_abb_something")
```

The output is as follows:

```
a
ab
abbb
No match
ab
abb
```

2. Using + causes the resulting RE to match 1 or more repetitions of the preceding RE:

```
prog = re.compile(r'ab+')

print_match("a")
print_match("ab")
print_match("abbb")
print_match("b")
print_match("bbab")
print_match("something_abb_something")
```

The output is as follows:

```
No match
ab
abbb
No match
ab
abb
```

3. **?** causes the resulting RE to match precisely 0 or 1 repetitions of the preceding RE:

```
prog = re.compile(r'ab?')

print_match("a")
print_match("ab")
print_match("abbb")
print_match("b")
print_match("bbab")
print_match("something_abb_something")
```

The output is as follows:

```
a
ab
ab
No match
ab
ab
```

Exercise 103: Greedy versus Non-Greedy Matching

The standard (default) mode of pattern matching in regex is greedy, that is, the program tries to match as much as it can. Sometimes, this behavior is natural, but, in some cases, you may want to match minimally:

1. The greedy way of matching a string is as follows:

```
prog = re.compile(r'<.*>')
print_match('<a> b <c>')
```

The output is as follows:

```
<a> b <c>
```

2. So, the preceding regex found both tags with the <> pattern, but what if we wanted to match the first tag only and stop there. We can use **?** by inserting it after any regex expression to make it non-greedy:

```
prog = re.compile(r'<.*?>')
print_match('<a> b <c>')
```

The output is as follows:

```
<a>
```

Exercise 104: Controlling Repetitions to Match

In many situations, we want to have precise control over how many repetitions of the pattern we want to match in a text. This can be done in a few ways, which we will show examples of here:

1. **{m}** specifies exactly **m** copies of RE to match. Fewer matches cause a non-match and returns **None**:

```
prog = re.compile(r'A{3}')

print_match("ccAAAdd")
print_match("ccAAAAdd")
print_match("ccAAdd")
```

The output is as follows:

```
AAA
AAA
No match
```

2. **{m,n}** specifies exactly **m** to **n** copies of **RE** to match:

```
prog = re.compile(r'A{2,4}B')

print_match("ccAAABdd")
print_match("ccABdd")
print_match("ccAABBBdd")
print_match("ccAAAAAAABdd")
```

The output is as follows:

```
AAAB
No match
AAB
AAAAB
```

3. Omitting **m** specifies a lower bound of zero:

```
prog = re.compile(r'A{,3}B')

print_match("ccAAABdd")
print_match("ccABdd")
print_match("ccAABBBdd")
print_match("ccAAAAAAABdd")
```

The output is as follows:

```
AAAB
AB
AAB
AAAB
```

4. Omitting **n** specifies an infinite upper bound:

    ```
    prog = re.compile(r'A{3,}B')

    print_match("ccAAABdd")
    print_match("ccABdd")
    print_match("ccAABBBdd")
    print_match("ccAAAAAAABdd")
    ```

    The output is as follows:

    ```
    AAAB
    No match
    No match
    AAAAAAAB
    ```

5. **{m,n}?** specifies **m** to **n** copies of RE to match in a non-greedy fashion:

    ```
    prog = re.compile(r'A{2,4}')
    print_match("AAAAAAA")

    prog = re.compile(r'A{2,4}?')
    print_match("AAAAAAA")
    ```

    The output is as follows:

    ```
    AAAA
    AA
    ```

Exercise 105: Sets of Matching Characters

To match an arbitrarily complex pattern, we need to be able to include a logical combination of characters together as a bunch. Regex gives us that kind of capability:

1. The following examples demonstrate such uses of regex. **[x,y,z]** matches x, y, or z:

    ```
    prog = re.compile(r'[A,B]')
    print_match("ccAd")
    print_match("ccABd")
    print_match("ccXdB")
    print_match("ccXdZ")
    ```

    The output will be as follows:

    ```
    A
    A
    B
    No match
    ```

    A range of characters can be matched inside the set using -. This is one of the most widely used regex techniques!

2. Suppose we want to pick out an email address from a text. Email addresses are generally of the form **<some name>@<some domain name>.<some domain identifier>**:

    ```
    prog = re.compile(r'[a-zA-Z]+@+[a-zA-Z]+\.com')

    print_match("My email is coolguy@xyz.com")
    print_match("My email is coolguy12@xyz.com")
    ```

    The output is as follows:

    ```
    coolguy@xyz.com
    No match
    ```

Look at the regex pattern inside the [...]. It is **'a-zA-Z'**. This covers all alphabets, including lowercase and uppercase! With this one simple regex, you are able to match any (pure) alphabetical string for that part of the email. Now, the next pattern is **'@'**, which is added to the previous regex by a **'+'** character. This is the way to build up a complex regex: by adding/stacking up individual regex patterns. We also use the same **[a-zA-Z]** for the email domain name and add a '**.com**' at the end to complete the pattern as a valid email address. Why \.? Because, by itself, DOT (.) is used as a special modifier in regex, but here we want to use DOT (.) just as DOT (.), not as a modifier. So, we need to precede it by a '\'.

3. So, with this regex, we could extract the first email address perfectly but got 'No match' with the second one.

4. What happened with the second email ID?

5. The regex could not capture it because it had the number '12' in the name! That pattern is not captured by the expression [a-zA-Z].

6. Let's change that and add the digits as well:

```
prog = re.compile(r'[a-zA-Z0-9]+@+[a-zA-Z]+\.com')


print_match("My email is coolguy12@xyz.com")
print_match("My email is coolguy12@xyz.org")
```

The output is as follows:

```
coolguy12@xyz.com
No match
```

Now, we catch the first email ID perfectly. But what's going on with the second one? Again, we got a mismatch. The reason is that we changed the .com to .org in that email, and in our regex expression, that portion was hardcoded as .com, so it did not find a match.

7. Let's try to address this in the following regex:

```
prog = re.compile(r'[a-zA-Z0-9]+@+[a-zA-Z]+\.+[a-zA-Z]{2,3}')
print_match("My email is coolguy12@xyz.org")
print_match("My email is coolguy12[AT]xyz[DOT]org")
```

The output is as follows:

```
coolguy12@xyz.org
No match
```

8. In this regex, we used the fact that most domain identifiers have 2 or 3 characters, so we used [a-zA-Z]{2,3} to capture that.

What happened with the second email ID? This is an example of the small tweaks that you can make to stay ahead of telemarketers who want to scrape online forums or any other corpus of text and extract your email ID. If you do not want your email to be found, you can change @ to [AT] and . to [DOT] ,and hopefully that can beat some regex techniques (but not all)!

Exercise 106: The use of OR in Regex using the OR Operator

Because regex patterns are like complex and compact logical constructors themselves, it makes perfect sense that we want to combine them to construct even more complex programs when needed. We can do that by using the | operator:

1. The following example demonstrates the use of the OR operator:

```
prog = re.compile(r'[0-9]{10}')
print_match("3124567897")
print_match("312-456-7897")
```

The output is as follows:

```
3124567897
No match
```

So, here, we are trying to extract patterns of 10-digit numbers that could be phone numbers. Note the use of **{10}** to denote exactly 10-digit numbers in the pattern. But the second number could not be matched for obvious reasons – it had '-' symbols inserted in between groups of numbers.

2. Use multiple smaller regexes and logically combine them by using the following command:

```
prog = re.compile(r'[0-9]{10}|[0-9]{3}-[0-9]{3}-[0-9]{4}')

print_match("3124567897")
print_match("312-456-7897")
```

The output is as follows:

```
3124567897
312-456-7897
```

Phone numbers are written in a myriad of ways and if you search on the web, you will see examples of very complex regexes (written not only in Python but other widely used languages, for web apps such as JavaScript, C++, PHP, Perl, and so on) for capturing phone numbers.

3. Create four strings and execute **print_match** on them:

```
p1= r'[0-9]{10}'
p2=r'[0-9]{3}-[0-9]{3}-[0-9]{4}'
p3 = r'\([0-9]{3}\)[0-9]{3}-[0-9]{4}'
p4 = r'[0-9]{3}\.[0-9]{3}\.[0-9]{4}'
pattern= p1+'|'+p2+'|'+p3+'|'+p4
prog = re.compile(pattern)

print_match("3124567897")
print_match("312-456-7897")
print_match("(312)456-7897")
print_match("312.456.7897")
```

The output is as follows:

```
3124567897
312-456-7897
(312)456-7897
312.456.7897
```

The findall Method

The last regex method that we will learn in this chapter is **findall**. Essentially, it is a **search-and-aggregate** method, that is, it puts all the instances that match with the regex pattern in a given text and returns them in a list. This is extremely useful, as we can just count the length of the returned list to count the number of occurrences or pick and use the returned pattern-matched words one by one as we see fit.

Note that, although we are giving short examples of single sentences in this chapter, you will often deal with a large corpus of text when using a RegEx.

In those cases you are likely to get many matches from a single regex pattern search. For all of those cases, the **findall** method is going to be the most useful:

```
ph_numbers = """Here are some phone numbers.

Pick out the numbers with 312 area code:

312-423-3456, 456-334-6721, 312-5478-9999,

312-Not-a-Number,777.345.2317, 312.331.6789"""

print(ph_numbers)

re.findall('312+[-\.][0-9-\.]+',ph_numbers)
```

The output is as follows:

```
Here are some phone numbers.

Pick out the numbers with 312 area code:

312-423-3456, 456-334-6721, 312-5478-9999,

312-Not-a-Number,777.345.2317, 312.331.6789


['312-423-3456', '312-5478-9999', '312.331.6789']
```

Activity 9: Extracting the Top 100 eBooks from Gutenberg

Project Gutenberg encourages the creation and distribution of eBooks by encouraging volunteer efforts to digitize and archive cultural works. This activity aims to scrape the URL of Project Gutenberg's Top 100 eBooks to identify the eBooks' links. It uses BeautifulSoup4 to parse the HTML and regular expression code to identify the Top 100 eBook file numbers.

You can use those book ID numbers to download the book into your local drive if you want.

Head over to the supplied Jupyter notebook (in the GitHub repository) to work on this activity.

These are the steps that will help you solve this activity:

1. Import the necessary libraries, including **regex** and **beautifulsoup**.

2. Check the SSL certificate.

3. Read the HTML from the URL.

4. Write a small function to check the status of the web request.

5. Decode the response and pass this on to BeautifulSoup for HTML parsing.

6. Find all the **href** tags and store them in the list of links. Check what the list looks like – print the first 30 elements.

7. Use a regular expression to find the numeric digits in these links. These are the file numbers for the top 100 eBooks.

8. Initialize the empty list to hold the file numbers over an appropriate range and use **regex** to find the numeric digits in the link **href** string. Use the **findall** method.

9. What does the **soup** object's text look like? Use the **.text** method and print only the first 2,000 characters (do not print the whole thing, as it is too long).

10. Search in the extracted text (using a regular expression) from the soup object to find the names of the top 100 eBooks (yesterday's ranking).

11. Create a starting index. It should point at the text *Top 100 Ebooks yesterday*. Use the **splitlines** method of soup.text. It splits the lines of text of the soup object.

12. Loop 1-100 to add the strings of the next 100 lines to this temporary list. Hint: use the **splitlines** method.

13. Use a regular expression to extract only text from the name strings and append it to an empty list. Use **match** and **span** to find the indices and use them.

> **Note**
>
> The solution for this activity can be found on page 315.

Activity 10: Building Your Own Movie Database by Reading an API

In this activity, you will build a complete movie database by communicating and interfacing with a free API. You will learn about obtaining a unique user key that must be used when your program tries to access the API. This activity will teach you general chapters about working with an API, which are fairly common for other highly popular API services such as Google or Twitter. Therefore, after doing this exercise, you will be confident about writing more complex programs to scrape data from such services.

The aims of this activity are as follows:

- To retrieve and print basic data about a movie (the title is entered by the user) from the web (OMDb database)

- If a poster of the movie can be found, it downloads the file and saves it at a user-specified location

These are the steps that will help you solve this activity:

1. Import **urllib.request**, **urllib.parse**, **urllib.error**, and **json**.

2. Load the secret API key (you have to get one from the OMDb website and use that; it has a daily limit of 1,000) from a JSON file stored in the same folder in a variable, by using **json.loads**.

3. Obtain a key and store it in JSON as **APIkeys.json**.

4. Open the **APIkeys.json** file.

5. Assign the OMDb portal (http://www.omdbapi.com/?) as a string to a variable.

6. Create a variable called **apikey** with the last portion of the URL (**&apikey=secretapikey**), where **secretapikey** is your own API key.

7. Write a utility function called **print_json** to print the movie data from a JSON file (which we will get from the portal).

8. Write a utility function to download a poster of the movie based on the information from the JSON dataset and save it in your local folder. Use the **os** module. The poster data is stored in the JSON key **Poster**. Use the Python command to open a file and write the poster data. Close the file after you're done. This function will save the poster data as an image file.

9. Write a utility function called **search_movie** to search for a movie by its name, print the downloaded **JSON** data, and save the movie poster in the local folder. Use a **try-except** loop for this. Use the previously created **serviceurl** and **apikey** variables. You have to pass on a dictionary with a key, **t**, and the movie name as the corresponding value to the **urllib.parse.urlencode()** function and then add the **serviceurl** and **apikey** to the output of the function to construct the full URL. This URL will be used to access the data. The **JSON** data has a key called **Response**. If it is **True**, that means the read was successful. Check this before processing the data. If it's not successful, then print the **JSON** key **Error**, which will contain the appropriate error message returned by the movie database.

10. Test the **search_movie** function by entering **Titanic**.

11. Test the **search_movie** function by entering **"Random_error"** (obviously, this will not be found, and you should be able to check whether your error catching code is working properly).

> **Note:**
> The solution for this activity can be found on page 320.

Summary

In this chapter, we went through several important concepts and learning modules related to advanced data gathering and web scraping. We started by reading data from web pages using two of the most popular Python libraries – `requests` and `BeautifulSoup`. In this task, we utilized the previous chapter's knowledge about the general structure of HTML pages and their interaction with Python code. We extracted meaningful data from the Wikipedia home page during this process.

Then, we learned how to read data from XML and JSON files, two of the most widely used data streaming/exchange formats on the web. For the XML part, we showed you how to traverse the tree-structure data string efficiently to extract key information. For the JSON part, we mixed it with reading data from the web using an API (Application Program Interface). The API we consumed was RESTful, which is one of the major standards in Web API.

At the end of this chapter, we went through a detailed exercise of using regex techniques in tricky string-matching problems to scrape useful information from a large and messy text corpus, parsed from HTML. This chapter should come in extremely handy for string and text processing tasks in your data wrangling career.

In the next chapter, we will learn about databases with Python.

8

RDBMS and SQL

Learning Objectives

By the end of this chapter, you will be able to:

- Apply the basics of RDBMS to query databases using Python

- Convert data from SQL into a pandas DataFrame

This chapter explains the concepts of databases, including their creation, manipulation and control, and transforming tables into pandas DataFrames.

Introduction

This chapter of our data journey is focused on **RDBMS** (Relational Database Management Systems) and **SQL** (Structured Query Language). In the previous chapter, we stored and read data from a file. In this chapter, we will read structured data, design access to the data, and create query interfaces for databases.

Data has been stored in RDBMS format for years. The reasons behind it are as follows:

- RDBMS is one of the safest ways to store, manage, and retrieve data.

- They are backed by a solid mathematical foundation (relational algebra and calculus) and they expose an efficient and intuitive declarative language – SQL – for easy interaction.

- Almost every language has a rich set of libraries to interact with different RDBMS and the tricks and methods of using them are well tested and well understood.

- Scaling an RDBMS is a pretty well-understood task and there are a bunch of well trained, experienced professionals to do this job (DBA or database administrator).

As we can see in the following chart, the market of DBMS is big. This chart was produced based on market research that was done by **Gartner, Inc.** in **2016**:

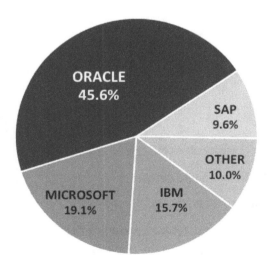

Figure 8.1 Commercial database market share in 2016

We will learn and play around with some basic and fundamental concepts of database and database management systems in this chapter.

Refresher of RDBMS and SQL

An RDBMS is a piece of software that manages data (represented for the end user in a tabular form) on physical hard disks and is built using the Codd's relational model. Most of the databases that we encounter today are RDBMS. In recent years, there has been a huge industry shift toward a newer kind of database management system, called **NoSQL** (**MongoDB**, **CouchDB**, **Riak**, and so on). These systems, although in some aspects they follow some of the rules of RDBMS, in most cases reject or modify them.

How is an RDBMS Structured?

The RDBMS structure consists of three main elements, namely the storage engine, query engine, and log management. Here is a diagram that shows the structure of a RDBMS:

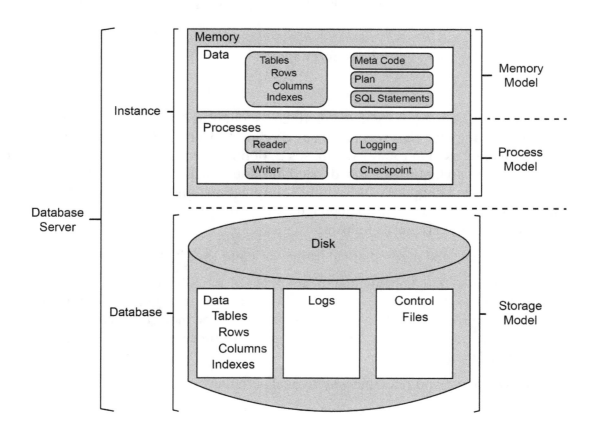

Figure 8.2 RDBMS structure

The following are the main concepts of any RDBMS structure:

- **Storage engine**: This is the part of the RDBMS that is responsible for storing the data in an efficient way and also to give it back when asked for, in an efficient way. As an end user of the RDBMS system (an application developer is considered an end user of an RDBMS), we will never need to interact with this layer directly.

- **Query engine**: This is the part of the RDBMS that allows us to create data objects (tables, views, and so on), manipulate them (create and delete columns, create/delete/update rows, and so on), and query them (read rows) using a simple yet powerful language.

- **Log management**: This part of the RDBMS is responsible for creating and maintaining the logs. If you are wondering why the log is such an important thing, then you should look into how replication and partitions are handled in a modern RDBMS (such as PostgreSQL) using something called **Write Ahead Log** (or WAL for short).

We will focus on the query engine in this chapter.

SQL

Structured **Q**uery **L**anguage or **SQL** (pronounced sequel), as it is commonly known, is a domain-specific language that was originally designed based on E.F. Codd's relational model and is widely used in today's databases to define, insert, manipulate, and retrieve data from them. It can be further sub-divided into four smaller sub-languages, namely **DDL** (Data Definition Language), **DML** (Data Manipulation Language), **DQL** (Data Query Language), and **DCL** (Data Control Language). There are several advantages of using SQL, with some of them being as follows:

- It is based on a solid mathematical framework and thus it is easy to understand.

- It is a declarative language, which means that we actually never tell it how to do its job. We almost always tell it what to do. This frees us from a big burden of writing custom code for data management. We can be more focused on the actual query problem we are trying to solve instead of bothering about how to create and maintain a data store.

- It gives you a fast and readable way to deal with data.

- SQL gives you out-of-the-box ways to get multiple pieces of data with a single query.

The main areas of focus for the following topic will be DDL, DML, and DQL. The DCL part is more for database administrators.

- **DDL**: This is how we define our data structure in SQL. As RDBMS is mainly designed and built with structured data in mind, we have to tell an RDBMS engine beforehand what our data is going to look like. We can update this definition at a later point in time, but an initial one is a must. This is where we will write statements such as **CREATE TABLE** or **DROP TABLE** or **ALTER TABLE**.

> **Note**
>
> Notice the use of uppercase letters. It is not a specification and you can use lowercase letters, but it is a widely followed convention and we will use that in this book.

- **DML**: DML is the part of SQL that let us insert, delete, or update a certain data point (a row) in a previously defined data object (a table). This is the part of SQL which contains statements such as **INSERT INTO**, **DELETE FROM**, or **UPDATE**.

- **DQL**: With DQL, we enable ourselves to query the data stored in a RDBMS, which was defined by DDL and inserted using DML. It gives us enormous power and flexibility to not only query data out of a single object (table), but also to extract relevant data from all the related objects using queries. The frequently used query that's used to retrieve data is the **SELECT** command. We will also see and use the concepts of the primary key, foreign key, index, joins, and so on.

Once you define and insert data in a database, it can be represented as follows:

First Name	Last Name	Address	City	Age
Mickey	Mouse	123 Fantasy Way	Anaheim	73
Bat	Man	321 Cavern Ave	Gotham	54
Wonder	Woman	987 Truth Way	Paradise	39
Donald	Duck	555 Quack Street	Mallard	65
Bugs	Bunny	567 Carrot Street	Rascal	58
Wiley	Coyote	999 Acme Way	Canyon	61
Cat	Woman	234 Purrfect Street	Hairball	32
Tweety	Bird	543	Itotltaw	28

Figure 8.3 Table displaying sample data

Another thing to remember about RDBMS is relations. Generally, in a table, we have one or more columns that will have unique values for each row in the table. We call them **primary keys** for the table. We should be aware that we will encounter unique values across the rows, which are not primary keys. The main difference between them and primary keys is the fact that a primary key cannot be null.

By using the primary key of one table and mentioning it as a foreign key in another table, we can establish relations between two tables. A certain table can be related to any finite number of tables. The relations can be 1:1, which means that each row of the second table is uniquely related to one row of the first table, or 1 :N, N:1, or N: M. An example of relations is as follows:

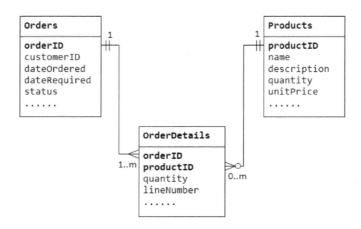

Figure 8.4 Diagram showing relations

With this brief refresher, we are now ready to jump into hands-on exercises and write some SQL to store and retrieve data.

Using an RDBMS (MySQL/PostgreSQL/SQLite)

In this topic, we will focus on how to write some basic SQL commands, as well as how to connect to a database from Python and use it effectively within Python. The database we will choose here is SQLite. There are other databases, such as **Oracle**, **MySQL**, **Postgresql**, and **DB2**. The main tricks that you are going to learn here will not change based on what database you are using. But for different databases, you will need to install different third-party Python libraries (such as **Psycopg2** for **Postgresql**, and so on). The reason they all behave the same way (apart for some small details) is the fact that they all adhere to **PEP249** (commonly known as Python DB API 2).

This is a good standardization and saves us a lot of headaches while porting from one RDBMS to another.

> **Note**
>
> Most of the industry standard projects which are written in Python and use some kind of RDBMS as the data store, most often relay on an ORM or Object Relational Mapper. An ORM is a high-level library in Python which makes many tasks, while dealing with RDBMS, easier. It also exposes a more Pythonic API than writing raw SQL inside Python code.

Exercise 107: Connecting to Database in SQLite

In this exercise, we will look into the first step toward using a RDBMS in Python code. All we are going to do is connect to a database and then close the connection. We will also learn about the best way to do this:

1. Import the **sqlite3** library of Python by using the following command:

    ```
    import sqlite3
    ```

2. Use the **connect** function to connect to a database. If you already have some experience with databases, then you will notice that we are not using any **server address**, **user name**, **password**, or other credentials to connect to a database. This is because these fields are not mandatory in **sqlite3,** unlike in **Postgresql** or **MySQL**. The main database engine of SQLite is embedded:

    ```
    conn = sqlite3.connect("chapter.db")
    ```

3. Close the connection, as follows:

    ```
    conn.close()
    ```

    This **conn** object is the main connection object, and we will need that to get a second type of object in the future once we want to interact with the database. We need to be careful about closing any open connection to our database.

4. Use the same **with** statement from Python, just like we did for files, and connect to the database, as follows:

    ```
    with sqlite3.connect("chapter.db") as conn:
        pass
    ```

In this exercise, we have connected to a database using Python.

Exercise 108: DDL and DML Commands in SQLite

In this exercise, we will look at how we can create a table, and we will also insert data in it.

As the name suggests, DDL (Data Definition Language) is the way to communicate to the database engine in advance to define what the data will look like. The database engine creates a table object based on the definition provided and prepares it.

To create a table in SQL, use the **CREATE TABLE** SQL clause. This will need the table name and the table definition. Table name is a unique identifier for the database engine to find and use the table for all future transactions. It can be anything (any alphanumeric string), as long as it is unique. We add the table definition in the form of (column_ name_1 data_type, column_name_2 data type, ...). For our purpose, we will use the **text** and **integer** datatypes, but usually a standard database engine supports many more datatypes, such as float, double, date time, Boolean, and so on. We will also need to specify a primary key. A primary key is a unique, non-null identifier that's used to uniquely identify a row in a table. In our case, we use email as a primary key. A primary key can be an integer or text.

The last thing you need to know is that unless you call a **commit** on the series of operations you just performed (together, we formally call them a **transaction**), nothing will be actually performed and reflected in the database. This property is called **atomicity**. In fact, for a database to be industry standard (to be useable in real life), it needs to follow the ACID (Atomicity, Consistency, Isolation, Durability) properties:

1. Use SQLite's **connect** function to connect to the **chapter.db** database, as follows:

   ```
   with sqlite3.connect("chapter.db") as conn:
   ```

   > **Note**
   >
   > This code will work once you add the snippet from step 3.

2. Create a cursor object by calling **conn.cursor()**. The cursor object acts as a medium to communicate with the database. Create a table in Python, as follows:

   ```
   cursor = conn.cursor()
   cursor.execute("CREATE TABLE IF NOT EXISTS user (email text, first_name
   text, last_name text, address text, age integer, PRIMARY KEY (email))")
   ```

3. Insert rows into the database that you created, as follows:

```
cursor.execute("INSERT INTO user VALUES ('bob@example.com', 'Bob', 'Codd',
'123 Fantasy lane, Fantasy City', 31)")
cursor.execute("INSERT INTO user VALUES ('tom@web.com', 'Tom', 'Fake', '456
Fantasy lane, Fantasu City', 39)")
```

4. Commit to the database:

```
conn.commit()
```

This will create the table and write two rows to it with data.

Reading Data from a Database in SQLite

In the preceding exercise, we created a table and stored data in it. Now, we will learn how to read the data that's stored in this database.

> The **SELECT** clause is immensely powerful, and it is really important for a data practitioner to master **SELECT** and everything related to it (such as conditions, joins, group-by, and so on).
>
> The * after **SELECT** tells the engine to select all of the columns from the table. It is a useful shorthand. We have not mentioned any condition for the selection (such as above a certain age, first name starting with a certain sequence of letters, and so on). We are practically telling the database engine to select all the rows and all the columns from the table. It is time-consuming and less effective if we have a huge table. Hence, we would want to use the **LIMIT** clause to limit the number of rows we want.

You can use the **SELECT** clause in SQL to retrieve data, as follows:

```
with sqlite3.connect("chapter.db") as conn:
    cursor = conn.cursor()
    rows = cursor.execute('SELECT * FROM user')
    for row in rows:
        print(row)
```

The output is as follows:

```
('bob@example.com', 'Bob', 'Codd', '123 Fantasy lane, Fantasu City', 31)
('tom@web.com', 'Tom', 'Fake', '456 Fantasy lane, Fantasu City', 39)
```

Figure 8.5: Output of the SELECT clause

The syntax to use the **SELECT** clause with a **LIMIT** as follows:

```
SELECT * FROM <table_name> LIMIT 50;
```

> **Note**
>
> This syntax is a sample code and will not work on Jupyter notebook.

This will select all the columns, but only the first 50 rows from the table.

Exercise 109: Sorting Values that are Present in the Database

In this exercise, we will use the **ORDER BY** clause to sort the rows of user table with respect to age:

1. Sort the **chapter.db** by **age** in descending order, as follows:

    ```
    with sqlite3.connect("chapter.db") as conn:
        cursor = conn.cursor()
        rows = cursor.execute('SELECT * FROM user ORDER BY age DESC')
        for row in rows:
            print(row)
    ```

    The output is as follows:

```
('tom@web.com', 'Tom', 'Fake', '456 Fantasy lane, Fantasu City', 39)
('bob@example.com', 'Bob', 'Codd', '123 Fantasy lane, Fantasu City', 31)
```

Figure 8.6: Output of data displaying age in descending order

2. Sort the **chapter.db** by **age** in ascending order, as follows:

```
with sqlite3.connect("chapter.db") as conn:
    cursor = conn.cursor()
    rows = cursor.execute('SELECT * FROM user ORDER BY age')
    for row in rows:
        print(row)
```

3. The output is as follows:

```
('bob@example.com', 'Bob', 'Codd', '123 Fantasy lane, Fantasu City', 31)
('tom@web.com', 'Tom', 'Fake', '456 Fantasy lane, Fantasu City', 39)
```

Figure 8.7: Output of data displaying age in ascending order

Notice that we don't need to specify the order as **ASC** to sort it into ascending order.

Exercise 110: Altering the Structure of a Table and Updating the New Fields

In this exercise, we are going to add a column using **ALTER** and **UPDATE** the values in the newly added column.

The **UPDATE** command is used to edit/update any row after it has been inserted. Be careful when using it because using **UPDATE** without selective clauses (such as **WHERE**) affects the entire table:

1. Establish the connection with the database by using the following command:

```
with sqlite3.connect("chapter.db") as conn:
    cursor = conn.cursor()
```

2. Add another column in the **user** table and fill it with **null** values by using the following command:

```
cursor.execute("ALTER TABLE user ADD COLUMN gender text")
```

3. Update all of the values of **gender** so that they are **M** by using the following command:

```
cursor.execute("UPDATE user SET gender='M'")
conn.commit()
```

4. To check the altered table, execute the following command:

```
rows = cursor.execute('SELECT * FROM user')
for row in rows:
        print(row)
```

```
('bob@example.com', 'Bob', 'Codd', '123 Fantasy lane, Fantasu City', 31, 'M')
('tom@web.com', 'Tom', 'Fake', '456 Fantasy lane, Fantasu City', 39, 'M')
```

Figure 8.8: Output after altering the table

We have updated the entire table by setting the gender of all the users as M, where M stands for male.

Exercise 111: Grouping Values in Tables

In this exercise, we will learn about a concept that we have already learned about in pandas. This is the **GROUP BY** clause. The **GROUP BY** clause is a technique that's used to retrieve distinct values from the database and place them in individual buckets.

The following diagram explains how the GROUP BY clause works:

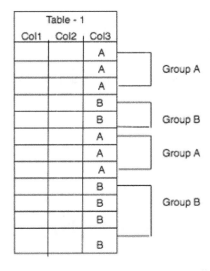

Figure 8.9: Illustration of the GROUP BY clause on a table

In the preceding diagram, we can see that the **Col3** column has only two unique values across all rows, A and B.

The command that's used to check the total number of rows belonging to each group is as follows:

```
SELECT count(*), col3 FROM table1 GROUP BY col3
```

Add female users to the table and group them based on the gender:

1. Add a female user to the table:

```
cursor.execute("INSERT INTO user VALUES ('shelly@www.com', 'Shelly',
'Milar', '123, Ocean View Lane', 39, 'F')")
```

2. Run the following code to see the count by each gender:

```
rows = cursor.execute("SELECT COUNT(*), gender FROM user GROUP BY gender")
for row in rows:
        print(row)
```

The output is as follows:

```
(1, 'F')
(2, 'M')
```

Figure 8.10: Output of the GROUP BY clause

Relation Mapping in Databases

We have been working with a single table and altering it, as well as reading back the data. However, the real power of an RDBMS comes from the handling of relationships among different objects (tables). In this section, we are going to create a new table called **comments** and link it with the user table in a 1: N relationship. This means that one user can have multiple comments. The way we are going to do this is by adding the **user** table's primary key as a foreign key in the **comments** table. This will create a 1: N relationship.

When we link two tables, we need to specify to the database engine what should be done if the parent row is deleted, which has many children in the other table. As we can see in the following diagram, we are asking what happens at the place of the question marks when we delete row1 of the user table:

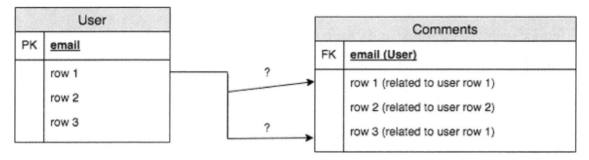

Figure 8.11: Illustration of relations

In a non-RDBMS situation, this situation can quickly become difficult and messy to manage and maintain. However, with an RDBMS, all we have to tell the database engine, in very precise ways, is what to do when a situation like this occurs. The database engine will do the rest for us. We use **ON DELETE** to tell the engine what we do with all the rows of a table when the parent row gets deleted. The following code illustrates these concepts:

```
with sqlite3.connect("chapter.db") as conn:

    cursor = conn.cursor()

    cursor.execute("PRAGMA foreign_keys = 1")

    sql = """

        CREATE TABLE comments (

            user_id text,

            comments text,

            FOREIGN KEY (user_id) REFERENCES user (email)

            ON DELETE CASCADE ON UPDATE NO ACTION

        )

    """

    cursor.execute(sql)

    conn.commit()
```

The **ON DELETE CASCADE** line informs the database engine that we want to delete all the children rows when the parent gets deleted. We can also define actions for **UPDATE**. In this case, there is nothing to do on **UPDATE**.

The **FOREIGN KEY** modifier modifies a column definition (**user_id**, in this case) and marks it as a foreign key, which is related to the primary key (**email**, in this case) of another table.

You may notice the strange looking **cursor.execute("PRAGMA foreign_keys = 1")** line in the code. It is there just because SQLite does not use the normal foreign key features by default. It is this line that enables that feature. It is typical to SQLite and we won't need it for any other databases.

Adding Rows in the comments Table

We have created a table called comments. In this section, we will dynamically generate an insert query, as follows:

```
with sqlite3.connect("chapter.db") as conn:

    cursor = conn.cursor()

    cursor.execute("PRAGMA foreign_keys = 1")

    sql = "INSERT INTO comments VALUES ('{}', '{}')"

    rows = cursor.execute('SELECT * FROM user ORDER BY age')

    for row in rows:

        email = row[0]

        print("Going to create rows for {}".format(email))

        name = row[1] + " " + row[2]

        for i in range(10):

            comment = "This is comment {} by {}".format(i, name)

            conn.cursor().execute(sql.format(email, comment))

    conn.commit()
```

Pay attention to how we dynamically generate the insert query so that we can insert 10 comments for each user.

Joins

In this exercise, we will learn how to exploit the relationship we just built. This means that if we have the primary key from one table, we can recover all the data needed from that table and also all the linked rows from the child table. To achieve this, we will use something called a **join**.

A join is basically a way to retrieve linked rows from two tables using any kind of primary key - foreign key relation that they have. There are many types of join, such as **INNER**, **LEFT OUTER**, **RIGHT OUTER**, **FULL OUTER**, and **CROSS**. They are used in different situations. However, most of the time, in simple 1: N relations, we end up using an **INNER** join. In *Chapter 1: Introduction to Data Wrangling with Python*, we learned about sets, then we can view an **INNER JOIN** as an intersection of two sets. The following diagram illustrate the concepts:

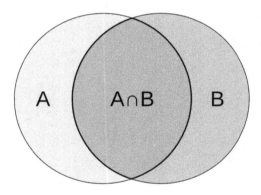

Figure 8.12: Intersection Join

Here, A represents one table and B represents another. The meaning of having common members is to have a relationship between them. It takes all of the rows of A and compares them with all of the rows of B to find the matching rows that satisfy the join predicate. This can quickly become a complex and time-consuming operation. Joins can be very expensive operations. Usually, we use some kind of **where** clause, after we specify the join, to shorten the scope of rows that are fetched from table A or B to perform the matching.

In our case, our first table, **user**, has three entries, with the primary key being the **email**. We can make use of this in our query to get comments just from **Bob**:

```
with sqlite3.connect("chapter.db") as conn:

    cursor = conn.cursor()s

    cursor.execute("PRAGMA foreign_keys = 1")

    sql = """
```

```
    SELECT * FROM comments

    JOIN user ON comments.user_id = user.email

    WHERE user.email='bob@example.com'

"""

rows = cursor.execute(sql)

for row in rows:

    print(row)
```

The output is as follows:

```
('bob@example.com', 'This is comment 0 by Bob Codd', 'bob@example.com',
'Bob', 'Codd', '123 Fantasy lane, Fantasu City', 31, None)

('bob@example.com', 'This is comment 1 by Bob Codd', 'bob@example.com',
'Bob', 'Codd', '123 Fantasy lane, Fantasu City', 31, None)

('bob@example.com', 'This is comment 2 by Bob Codd', 'bob@example.com',
'Bob', 'Codd', '123 Fantasy lane, Fantasu City', 31, None)

('bob@example.com', 'This is comment 3 by Bob Codd', 'bob@example.com',
'Bob', 'Codd', '123 Fantasy lane, Fantasu City', 31, None)

('bob@example.com', 'This is comment 4 by Bob Codd', 'bob@example.com',
'Bob', 'Codd', '123 Fantasy lane, Fantasu City', 31, None)

('bob@example.com', 'This is comment 5 by Bob Codd', 'bob@example.com',
'Bob', 'Codd', '123 Fantasy lane, Fantasu City', 31, None)

('bob@example.com', 'This is comment 6 by Bob Codd', 'bob@example.com',
'Bob', 'Codd', '123 Fantasy lane, Fantasu City', 31, None)

('bob@example.com', 'This is comment 7 by Bob Codd', 'bob@example.com',
'Bob', 'Codd', '123 Fantasy lane, Fantasu City', 31, None)

('bob@example.com', 'This is comment 8 by Bob Codd', 'bob@example.com',
'Bob', 'Codd', '123 Fantasy lane, Fantasu City', 31, None)

('bob@example.com', 'This is comment 9 by Bob Codd', 'bob@example.com',
'Bob', 'Codd', '123 Fantasy lane, Fantasu City', 31, None)
```

Figure 8.13: Output of the Join query

Retrieving Specific Columns from a JOIN query

In the previous exercise, we saw that we can use a JOIN to fetch the related rows from two tables. However, if we look at the results, we will see that it returned all the columns, thus combining both tables. This is not very concise. What about if we only want to see the emails and the related comments, and not all the data?

There is some nice shorthand code that lets us do this:

```python
with sqlite3.connect("chapter.db") as conn:

    cursor = conn.cursor()

    cursor.execute("PRAGMA foreign_keys = 1")

    sql = """

        SELECT comments.* FROM comments

        JOIN user ON comments.user_id = user.email

        WHERE user.email='bob@example.com'

    """

    rows = cursor.execute(sql)

    for row in rows:

        print(row)
```

Just by changing the **SELECT** statement, we made our final result look as follows:

```
('bob@example.com', 'This is comment 0 by Bob Codd')

('bob@example.com', 'This is comment 1 by Bob Codd')

('bob@example.com', 'This is comment 2 by Bob Codd')

('bob@example.com', 'This is comment 3 by Bob Codd')

('bob@example.com', 'This is comment 4 by Bob Codd')

('bob@example.com', 'This is comment 5 by Bob Codd')

('bob@example.com', 'This is comment 6 by Bob Codd')

('bob@example.com', 'This is comment 7 by Bob Codd')

('bob@example.com', 'This is comment 8 by Bob Codd')

('bob@example.com', 'This is comment 9 by Bob Codd')
```

Exercise 112: Deleting Rows

In this exercise, we are going to delete a row from the user table and observe the effects it will have on the **comments** table. Be very careful when running this command as it can have a destructive effect on the data. Please keep in mind that it has to almost always be run accompanied by a **WHERE** clause so that we delete just a part of the data and not everything:

1. To delete a row from a table, we use the **DELETE** clause in **SQL**. To run delete on the **user** table, we are going to use the following code:

```
with sqlite3.connect("chapter.db") as conn:
    cursor = conn.cursor()
    cursor.execute("PRAGMA foreign_keys = 1")
    cursor.execute("DELETE FROM user WHERE email='bob@example.com'")
    conn.commit()
```

2. Perform the **SELECT** operation on the user table:

```
with sqlite3.connect("chapter.db") as conn:
    cursor = conn.cursor()
    cursor.execute("PRAGMA foreign_keys = 1")
    rows = cursor.execute("SELECT * FROM user")
    for row in rows:
        print(row)
```

Observe that the user Bob has been deleted.

Now, moving on to the **comments** table, we have to remember that we had mentioned **ON DELETE CASCADE** while creating the table. The database engine knows that if a row is deleted from the parent table (**user**), all the related rows from the child tables (**comments**) will have to be deleted.

3. Perform a select operation on the comments table by using the following command:

```
with sqlite3.connect("chapter.db") as conn:
    cursor = conn.cursor()
    cursor.execute("PRAGMA foreign_keys = 1")
    rows = cursor.execute("SELECT * FROM comments")
    for row in rows:
        print(row)
```

The output is as follows:

```
('tom@web.com', 'This is comment 0 by Tom Fake')
('tom@web.com', 'This is comment 1 by Tom Fake')
('tom@web.com', 'This is comment 2 by Tom Fake')
('tom@web.com', 'This is comment 3 by Tom Fake')
('tom@web.com', 'This is comment 4 by Tom Fake')
('tom@web.com', 'This is comment 5 by Tom Fake')
('tom@web.com', 'This is comment 6 by Tom Fake')
('tom@web.com', 'This is comment 7 by Tom Fake')
('tom@web.com', 'This is comment 8 by Tom Fake')
('tom@web.com', 'This is comment 9 by Tom Fake')
```

We can see that all of the rows related to Bob are deleted.

Updating Specific Values in a Table

In this exercise, we will see how we can update rows in a table. We have already looked at this in the past but, as we mentioned, at a table level only. Without WHERE, updating is often a bad idea.

Combine UPDATE with WHERE to selectively update the first name of the user with the email address **tom@web.com**:

```python
with sqlite3.connect("chapter.db") as conn:

    cursor = conn.cursor()

    cursor.execute("PRAGMA foreign_keys = 1")

    cursor.execute("UPDATE user set first_name='Chris' where email='tom@web.
com'")

    conn.commit()

    rows = cursor.execute("SELECT * FROM user")

    for row in rows:

        print(row)
```

The output is as follows:

```
('tom@web.com', 'Chris', 'Fake', '456 Fantasy lane, Fantasu City', 39, 'M')
('shelly@www.com', 'Shelly', 'Milar', '123, Ocean View Lane', 39, 'F')
```

Figure 8.14: Output of the update query

Exercise 113: RDBMS and DataFrames

We have looked into many fundamental aspects of storing and querying data from a database, but as a data wrangling expert, we need our data to be packed and presented as a DataFrame so that we can perform quick and convenient operations on them:

1. Import **pandas** using the following code:

   ```
   import pandas as pd
   ```

2. Create a columns list with **email**, **first name**, **last name**, **age**, **gender**, and **comments** as column names. Also, create an empty data list:

   ```
   columns = ["Email", "First Name", "Last Name", "Age", "Gender", "Comments"]
   data = []
   ```

3. Connect to **chapter.db** using **SQLite** and obtain a cursor, as follows:

   ```
   with sqlite3.connect("chapter.db") as conn:
       cursor = conn.cursor()
   ```
   Use the execute method from the cursor to set "PRAGMA foreign_keys = 1"
   ```
       cursor.execute("PRAGMA foreign_keys = 1")
   ```

4. Create a **sql** variable that will contain the **SELECT** command and use the **join** command to join the databases:

   ```
   sql = """
           SELECT user.email, user.first_name, user.last_name, user.age, user.
   gender, comments.comments FROM comments
           JOIN user ON comments.user_id = user.email
           WHERE user.email = 'tom@web.com'
       """
   ```

5. Use the **execute** method of cursor to execute the **sql** command:

```
rows = cursor.execute(sql)
```

6. Append the rows to the data list:

```
for row in rows:
    data.append(row)
```

7. Create a DataFrame using the data list:

```
df = pd.DataFrame(data, columns=columns)
```

8. We have created the DataFrame using the data list. You can print the values into the DataFrame using **df.head**.

Activity 11: Retrieving Data Correctly From Databases

In this activity, we have the persons table:

id	first_name	last_name	age	city	zip_code
1	Erica	NaN	22	south port	2345678
2	Jordi	NaN	73	east port	123456
3	Chasity	NaN	70	new port	76856785
4	Gregg	NaN	31	new port	76856785
5	Tony	Lindgren	7	west port	2345678

Figure 8.15: The persons table

We have the pets table:

owner_id	pet_name	pet_type	treatment_done
57	mani	1.0	0
80	tamari	NaN	0
25	raba	NaN	0
27	olga	NaN	0
60	raba	NaN	0

Figure 8.16: The pets table

As we can see, the **id** column in the persons table (which is an integer) serves as the primary key for that table and as a foreign key for the pet table, which is linked via the **owner_id** column.

The persons table has the following columns:

- **first_name**: The first name of the person
- **last_name**: The last name of the person (can be "null")
- **age**: The age of the person
- **city**: The city from where he/she is from
- **zip_code**: The zip code of the city

The pets table has the following columns:

- **pet_name**: The name of the pet.
- **pet_type**: What type of pet it is, for example, cat, dog, and so on. Due to a lack of further information, we do not know which number represents what, but it is an integer and can be null.
- **treatment_done**: It is also an integer column, and 0 here represents "No", whereas 1 represents "Yes".

The name of the SQLite DB is **petsdb** and it is supplied along with the Activity notebook.

These steps will help you complete this activity:

1. Connect to **petsDB** and check whether the connection has been successful.

2. Find the different age groups in the persons database.

3. Find the age group that has the maximum number of people.

4. Find the people who do not have a last name.

5. Find out how many people have more than one pet.

6. Find out how many pets have received treatment.

7. Find out how many pets have received treatment and the type of pet is known.

8. Find out how many pets are from the city called **east port**.

9. Find out how many pets are from the city called **east port** and who received a treatment.

> **Note**
>
> The solution for this activity can be found on page 324.

Summary

We have come to the end of the database chapter. We have learned how to connect to SQLite using Python. We have brushed up on the basics of relational databases and learned how to open and close a database. We then learned how to export this relational database into Python DataFrames.

In the next chapter, we will be performing data wrangling on real-world datasets.

Application of Data Wrangling in Real Life

Learning Objectives

By the end of this chapter, you will be able to:

- Perform data wrangling on multiple full-fledged datasets from renowned sources
- Create a unified dataset that can be passed on to a data science team for machine learning and predictive analytics
- Relate data wrangling to version control, containerization, cloud services for data analytics, and big data technologies such as Apache Spark and Hadoop

In this chapter, you will apply your gathered knowledge on real-life datasets and investigate various aspects of it.

Introduction

We learned about databases in the previous chapter, so now it is time to combine the knowledge of data wrangling and Python with a real-world scenario. In the real world, data from one source is often inadequate to perform analysis. Generally, a data wrangler has to distinguish between relevant and non-relevant data and combine data from different sources.

The primary job of a data wrangling expert is to pull data from multiple sources, format and clean it (impute the data if it is missing), and finally combine it in a coherent manner to prepare a dataset for further analysis by data scientists or machine learning engineers.

In this topic, we will try to mimic such a typical task flow by downloading and using two different datasets from reputed web portals. Each of the datasets contains partial data pertaining to the key question that is being asked. Let's examine it more closely.

Applying Your Knowledge to a Real-life Data Wrangling Task

Suppose you are asked this question: **In India, did the enrollment in primary/ secondary/tertiary education increase with the improvement of per capita GDP in the past 15 years?** The actual modeling and analysis will be done by some senior data scientist, who will use machine learning and data visualization for analysis. As a data wrangling expert, **your job will be to acquire and provide a clean dataset that contains educational enrollment and GDP data side by side**.

Suppose you have a link for a dataset from the United Nations and you can download the dataset of education (for all the nations around the world). But this dataset has some missing values and moreover it does not have any GDP information. Someone has also given you another separate CSV file (downloaded from the World Bank site) which contains GDP data but in a messy format.

In this activity, we will examine how to handle these two separate sources and clean the data to prepare a simple final dataset with the required data and save it to the local drive as a SQL database file:

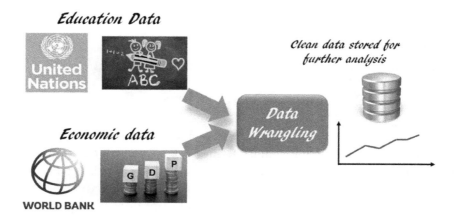

Figure 9.1: Pictorial representation of the merging of education and economic data

You are encouraged to follow along with the code and results in the notebook and try to understand and internalize the nature of the data wrangling flow. You are also encouraged to try extracting various data from these files and answer your own questions about a nations' socio-economic factors and their inter-relationships.

> **Note**
>
> Coming up with interesting questions about social, economic, technological, and geo-political topics and then answering them using freely available data and a little bit of programming knowledge is one of most fun ways to learn about any data science topic. You will get a flare of that process in this chapter.

Data Imputation

Clearly, we are missing some data. Let's say we decide to impute these data points by simple linear interpolation between the available data points. We can take out a pen and paper or a calculator and compute those values and manually create a dataset. But being a data wrangler, we will of course take advantage of Python programming, and use pandas imputation methods for this task.

But to do that, we first need to create a DataFrame with missing values in it, that is, we need to append another DataFrame with missing values to the current DataFrame.

Activity 12: Data Wrangling Task – Fixing UN Data

Suppose the agenda of the data analysis is to find out whether the enrolment in primary, secondary, or tertiary education has increased with the improvement of per capita GDP in the past 15 years. For this task, we will first need to clean or wrangle the two datasets, that is, the Education Enrolment and GDP data.

The UN data is available on https://github.com/TrainingByPackt/Data-Wrangling-with-Python/blob/master/Chapter09/Activity12-15/SYB61_T07_Education.csv.

> **Note**
>
> If you download the CSV file and open it using Excel, then you will see that the **Footnotes** column sometimes contains useful notes. We may not want to drop it in the beginning. If we are interested in a particular country's data (like we are in this task), then it may well turn out that **Footnotes** will be NaN, that is, blank. In that case, we can drop it at the end. But for some countries or regions, it may contain information.

These steps will guide you to find the solution:

1. Download the dataset from the UN data from GitHub from the following link: https://github.com/TrainingByPackt/Data-Wrangling-with-Python/blob/master/Lesson09/Activity12-15/India_World_Bank_Info.csv.

   The UN data has missing values. Clean the data to prepare a simple final dataset with the required data and save it to the local drive as a SQL database file.

2. Use the `pd.read_csv` method of pandas to create a DataFrame.

3. Since the first row does not contain useful information, skip it using the `skiprows` parameter.

4. Drop the column region/country/area and source.

5. Assign the following names as columns of DataFrame: Region/County/Area, Year, Data, Value, and Footnotes.

6. Check how many unique values are present in the **Footnotes** column.

7. Check the type of value column.

8. Create a function to convert the value column into a floating-point.

9. Use the **apply** method to apply this function to a value.

10. Print the unique values in the data column.

> **Note:**
>
> The solution for this activity can be found on page 338.

Activity 13: Data Wrangling Task – Cleaning GDP Data

The GDP data is available on https://data.worldbank.org/ and it is available on GitHub at https://github.com/TrainingByPackt/Data-Wrangling-with-Python/blob/master/Chapter09/Activity12-15/India_World_Bank_Info.csv.

In this activity, we will clean the GDP data.

1. Create three DataFrames from the original DataFrame using filtering. Create the **df_primary, df_secondary,** and **df_tertiary DataFrames** for students enrolled in primary education, secondary education, and tertiary education in thousands, respectively.

2. Plot bar charts of the enrollment of primary students in a low-income country like India and a higher-income country like the USA.

3. Since there is missing data, use pandas imputation methods to impute these data points by simple linear interpolation between data points. To do that, create a DataFrame with missing values inserted and append a new DataFrame with missing values to the current DataFrame.

4. (For India) Append the rows corresponding to the missing years - **2004 - 2009, 2011 – 2013**.

5. Create a dictionary of values with **np.nan**. Note that there are 9 missing data points, so we need to create a list with identical values repeated 9 times.

6. Create a DataFrame of missing values (from the preceding dictionary) that we can append.

7. Append the DataFrames together.

8. Sort by Year and reset the indices using **reset_index**. Use **inplace=True** to execute the changes on the DataFrame itself.

9. Use the interpolate method for linear interpolation. It fills all the NaNs by linearly interpolated values. See the following link for more details about this method: http://pandas.pydata.org/pandas-docs/version/0.17/generated/pandas.DataFrame.interpolate.html.

10. Repeat the same steps for USA (or other countries).

11. If there are values that are unfilled, use the `limit` and `limit_direction` parameters with the interpolate method to fill them in.

12. Plot the final graph using the new data.

13. Read the GDP data using the pandas `read_csv` method. It will generally throw an error.

14. To avoid errors, try the `error_bad_lines = False` option.

15. Since there is no delimiter in the file, add the `\t` delimiter.

16. Use the `skiprows` function to remove rows that are not useful.

17. Examine the dataset. Filter the dataset with information that states that it is similar to the previous education dataset.

18. Reset the index for this new dataset.

19. Drop the not useful rows and re-index the dataset.

20. Rename the columns properly. This is necessary for merging the two datasets.

21. We will concentrate only on the data from 2003 to 2016. Eliminate the remaining data.

22. Create a new DataFrame called `df_gdp` with rows 43 to 56.

> **Note**
>
> The solution for this activity can be found on page 338.

Activity 14: Data Wrangling Task – Merging UN Data and GDP Data

The steps to merge the databases is as follows:

1. Reset the indexes for merging.

2. Merge the two DataFrames, **primary_enrollment_india** and **df_gdp**, on the Year column.

3. Drop the data, footnotes, and region/county/area.

4. Rearrange the columns for proper viewing and presentation.

> **Note**
>
> The solution for this activity can be found on page 345.

Activity 15: Data Wrangling Task – Connecting the New Data to the Database

The steps to connect the data to the database is as follows:

1. Import the **sqlite3** module of Python and use the **connect** function to connect to the database. The main database engine is embedded. But for a different database like **Postgresql** or **MySQL**, we will need to connect to them using those credentials. We designate **Year** as the **PRIMARY KEY** of this table.

2. Then, run a loop with the dataset rows one by one to insert them into the table.

3. If we look at the current folder, we should see a file called **Education_GDP.db**, and if we examine that using a database viewer program, we can see the data transferred there.

> **Note**
>
> The solution for this activity can be found on page 347.

In this notebook, we examined a complete data wrangling flow, including reading data from the web and local drive, filtering, cleaning, quick visualization, imputation, indexing, merging, and writing back to a database table. We also wrote custom functions to transform some of the data and saw how to handle situations where we may get errors when reading the file.

An Extension to Data Wrangling

This is the concluding chapter of our book, where we want to give you a broad overview of some of the exciting technologies and frameworks that you may need to learn beyond data wrangling to work as a full-stack data scientist. Data wrangling is an essential part of the whole data science and analytics pipeline, but it is not the whole enterprise. You have learned invaluable skills and techniques in this book, but it is always good to broaden your horizons and look beyond to see what other tools that are out there can give you an edge in this competitive and ever-changing world.

Additional Skills Required to Become a Data Scientist

To practice as a fully qualified data scientist/analyst, you should have some basic skills in your repertoire, irrespective of the particular programming language you choose to focus on. These skills and know-hows are language agnostic and can be utilized with any framework that you have to embrace, depending on your organization and business needs. We describe them in brief here:

- **Git and version control**: Git to version control is what RDBMS is to data storage and query. It simply means that there is a huge gap between the pre and post Git era of version controlling your code. As you may have noticed, all the notebooks for this book/book are hosted on GitHub, and this was done to take advantage of the powerful Git VCS. It gives you, out of the box, version control, history, branching facilities for different code, merging different code branches, and advanced operations like cherry picking, diff, and so on. It is an very essential tool to master as you can be almost sure that you will face it at one point of time in your journey. Packt has a very good book on it. You can check that out for more information.

- **Linux command line**: People coming from a Windows background (or even Mac, if you have not done any development before) are not very familiar, usually, with the command line. The superior UI of those OSes hides the low level details of interaction with the OS using a command line. However, as a data professional, it is important that you know the command line well. There are so many operations that you can do by simply using the command line that it is astonishing.

- **SQL and basic relational database concepts**: We dedicated an entire chapter to SQL and RDBMS. However, as we already mentioned there, it was really not enough. This is a vast subject and needs years of study to master it. Try to read more about it (Including Theory and Practical) from books and online sources. Do not forget that, despite all the other sources of data being used nowadays, we still have hundreds of millions of bytes of structured data stored in legacy database systems. You can be sure to come across one, sooner or later.

- **Docker and containerization**: Since its first release in 2013, Docker has changed the way we distribute and deploy software in server-based applications. It gives you a clean and lightweight abstraction over the underlying OS and lets you iterate fast on development without the headache of creating and maintaining a proper environment. It is very useful in both the development and production phases. Without virtually no competitor present, they are becoming the default in the industry very fast. We strongly advise you to explore it in great detail.

Basic Familiarity with Big Data and Cloud Technologies

Big data and cloud platforms are the latest trend. We will introduce them here with one or two short sentences and we encourage you to go ahead and learn about them as much as you can. If you are planning to grow as a data professional, then you can be sure that without these necessary skills it will be hard for you to transition to the next level:

- **Fundamental characteristics of big data**: Big data is simply data that is very big in size. The term size is a bit ambiguous here. It can mean one static chunk of data (like the detail census data of a big country like India or the US) or data that is dynamically generated as time passes, and each time it is huge. To give an example for the second category, we can think of how much data is generated by Facebook per day. It's about 500+ Terabytes per day. You can easily imagine that we will need specialized tools to deal with that amount of data. There are three different categories of big data, that is, Structured, Unstructured, and Semi-Structured. The main features that define big data are Volume, Variety, Velocity, and Variability.

- **Hadoop ecosystem**: Apache Hadoop (and the related ecosystem) is a software framework that aims to use the Map-Reduce programming model to simplify the storage and processing of big data. It has since become one of the backbones of big data processing in the industry. The modules in Hadoop are designed keeping in mind that hardware failures are common occurrences, and they should be automatically handled by the framework. The four base modules of Hadoop are common, HDFS, YARN, and MapReduce. The Hadoop ecosystem consists of Apache Pig, Apache Hive, Apache Impala, Apache Zookeeper, Apache HBase, and more. They are very important bricks in many high demand and cutting-edge data pipelines. We encourage you to study more about them. They are essential in any industry that aims to leverage data.

- **Apache Spark**: Apache Spark is a general purpose Cluster Computing framework that was initially developed at the University of California, Barkley, and released in 2014. It gives you an interface to program an entire cluster of computers with built-in data parallelism and fault tolerance. It contains Spark Core, Spark SQL, Spark Streaming, MLib (for machine learning), and GraphX. It is now one of the main frameworks that's used in the industry to process a huge amount of data in real time based on streaming data. We encourage you to read and master it if you want to go toward real time data engineering.

- **Amazon Web service (AWS)**: Amazon Web Services (often abbreviated as AWS) are a bunch of managed services offered by Amazon ranging from infrastructure-as-a-Service, Database-as-a-Service, MachineLearning-as-a-Service, Cache, Load Balancer, NoSQL database, to Message Queues and several other types. They are very useful for all sorts of applications. It can be a simple web app or a multi-cluster data pipeline. Many famous companies run their entire infrastructure on AWS (such as Netflix). They give us on-demand provision, easy scaling, a managed environment, a slick UI to control everything, and also a very powerful command-line client. They also expose a rich set of APIs and we can find an AWS API client in virtually any programming language. The Python one is called Boto3. If you are planning to become a data professional, then it can be said with near certainty that you will end up using many of their services at one point or another.

What Goes with Data Wrangling?

We learned in *Chapter 1, Introduction to Data Wrangling with Python*, that the process of data wrangling lies in-between data gathering and advanced analytics, including visualization and machine learning. However, the boundaries that exist in-between these processes may not always be strict and rigid. It depends largely on the organizational culture and team composition.

Therefore, we need to not only be aware of the data wrangling but also the other components of the data science platform to wrangle data effectively. Even if you are performing pure data wrangling tasks, having a good grasp over how data is sourced and utilized will give you an edge for coming up with unique and efficient solutions to complex data wrangling problems and enhance the value of those solutions to the machine learning scientist or the business domain expert:

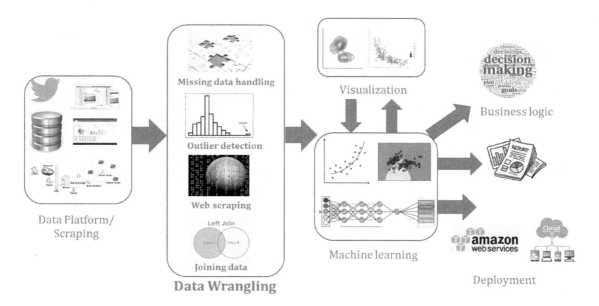

Figure 9.2: Process of data wrangling

Now, we have, in fact, already laid out a solid groundwork in this book for the data platform part, assuming that it is an integral part of data wrangling workflow. For example, we have covered web scraping, working with RESTful APIs, and database access and manipulation using Python libraries in detail.

We have also touched on basic visualization techniques and plotting functions in Python using matplotlib. However, there are other advanced statistical plotting libraries such as **Seaborn** that you can master for more sophisticated visualization for data science tasks.

Business logic and domain expertise is the most varied topic and it can only be learned on the job, however it will come eventually with experience. If you have an academic background and/or work experience in any domain such as finance, medicine and healthcare, and engineering, that knowledge will come in handy in your data science career.

The fruit of the hard work of data wrangling is realized fully in the domain of machine learning. It is the science and engineering of making machines learn patterns and insights from data for predictive analytics and intelligent, automated decision-making with a deluge of data, which cannot be analyzed efficiently by humans. Machine learning has become one of the most sought-after skills in the modern technology landscape. It has truly become one of the most exciting and promising intellectual fields, with applications ranging from e-commerce to healthcare and virtually everything in-between. Data wrangling is intrinsically linked with machine learning as it prepares the data so that it's suitable for intelligent algorithms to process. Even if you start your career in data wrangling, it could be a natural progression to move to machine learning.

Packt has published numerous books and books on this topic that you should explore. In the next section, we will touch upon some approaches to adopt and Python libraries to check out for giving you a boost in your learning.

Tips and Tricks for Mastering Machine Learning

Machine learning is difficult to start with. We have listed some structured MOOCs and incredible free resources that are available so that you can begin your journey:

- Understand the definition of and differentiation between the buzzwords—artificial intelligence, machine learning, deep learning, and data science. Cultivate the habit of reading great posts or listening to the expert talks, on these topics, and understand their true reach and applicability in some business problem.

- Stay updated with the recent trends by watching videos, reading books like *The Master Algorithm: How the Quest for the Ultimate Learning Machine Will Remake Our World*, and articles and following influential blogs like KDnuggets, Brandon Rohrer's blog, Open AI's blog about their research, Towards Data Science publication on Medium, and so on.

- As you learn new algorithms or concepts, pause and analyze how you can apply these machine learning concepts or algorithm in your daily work. This is the best method for learning and expanding your knowledge base.

- If you choose Python as your preferred language for machine learning tasks, you have a great ML library in **scikit-learn**. It is the most widely used general machine learning package in the Python ecosystem. scikit-learn has a wide variety of supervised and unsupervised learning algorithms, which are exposed via a stable consistent interface. Moreover, it is specifically designed to interface seamlessly with other popular data wrangling and numerical libraries such as NumPy and pandas.

- Another hot skill in today's job market is deep learning. Packt has many books and books on this topic and there are excellent MOOC books from Bookra where you can study deep learning. For Python libraries, you can learn and practice with **TensorFlow**, **Keras**, or **PyTorch** for deep learning.

Summary

Data is everywhere and it is all around us. In these nine chapters, we have learned about how data from different types and sources can be cleaned, corrected, and combined. Using the power of Python and the knowledge of data wrangling and applying the tricks and tips that you have studied in this book, you are ready to be a data wrangler.

Appendix

About

This section is included to assist the students to perform the activities in the book.
It includes detailed steps that are to be performed by the students to achieve the objectives of
the activities.

Solution of Activity 1: Handling Lists

These are the steps to complete this activity:

1. Import the **random** library:

    ```
    import random
    ```

2. Set the maximum number of random numbers:

    ```
    LIMIT = 100
    ```

3. Use the **randint** function from the **random** library to create 100 random numbers. Tip: try getting a list with the least number of duplicates:

    ```
    random_number_list = [random.randint(0, LIMIT) for x in range(0, LIMIT)]
    ```

4. Print **random_number_list**:

    ```
    random_number_list
    ```

    The sample output is as follows:

    ```
    [5,
    72,
    7,
    24,
    90,
    52,
    26,
    80,
    75,
    74,
    3,
    46,
    99,
    78,
    18,
    8,
    62,
    18,
    95,
    23,
    47,
    26,
    92,
    84,
    62,
    34,
    89,
    84,
    32,
    41,
    73,
    58,
    7,
    16,
    87,
    ```

Figure 1.16: Section of output for random_number_list

5. Create a **list_with_divisible_by_3** list from **random_number_list**, which will contain only numbers that are divisible by **3**:

```
list_with_divisible_by_3 = [a for a in random_number_list if a % 3 == 0]
list_with_divisible_by_3
```

The sample output is as follows:

```
[72,
 24,
 90,
 75,
 3,
 99,
 78,
 18,
 18,
 84,
 84,
 87,
 18,
 39,
 90,
 54,
 27,
 24,
 66,
 48,
 18,
 96,
 9,
 99,
 54,
 90,
 18,
 36,
 33,
 72,
 75,
 21,
 75,
 12,
```

Figure 1.17: Section of output for random_number_list divisible by 3

6. Use the **len** function to measure the length of the first list and the second list, and store them in two different variables, **length_of_random_list** and **length_of_3_divisible_list**. Calculate the difference in length in a variable called **difference**:

```
length_of_random_list = len(random_number_list)
length_of_3_divisible_list = len(list_with_divisible_by_3)
difference = length_of_random_list - length_of_3_divisible_list
difference
```

The sample output is as follows:

```
62
```

7. Combine the tasks we have performed so far and add a while loop to it. Run the loop 10 times and add the values of the difference variables to a list:

```
NUMBER_OF_EXPERIMENTS = 10
difference_list = []
for i in range(0, NUMBER_OF_EXPERIEMENTS):
    random_number_list = [random.randint(0, LIMIT) for x in range(0, LIMIT)]
    list_with_divisible_by_3 = [a for a in random_number_list if a % 3 == 0]

    length_of_random_list = len(random_number_list)
    length_of_3_divisible_list = len(list_with_divisible_by_3)
    difference = length_of_random_list - length_of_3_divisible_list

    difference_list.append(difference)
difference_list
```

The sample output is as follows:

```
[64, 61, 67, 60, 73, 66, 66, 75, 70, 61]
```

8. Then, calculate the arithmetic mean (common average) for the differences in the lengths that you have:

```
avg_diff = sum(difference_list) / float(len(difference_list))
avg_diff
```

The sample output is as follows:

```
66.3
```

Solution of Activity 2: Analyze a Multiline String and Generate the Unique Word Count

These are the steps to complete this activity:

1. Create a string called **multiline_text** and copy the text present in the first chapter of *Pride and Prejudice*. Use *Ctrl + A* to select the entire text and then *Ctrl + C* to copy it and paste the text you just copied into it:

```
multiline_text = """"It is a truth universally acknowledged, that a single man in possession of a good fortune, must be in want of

However little known the feelings or views of such a man may be on his first entering a neighbourhood, this truth is so well fixed

"My dear Mr. Bennet," said his lady to him one day, "have you heard that Netherfield Park is let at last?"

Mr. Bennet replied that he had not.

"But it is," returned she; "for Mrs. Long has just been here, and she told me all about it."

Mr. Bennet made no answer.

"Do you not want to know who has taken it?" cried his wife impatiently.

"You want to tell me, and I have no objection to hearing it."

This was invitation enough.

"Why, my dear, you must know, Mrs. Long says that Netherfield is taken by a young man of large fortune from the north of England;

"What is his name?"

"Bingley."

"Is he married or single?"

"Oh! Single, my dear, to be sure! A single man of large fortune; four or five thousand a year. What a fine thing for our girls!"
```

Figure 1.18: Initializing the mutliline_text string

2. Find the type of the string using the **type** function:

```
type(multiline_text)
```

The output is as follows:

```
str
```

3. Now, find the length of the string, using the **len** function:

```
len(multiline_text)
```

The output is as follows:

```
4475
```

4. Use string methods to get rid of all the new lines (**\n** or **\r**),and symbols. Remove all new lines by replacing them with this:

```
multiline_text = multiline_text.replace('\n', "")
```

Then, we will print and check the output:

```
multiline_text
```

The output is as follows:

```
'It is a truth universally acknowledged, that a single man in possession of a good fortune, must be in want of a wife.However l
ittle known the feelings or views of such a man may be on his first entering a neighbourhood, this truth is so well fixed in th
e minds of the surrounding families, that he is considered the rightful property of some one or other of their daughters."My de
ar Mr. Bennet," said his lady to him one day, "have you heard that Netherfield Park is let at last?"Mr. Bennet replied that he
had not."But it is," returned she; "for Mrs. Long has just been here, and she told me all about it."Mr. Bennet made no answe
r."Do you not want to know who has taken it?" cried his wife impatiently."You want to tell me, and I have no objection to heari
ng it."This was invitation enough."Why, my dear, you must know, Mrs. Long says that Netherfield is taken by a young man of larg
e fortune from the north of England; that he came down on Monday in a chaise and four to see the place, and was so much delight
ed with it, that he agreed with Mr. Morris immediately; that he is to take possession before Michaelmas, and some of his servan
ts are to be in the house by the end of next week.""What is his name?""Bingley.""Is he married or single?""Oh! Single, my dear,
to be sure! A single man of large fortune; four or five thousand a year. What a fine thing for our girls!""How so? How can it a
ffect them?""My dear Mr. Bennet," replied his wife, "how can you be so tiresome! You must know that I am thinking of his marryi
ng one of them.""Is that his design in settling here?""Design! Nonsense, how can you talk so! But it is very likely that he may
fall in love with one of them, and therefore you must visit him as soon as he comes.""I see no occasion for that. You and the g
irls may go, or you may send them by themselves, which perhaps will be still better, for as you are as handsome as any of them,
Mr. Bingley may like you the best of the party.""My dear, you flatter me. I certainly have had my share of beauty, but I do not
pretend to be anything extraordinary now. When a woman has five grown-up daughters, she ought to give over thinking of her own
beauty.""In such cases, a woman has not often much beauty to think of.""But, my dear, you must indeed go and see Mr. Bingley wh
en he comes into the neighbourhood.""It is more than I engage for, I assure you.""But consider your daughters. Only think what
an establishment it would be for one of them. Sir William and Lady Lucas are determined to go, merely on that account, for in g
eneral, you know, they visit no newcomers. Indeed you must go, for it will be impossible for us to visit him if you do not.""Yo
u are over-scrupulous, surely. I dare say Mr. Bingley will be very glad to see you; and I will send a few lines by you to assur
e him of my hearty consent to his marrying whichever he chooses of the girls; though I must throw in a good word for my little
```

Figure 1.19: The multiline_text string after removing the new lines

5. Removing the special characters and punctuation:

```
# remove special chars, punctuation etc.
cleaned_multiline_text = ""
for char in multiline_text:
    if char == " ":
        cleaned_multiline_text += char
    elif char.isalnum():  # using the isalnum() method of strings.
        cleaned_multiline_text += char
    else:
        cleaned_multiline_text += " "
```

6. Check the content of **cleaned_multiline_text**:

```
cleaned_multiline_text
```

The output is as follows:

'It is a truth universally acknowledged that a single man in possession of a good fortune must be in want of a wife However l
ittle known the feelings or views of such a man may be on his first entering a neighbourhood this truth is so well fixed in th
e minds of the surrounding families that he is considered the rightful property of some one or other of their daughters My de
ar Mr Bennet   said his lady to him one day   have you heard that Netherfield Park is let at last Mr Bennet replied that he
had not But it is   returned she   for Mrs Long has just been here and she told me all about it Mr Bennet made no answer
Do you not want to know who has taken it   cried his wife impatiently You want to tell me and I have no objection to hearing
it This was invitation enough Why my dear   you must know Mrs Long says that Netherfield is taken by a young man of large f
ortune from the north of England that he came down on Monday in a chaise and four to see the place and was so much delighted
with it that he agreed with Mr Morris immediately that he is to take possession before Michaelmas and some of his servants
are to be in the house by the end of next week   What is his name   Bingley Is he married or single   Oh Single my dear to
be sure A single man of large fortune four or five thousand a year What a fine thing for our girls   How so How can it affe
ct them   My dear Mr Bennet   replied his wife   how can you be so tiresome You must know that I am thinking of his marrying
one of them   Is that his design in settling here   Design Nonsense how can you talk so But it is very likely that he may fa
ll in love with one of them and therefore you must visit him as soon as he comes   I see no occasion for that You and the gir
ls may go or you may send them by themselves which perhaps will be still better for as you are as handsome as any of them M
r Bingley may like you the best of the party   My dear you flatter me I certainly have had my share of beauty but I do not
pretend to be anything extraordinary now When a woman has five grown up daughters she ought to give over thinking of her own
beauty In such cases a woman has not often much beauty to think of   But my dear you must indeed go and see Mr Bingley wh
en he comes into the neighbourhood   It is more than I engage for I assure you   But consider your daughters Only think what
an establishment it would be for one of them Sir William and Lady Lucas are determined to go merely on that account for in g
eneral you know they visit no newcomers Indeed you must go for it will be impossible for us to visit him if you do not   Yo
u are over scrupulous surely I dare say Mr Bingley will be very glad to see you and I will send a few lines by you to assur
e him of my hearty consent to his marrying whichever he chooses of the girls though I must throw in a good word for my little

Figure 1.20: The cleaned_multiline_text string

7. Generate a list of all the words from the cleaned string using the following command:

```
list_of_words = cleaned_multiline_text.split()
list_of_words
```

The output is as follows:

```
['It',
 'is',
 'a',
 'truth',
 'universally',
 'acknowledged',
 'that',
 'a',
 'single',
 'man',
 'in',
 'possession',
 'of',
 'a',
 'good',
 'fortune',
 'must',
 'be',
 'in',
```

Figure 1.21: The section of output displaying the list_of_words

8. Find the number of words:

    ```
    len(list_of_words)
    ```

    The output is **852**.

9. Create a list from the list you just created, which includes only unique words:

    ```
    unique_words_as_dict = dict.fromkeys(list_of_words)
    len(list(unique_words_as_dict.keys()))
    ```

    The output is **340**.

10. Count the number of times each of the unique words appeared in the cleaned text:

    ```
    for word in list_of_words:
        if unique_words_as_dict[word] is None:
            unique_words_as_dict[word] = 1
        else:
            unique_words_as_dict[word] += 1
    unique_words_as_dict
    ```

    The output is as follows:

    ```
    {'It': 3,
     'is': 12,
     'a': 20,
     'truth': 2,
     'universally': 1,
     'acknowledged': 1,
     'that': 15,
     'single': 3,
     'man': 4,
     'in': 11,
     'possession': 2,
     'of': 29,
     'good': 3,
     'fortune': 3,
     'must': 7,
     'be': 11,
     'want': 3,
     'wife': 4,
     'However': 1,
    ```

Figure 1.22: Section of output showing unique_words_as_dict

You just created, step by step, a unique word counter using all the neat tricks that you just learned.

11. Find the top 25 words from the **unique_words_as_dict**.

```
top_words = sorted(unique_words_as_dict.items(), key=lambda key_val_tuple:
key_val_tuple[1], reverse=True)
top_words[:25]
```

These are the steps to complete this activity:

```
[('of', 29),
 ('you', 24),
 ('to', 22),
 ('a', 20),
 ('the', 17),
 ('and', 17),
 ('I', 17),
 ('that', 15),
 ('is', 12),
 ('for', 12),
 ('in', 11),
 ('be', 11),
 ('his', 11),
 ('he', 11),
 ('it', 11),
 ('them', 11),
 ('Mr', 10),
 ('my', 10),
 ('not', 9),
 ('will', 9),
 ('so', 8),
 ('dear', 8),
 ('was', 8),
 ('are', 8),
 ('must', 7)]
```

Figure 1.23: Top 25 unique words from multiline_text

Solution of Activity 3: Permutation, Iterator, Lambda, List

These are the steps to solve this activity:

1. Look up the definition of **permutations** and **dropwhile** from **itertools**. There is a way to look up the definition of a function inside Jupyter itself. Just type the function name, followed by ?, and press *Shift + Enter*:

```
from itertools import permutations, dropwhile
permutations?
dropwhile?
```

You will see a long list of definitions after each ?. We will skip it here.

2. Write an expression to generate all the possible three-digit numbers using 1, 2, and 3:

```
permutations(range(3))
```

The output is as follows:

```
<itertools.permutations at 0x7f6c6c077af0>
```

3. Loop over the iterator expression you generated before. Use print to print each element returned by the iterator. Use **assert** and **isinstance** to make sure that the elements are tuples:

```
for number_tuple in permutations(range(3)):
    print(number_tuple)
    assert isinstance(number_tuple, tuple)
```

The output is as follows:

```
(0, 1, 2)
(0, 2, 1)
(1, 0, 2)
(1, 2, 0)
(2, 0, 1)
(2, 1, 0)
```

4. Write the loop again. But this time, use **dropwhile** with a lambda expression to drop any leading zeros from the tuples. As an example, **(0, 1, 2)** will become **[0, 2]**. Also, cast the output of the **dropwhile** to a list.

An extra task can be to check the actual type that **dropwhile** returns without casting:

```
for number_tuple in permutations(range(3)):
    print(list(dropwhile(lambda x: x <= 0, number_tuple)))
```

The output is as follows:

```
[1, 2]
[2, 1]
[1, 0, 2]
[1, 2, 0]
[2, 0, 1]
[2, 1, 0]
```

5. Write all the logic you wrote before, but this time write a separate function where you will be passing the list generated from **dropwhile**, and the function will return the whole number contained in the list. As an example, if you pass [1, 2] to the function, it will return 12. Make sure that the return type is indeed a number and not a string. Although this task can be achieved using other tricks, we require that you treat the incoming list as a stack in the function and generate the number there:

```
import math
def convert_to_number(number_stack):
    final_number = 0
    for i in range(0, len(number_stack)):
        final_number += (number_stack.pop() * (math.pow(10, i)))
    return final_number


for number_tuple in permutations(range(3)):
    number_stack = list(dropwhile(lambda x: x <= 0, number_tuple))
    print(convert_to_number(number_stack))
```

The output is as follows:

```
12.0
21.0
102.0
120.0
201.0
210.0
```

Solution of Activity 4: Design Your Own CSV Parser

These are the steps to complete this activity:

1. Import **zip_longest** from **itertools**:

```
from itertools import zip_longest
```

2. Define the **return_dict_from_csv_line** function so that it contains **header**, **line**, and **fillvalue** as **None**, and add it to a **dict**:

```
def return_dict_from_csv_line(header, line):
    # Zip them
    zipped_line = zip_longest(header, line, fillvalue=None)
    # Use dict comprehension to generate the final dict
    ret_dict = {kv[0]: kv[1] for kv in zipped_line}
    return ret_dict
```

3. Open the accompanying **sales_record.csv** file using **r** mode inside a with block. First, check that it is opened, read the first line, and use string methods to generate a list of all the column names with **open("sales_record.csv", "r") as fd**. When you read each line, pass that line to a function along with the list of the headers. The work of the function is to construct a dict out of these two and fill up the **key:values**. Keep in mind that a missing value should result in a **None**:

```
first_line = fd.readline()
header = first_line.replace("\n", "").split(",")
for i, line in enumerate(fd):
    line = line.replace("\n", "").split(",")
    d = return_dict_from_csv_line(header, line)
    print(d)
    if i > 10:
        break
```

The output is as follows:

```
{'Region': 'Central America and the Caribbean', 'Country': 'Antigua and Barbuda ', 'Item Type': 'Baby Food', 'Sales Channel':
'Online', 'Order Priority': 'M', 'Order Date': '12/20/2013', 'Order ID': '957081544', 'Ship Date': '1/11/2014', 'Units Sold':
'552', 'Unit Price': '255.28', 'Unit Cost': '159.42', 'Total Revenue': '140914.56', 'Total Cost': '87999.84', 'Total Profit':
'52914.72'}
{'Region': 'Central America and the Caribbean', 'Country': 'Panama', 'Item Type': 'Snacks', 'Sales Channel': 'Offline', 'Order
Priority': 'C', 'Order Date': '7/5/2010', 'Order ID': '301644504', 'Ship Date': '7/26/2010', 'Units Sold': '2167', 'Unit Pric
e': '152.58', 'Unit Cost': '97.44', 'Total Revenue': '330640.86', 'Total Cost': '211152.48', 'Total Profit': '119488.38'}
```

Figure 2.10: Section of output

Solution of Activity 5: Generating Statistics from a CSV File

These are the steps to complete this activity:

1. Load the necessary libraries:

```
import numpy as np
import pandas as pd
import matplotlib.pyplot as plt
```

2. Read in the Boston housing dataset (given as a `.csv` file) from the local direction:

```
# Hint: The Pandas function for reading a CSV file is 'read_csv'.
# Don't forget that all functions in Pandas can be accessed by syntax like
pd.{function_name}
df=pd.read_csv("Boston_housing.csv")
```

3. Check the first 10 records:

```
df.head(10)
```

The output is as follows:

	CRIM	ZN	INDUS	CHAS	NOX	RM	AGE	DIS	RAD	TAX	PTRATIO	B	LSTAT	PRICE
0	0.00632	18.0	2.31	0	0.538	6.575	65.2	4.0900	1	296	15.3	396.90	4.98	24.0
1	0.02731	0.0	7.07	0	0.469	6.421	78.9	4.9671	2	242	17.8	396.90	9.14	21.6
2	0.02729	0.0	7.07	0	0.469	7.185	61.1	4.9671	2	242	17.8	392.83	4.03	34.7
3	0.03237	0.0	2.18	0	0.458	6.998	45.8	6.0622	3	222	18.7	394.63	2.94	33.4
4	0.06905	0.0	2.18	0	0.458	7.147	54.2	6.0622	3	222	18.7	396.90	5.33	36.2
5	0.02985	0.0	2.18	0	0.458	6.430	58.7	6.0622	3	222	18.7	394.12	5.21	28.7
6	0.08829	12.5	7.87	0	0.524	6.012	66.6	5.5605	5	311	15.2	395.60	12.43	22.9
7	0.14455	12.5	7.87	0	0.524	6.172	96.1	5.9505	5	311	15.2	396.90	19.15	27.1
8	0.21124	12.5	7.87	0	0.524	5.631	100.0	6.0821	5	311	15.2	386.63	29.93	16.5
9	0.17004	12.5	7.87	0	0.524	6.004	85.9	6.5921	5	311	15.2	386.71	17.10	18.9

Figure 3.23: Output displaying the first 10 records

4. Find the total number of records:

```
df.shape
```

The output is as follows:

```
(506, 14)
```

5. Create a smaller DataFrame with columns that do not include **CHAS**, **NOX**, **B**, and **LSTAT**:

```
df1=df[['CRIM','ZN','INDUS','RM','AGE','DIS',
'RAD','TAX','PTRATIO','PRICE']]
```

6. Check the last 7 records of the new DataFrame you just created:

```
df1.tail(7)
```

The output is as follows:

	CRIM	ZN	INDUS	RM	AGE	DIS	RAD	TAX	PTRATIO	PRICE
499	0.17783	0.0	9.69	5.569	73.5	2.3999	6	391	19.2	17.5
500	0.22438	0.0	9.69	6.027	79.7	2.4982	6	391	19.2	16.8
501	0.06263	0.0	11.93	6.593	69.1	2.4786	1	273	21.0	22.4
502	0.04527	0.0	11.93	6.120	76.7	2.2875	1	273	21.0	20.6
503	0.06076	0.0	11.93	6.976	91.0	2.1675	1	273	21.0	23.9
504	0.10959	0.0	11.93	6.794	89.3	2.3889	1	273	21.0	22.0
505	0.04741	0.0	11.93	6.030	80.8	2.5050	1	273	21.0	11.9

Figure 3.24: Last seven records of the DataFrame

7. Plot histograms of all the variables (columns) in the new DataFrame by using a **for** loop:

```
for c in df1.columns:
    plt.title("Plot of "+c,fontsize=15)
    plt.hist(df1[c],bins=20)
    plt.show()
```

The output is as follows:

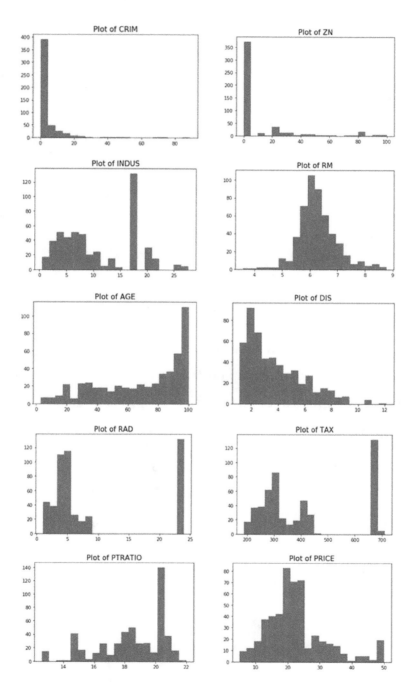

Figure 3.25: Plot of all variables using a for loop

8. Crime rate could be an indicator of house price (people don't want to live in high-crime areas). Create a scatter plot of crime rate versus price:

```
plt.scatter(df1['CRIM'],df1['PRICE'])
plt.show()
```

The output is as follows:

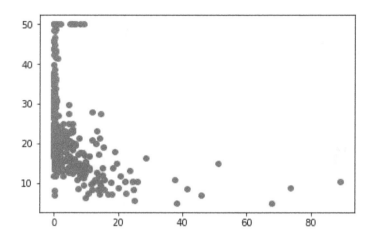

Figure 3.26: Scatter plot of crime rate versus price

We can understand the relationship better if we plot log10(crime) versus price.

9. Create that plot of log10(crime) versus price:

```
plt.scatter(np.log10(df1['CRIM']),df1['PRICE'],c='red')
plt.title("Crime rate (Log) vs. Price plot", fontsize=18)
plt.xlabel("Log of Crime rate",fontsize=15)
plt.ylabel("Price",fontsize=15)
plt.grid(True)
plt.show()
```

The output is as follows:

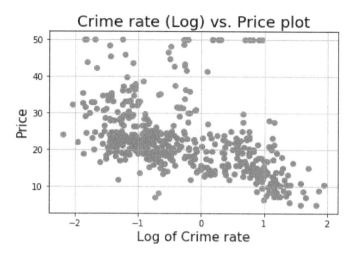

Figure 3.27: Scatter plot of crime rate (Log) versus price

10. Calculate the mean rooms per dwelling:

```
df1['RM'].mean()
```

The output is **6.284634387351788**.

11. Calculate the median age:

```
df1['AGE'].median()
```

The output is **77.5**.

12. Calculate the average (mean) distances to five Boston employment centers:

```
df1['DIS'].mean()
```

The output is **3.795042687747034**.

13. Calculate the percentage of houses with low price (< $20,000):

```
# Create a Pandas series and directly compare it with 20
# You can do this because Pandas series is basically NumPy array and you
have seen how to filter NumPy array
low_price=df1['PRICE']<20
# This creates a Boolean array of True, False
print(low_price)
# True = 1, False = 0, so now if you take an average of this NumPy array,
you will know how many 1's are there.
# That many houses are priced below 20,000. So that is the answer.
# You can convert that into percentage by multiplying with 100
pcnt=low_price.mean()*100
print("\nPercentage of house with <20,000 price is: ",pcnt)
```

The output is as follows:

```
0       False
1       False
2       False
3       False
4       False
5       False
6       False
7       False
8        True
9        True
10       True
...
500      True
501     False
502     False
503     False
504     False
505      True
Name: PRICE, Length: 506, dtype: bool

Percentage of house with <20,000 price is:  41.50197628458498
```

Solution of Activity 6: Working with the Adult Income Dataset (UCI)

These are the steps to complete this activity:

1. Load the necessary libraries:

```
import numpy as np
import pandas as pd
import matplotlib.pyplot as plt
```

2. Read in the adult income dataset (given as a **.csv** file) from the local directory and check the first 5 records:

```
df = pd.read_csv("adult_income_data.csv")
df.head()
```

The output is as follows:

	39	State-gov	77516	Bachelors	13	Never-married	Adm-clerical	Not-in-family	Male	2174	0	40	United-States	<=50K
0	50	Self-emp-not-inc	83311	Bachelors	13	Married-civ-spouse	Exec-managerial	Husband	Male	0	0	13	United-States	<=50K
1	38	Private	215646	HS-grad	9	Divorced	Handlers-cleaners	Not-in-family	Male	0	0	40	United-States	<=50K
2	53	Private	234721	11th	7	Married-civ-spouse	Handlers-cleaners	Husband	Male	0	0	40	United-States	<=50K
3	28	Private	338409	Bachelors	13	Married-civ-spouse	Prof-specialty	Wife	Female	0	0	40	Cuba	<=50K
4	37	Private	284582	Masters	14	Married-civ-spouse	Exec-managerial	Wife	Female	0	0	40	United-States	<=50K

Figure 4.61: DataFrame displaying the first five records from the .csv file

3. Create a script that will read a text file line by line and extracts the first line, which is the header of the .csv file:

```
names = []
with open('adult_income_names.txt','r') as f:
    for line in f:
        f.readline()
        var=line.split(":")[0]
        names.append(var)
names
```

The output is as follows:

```
['age',
 'workclass',
 'fnlwgt',
 'education',
 'education-num',
 'marital-status',
 'occupation',
 'relationship',
 'sex',
 'capital-gain',
 'capital-loss',
 'hours-per-week',
 'native-country']
```

Figure 4.62: Names of the columns in the database

4. Add a name of **Income** for the response variable (last column) to the dataset by using the **append** command:

```
names.append('Income')
```

5. Read the new file again using the following command:

```
df = pd.read_csv("adult_income_data.csv",names=names)
df.head()
```

The output is as follows:

	age	workclass	fnlwgt	education	education-num	marital-status	occupation	relationship	sex	capital-gain	capital-loss	hours-per-week	native-country
0	39	State-gov	77516	Bachelors	13	Never-married	Adm-clerical	Not-in-family	Male	2174	0	40	United States
1	50	Self-emp-not-inc	83311	Bachelors	13	Married-civ-spouse	Exec-managerial	Husband	Male	0	0	13	United States
2	38	Private	215646	HS-grad	9	Divorced	Handlers-cleaners	Not-in-family	Male	0	0	40	United States
3	53	Private	234721	11th	7	Married-civ-spouse	Handlers-cleaners	Husband	Male	0	0	40	United States
4	28	Private	338409	Bachelors	13	Married-civ-spouse	Prof-specialty	Wife	Female	0	0	40	Cuba

Figure 4.63: DataFrame with the income column added

6. Use the **describe** command to get the statistical summary of the dataset:

```
df.describe()
```

The output is as follows:

	age	fnlwgt	education-num	capital-gain	capital-loss	hours-per-week
count	32561.000000	3.256100e+04	32561.000000	32561.000000	32561.000000	32561.000000
mean	38.581647	1.897784e+05	10.080679	1077.648844	87.303830	40.437456
std	13.640433	1.055500e+05	2.572720	7385.292085	402.960219	12.347429
min	17.000000	1.228500e+04	1.000000	0.000000	0.000000	1.000000
25%	28.000000	1.178270e+05	9.000000	0.000000	0.000000	40.000000
50%	37.000000	1.783560e+05	10.000000	0.000000	0.000000	40.000000
75%	48.000000	2.370510e+05	12.000000	0.000000	0.000000	45.000000
max	90.000000	1.484705e+06	16.000000	99999.000000	4356.000000	99.000000

Figure 4.64: Statistical summary of the dataset

Note that only a small number of columns are included. Many variables in the dataset have multiple factors or classes.

7. Make a list of all the variables in the classes by using the following command:

```
# Make a list of all variables with classes
vars_class = ['workclass','education','marital-status',
              'occupation','relationship','sex','native-country']
```

8. Create a loop to count and print them by using the following command:

```
for v in vars_class:
    classes=df[v].unique()
    num_classes = df[v].nunique()
    print("There are {} classes in the \"{}\" column. They are: {}".
format(num_classes,v,classes))
    print("-"*100)
```

The output is as follows:

```
There are 9 classes in the "workclass" column. They are: [' State-gov' ' Self-emp-not-inc' ' Privat
e' ' Federal-gov' ' Local-gov'
 ' ?' ' Self-emp-inc' ' Without-pay' ' Never-worked']
--------------------------------------------------------------------------------
There are 16 classes in the "education" column. They are: [' Bachelors' ' HS-grad' ' 11th' ' Master
s' ' 9th' ' Some-college'
 ' Assoc-acdm' ' Assoc-voc' ' 7th-8th' ' Doctorate' ' Prof-school'
 ' 5th-6th' ' 10th' ' 1st-4th' ' Preschool' ' 12th']
--------------------------------------------------------------------------------
There are 7 classes in the "marital-status" column. They are: [' Never-married' ' Married-civ-spous
e' ' Divorced'
 ' Married-spouse-absent' ' Separated' ' Married-AF-spouse' ' Widowed']
--------------------------------------------------------------------------------
There are 15 classes in the "occupation" column. They are: [' Adm-clerical' ' Exec-managerial' ' Han
dlers-cleaners' ' Prof-specialty'
 ' Other-service' ' Sales' ' Craft-repair' ' Transport-moving'
 ' Farming-fishing' ' Machine-op-inspct' ' Tech-support' ' ?'
 ' Protective-serv' ' Armed-Forces' ' Priv-house-serv']
--------------------------------------------------------------------------------
There are 6 classes in the "relationship" column. They are: [' Not-in-family' ' Husband' ' Wife' ' O
wn-child' ' Unmarried'
 ' Other-relative']
--------------------------------------------------------------------------------
There are 2 classes in the "sex" column. They are: [' Male' ' Female']
--------------------------------------------------------------------------------
There are 42 classes in the "native-country" column. They are: [' United-States' ' Cuba' ' Jamaica'
 ' India' ' ?' ' Mexico' ' South'
 ' Puerto-Rico' ' Honduras' ' England' ' Canada' ' Germany' ' Iran'
 ' Philippines' ' Italy' ' Poland' ' Columbia' ' Cambodia' ' Thailand'
 ' Ecuador' ' Laos' ' Taiwan' ' Haiti' ' Portugal' ' Dominican-Republic'
 ' El-Salvador' ' France' ' Guatemala' ' China' ' Japan' ' Yugoslavia'
 ' Peru' ' Outlying-US(Guam-USVI-etc)' ' Scotland' ' Trinadad&Tobago'
 ' Greece' ' Nicaragua' ' Vietnam' ' Hong' ' Ireland' ' Hungary'
 ' Holand-Netherlands']
--------------------------------------------------------------------------------
```

Figure 4.65: Output of different factors or classes

9. Find the missing values by using the following command:

```
df.isnull().sum()
```

The output is as follows:

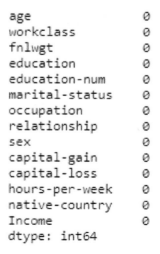

```
age                0
workclass          0
fnlwgt             0
education          0
education-num      0
marital-status     0
occupation         0
relationship       0
sex                0
capital-gain       0
capital-loss       0
hours-per-week     0
native-country     0
Income             0
dtype: int64
```

Figure 4.66: Finding the missing values

10. Create a DataFrame with only age, education, and occupation by using subsetting:

```
df_subset = df[['age','education','occupation']]
df_subset.head()
```

The output is as follows:

	age	education	occupation
0	39	Bachelors	Adm-clerical
1	50	Bachelors	Exec-managerial
2	38	HS-grad	Handlers-cleaners
3	53	11th	Handlers-cleaners
4	28	Bachelors	Prof-specialty

Figure 4.67: Subset DataFrame

11. Plot a histogram of age with a bin size of 20:

```
df_subset['age'].hist(bins=20)
```

The output is as follows:

```
<matplotlib.axes._subplots.AxesSubplot at 0x19dea8d0>
```

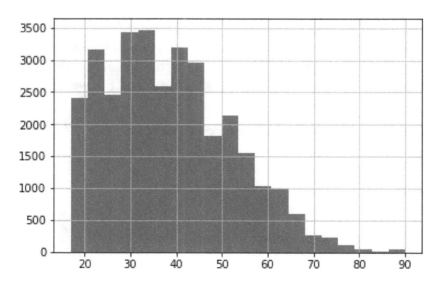

Figure 4.68: Histogram of age with a bin size of 20

12. Plot boxplots for **age** grouped by **education** (use a long figure size 25x10 and make x ticks font size 15):

```
df_subset.boxplot(column='age',by='education',figsize=(25,10))
plt.xticks(fontsize=15)
plt.xlabel("Education",fontsize=20)
plt.show()
```

The output is as follows:

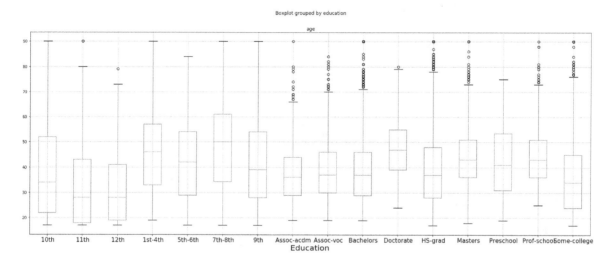

Figure 4.69: Boxplot of age grouped by education

Before doing any further operations, we need to use the **apply** method we learned in this chapter. It turns out that when reading the dataset from the CSV file, all the strings came with a whitespace character in front. So, we need to remove that whitespace from all the strings.

13. Create a function to strip the whitespace characters:

```
def strip_whitespace(s):
    return s.strip()
```

14. Use the **apply** method to apply this function to all the columns with string values, create a new column, copy the values from this new column to the old column, and drop the new column. This is the preferred method so that you don't accidentally delete valuable data. Most of the time, you will need to create a new column with a desired operation and then copy it back to the old column if necessary. Ignore any warning messages that are printed:

```
# Education column
df_subset['education_stripped']=df['education'].apply(strip_whitespace)
df_subset['education']=df_subset['education_stripped']
df_subset.drop(labels=['education_stripped'],axis=1,inplace=True)


# Occupation column
df_subset['occupation_stripped']=df['occupation'].apply(strip_whitespace)
df_subset['occupation']=df_subset['occupation_stripped']
df_subset.drop(labels=['occupation_stripped'],axis=1,inplace=True)
```

This is the sample warning message, which you should ignore:

```
C:\Users\user\Anaconda3\lib\site-packages\ipykernel_launcher.py:2: SettingWithCopyWarning:
A value is trying to be set on a copy of a slice from a DataFrame.
Try using .loc[row_indexer,col_indexer] = value instead

See the caveats in the documentation: http://pandas.pydata.org/pandas-docs/stable/indexing.html#indexing-view-versus-copy

C:\Users\user\Anaconda3\lib\site-packages\ipykernel_launcher.py:3: SettingWithCopyWarning:
A value is trying to be set on a copy of a slice from a DataFrame.
Try using .loc[row_indexer,col_indexer] = value instead

See the caveats in the documentation: http://pandas.pydata.org/pandas-docs/stable/indexing.html#indexing-view-versus-copy
  This is separate from the ipykernel package so we can avoid doing imports until
C:\Users\user\Anaconda3\lib\site-packages\pandas\core\frame.py:3697: SettingWithCopyWarning:
A value is trying to be set on a copy of a slice from a DataFrame

See the caveats in the documentation: http://pandas.pydata.org/pandas-docs/stable/indexing.html#indexing-view-versus-copy
  errors=errors)
C:\Users\user\Anaconda3\lib\site-packages\ipykernel_launcher.py:7: SettingWithCopyWarning:
A value is trying to be set on a copy of a slice from a DataFrame.
Try using .loc[row_indexer,col_indexer] = value instead

See the caveats in the documentation: http://pandas.pydata.org/pandas-docs/stable/indexing.html#indexing-view-versus-copy
  import sys
C:\Users\user\Anaconda3\lib\site-packages\ipykernel_launcher.py:8: SettingWithCopyWarning:
A value is trying to be set on a copy of a slice from a DataFrame.
Try using .loc[row_indexer,col_indexer] = value instead
```

Figure 4.70: Warning message to be ignored

15. Find the number of people who are aged between 30 and 50 (inclusive) by using the following command:

```
# Conditional clauses and join them by & (AND)
df_filtered=df_subset[(df_subset['age']>=30) & (df_subset['age']<=50)]
```

Check the contents of the new dataset:

```
df_filtered.head()
```

The output is as follows:

	age	education	occupation	race
6	49	9th	Other-service	Black
10	37	Some-college	Exec-managerial	Black
13	32	Assoc-acdm	Sales	Black
22	35	9th	Farming-fishing	Black
71	31	Bachelors	Sales	Black

Figure 4.71: Contents of new DataFrame

16. Find the **shape** of the filtered DataFrame and specify the index of the tuple as 0 to return the first element:

```
answer_1=df_filtered.shape[0]
answer_1
```

The output is as follows:

```
1630
```

17. Print the number of black people aged between 30 and 50 using the following command:

```
print("There are {} people of age between 30 and 50 in this
dataset.".format(answer_1))
```

The output is as follows:

```
There are 1630 black of age between 30 and 50 in this dataset.
```

18. Group the records based on occupation to find how the mean age is distributed:

```
df_subset.groupby('occupation').describe()['age']
```

The output is as follows:

occupation	count	mean	std	min	25%	50%	75%	max
?	1843.0	40.882800	20.336350	17.0	21.0	35.0	61.0	90.0
Adm-clerical	3770.0	36.964456	13.362998	17.0	26.0	35.0	46.0	90.0
Armed-Forces	9.0	30.222222	8.089774	23.0	24.0	29.0	34.0	46.0
Craft-repair	4099.0	39.031471	11.606436	17.0	30.0	38.0	47.0	90.0
Exec-managerial	4066.0	42.169208	11.974548	17.0	33.0	41.0	50.0	90.0
Farming-fishing	994.0	41.211268	15.070283	17.0	29.0	39.0	52.0	90.0
Handlers-cleaners	1370.0	32.165693	12.372635	17.0	23.0	29.0	39.0	90.0
Machine-op-inspct	2002.0	37.715285	12.068266	17.0	28.0	36.0	46.0	90.0
Other-service	3295.0	34.949621	14.521508	17.0	22.0	32.0	45.0	90.0
Priv-house-serv	149.0	41.724832	18.633688	17.0	24.0	40.0	57.0	81.0
Prof-specialty	4140.0	40.517633	12.016676	17.0	31.0	40.0	48.0	90.0
Protective-serv	649.0	38.953775	12.822062	17.0	29.0	36.0	47.0	90.0
Sales	3650.0	37.353973	14.186352	17.0	25.0	35.0	47.0	90.0
Tech-support	928.0	37.022629	11.316594	17.0	28.0	36.0	44.0	73.0
Transport-moving	1597.0	40.197871	12.450792	17.0	30.0	39.0	49.0	90.0

Figure 4.72: DataFrame with data grouped by age and education

The code returns **79 rows × 1 columns**.

19. Group by occupation and show the summary statistics of age. Find which profession has the oldest workers on average and which profession has its largest share of workforce above the 75th percentile:

```
df_subset.groupby('occupation').describe()['age']
```

The output is as follows:

occupation	count	mean	std	min	25%	50%	75%	max
?	1843.0	40.882800	20.336350	17.0	21.0	35.0	61.0	90.0
Adm-clerical	3770.0	36.964456	13.362998	17.0	26.0	35.0	46.0	90.0
Armed-Forces	9.0	30.222222	8.089774	23.0	24.0	29.0	34.0	46.0
Craft-repair	4099.0	39.031471	11.606436	17.0	30.0	38.0	47.0	90.0
Exec-managerial	4066.0	42.169208	11.974548	17.0	33.0	41.0	50.0	90.0
Farming-fishing	994.0	41.211268	15.070283	17.0	29.0	39.0	52.0	90.0
Handlers-cleaners	1370.0	32.165693	12.372635	17.0	23.0	29.0	39.0	90.0
Machine-op-inspct	2002.0	37.715285	12.068266	17.0	28.0	36.0	46.0	90.0
Other-service	3295.0	34.949621	14.521508	17.0	22.0	32.0	45.0	90.0
Priv-house-serv	149.0	41.724832	18.633688	17.0	24.0	40.0	57.0	81.0
Prof-specialty	4140.0	40.517633	12.016676	17.0	31.0	40.0	48.0	90.0
Protective-serv	649.0	38.953775	12.822062	17.0	29.0	36.0	47.0	90.0
Sales	3650.0	37.353973	14.186352	17.0	25.0	35.0	47.0	90.0
Tech-support	928.0	37.022629	11.316594	17.0	28.0	36.0	44.0	73.0
Transport-moving	1597.0	40.197871	12.450792	17.0	30.0	39.0	49.0	90.0

Figure 4.73: DataFrame showing summary statistics of age

Is there a particular occupation group that has very low representation? Perhaps we should remove those pieces of data because with very low data, the group won't be useful in analysis. Actually, just by looking at the preceding table, you should be able to see that the **Armed-Forces** group has only got a 9 count, that is, 9 data points. But how can we detect this? By plotting the count column in a bar chart. Note how the first argument to the **barh** function is the index of the DataFrame, which is the summary stats of the occupation groups. We can see that the **Armed-Forces** group has almost no data. This exercise teaches you that, sometimes, the outlier is not just a value, but can be a whole group. The data of this group is fine, but it is too small to be useful for any analysis. So, it can be treated as an outlier in this case. But always use your business knowledge and engineering judgement for such outlier detection and how to process them.

20. Use subset and groupby to find the outliers:

```
occupation_stats= df_subset.groupby(
    'occupation').describe()['age']
```

21. Plot the values on a bar chart:

```
plt.figure(figsize=(15,8))
plt.barh(y=occupation_stats.index,
         width=occupation_stats['count'])
plt.yticks(fontsize=13)
plt.show()
```

The output is as follows:

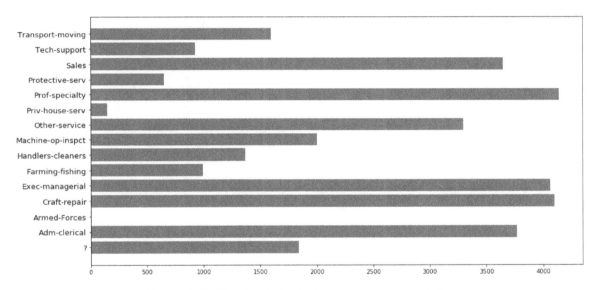

Figure 4.74: Bar chart displaying occupation statistics

22. Practice merging by common keys. Suppose you are given two datasets where the common key is **occupation**. First, create two such disjoint datasets by taking random samples from the full dataset and then try merging. Include at least two other columns, along with the common key column for each dataset. Notice how the resulting dataset, after merging, may have more data points than either of the two starting datasets if your common key is not unique:

```
df_1 = df[['age',
           'workclass',
           'occupation']].sample(5,random_state=101)
df_1.head()
```

The output is as follows:

	age	workclass	occupation
22357	51	Private	Machine-op-inspct
26009	19	Private	Sales
20734	40	Private	Exec-managerial
17695	17	Private	Handlers-cleaners
27908	61	Private	Craft-repair

Figure 4.75: Output after merging the common keys

The second dataset is as follows:

```
df_2 = df[['education',
          'occupation']].sample(5,random_state=101)
df_2.head()
```

The output is as follows:

	education	occupation
22357	HS-grad	Machine-op-inspct
26009	11th	Sales
20734	HS-grad	Exec-managerial
17695	10th	Handlers-cleaners
27908	7th-8th	Craft-repair

Figure 4.76: Output after merging the common keys

Merging the two datasets together:

```
df_merged = pd.merge(df_1,df_2,
                     on='occupation',
                     how='inner').drop_duplicates()
df_merged
```

The output is as follows:

	age	workclass	occupation	education
0	51	Private	Machine-op-inspct	HS-grad
1	19	Private	Sales	11th
2	40	Private	Exec-managerial	HS-grad
3	17	Private	Handlers-cleaners	10th
4	61	Private	Craft-repair	7th-8th

Figure 4.77: Output of distinct occupation values

Solution of Activity 7: Reading Tabular Data from a Web Page and Creating DataFrames

These are the steps to complete this activity:

1. Import BeautifulSoup and load the data by using the following command:

```
from bs4 import BeautifulSoup
import pandas as pd
```

2. Open the Wikipedia file by using the following command:

```
fd = open("List of countries by GDP (nominal) - Wikipedia.htm", "r")
soup = BeautifulSoup(fd)
fd.close()
```

3. Calculate the tables by using the following command:

```
all_tables = soup.find_all("table")
print("Total number of tables are {} ".format(len(all_tables)))
```

There are 9 tables in total.

4. Find the right table using the class attribute by using the following command:

```
data_table = soup.find("table", {"class": '"wikitable"|}'})
print(type(data_table))
```

The output is as follows:

```
<class 'bs4.element.Tag'>
```

5. Separate the source and the actual data by using the following command:

```
sources = data_table.tbody.findAll('tr', recursive=False)[0]
sources_list = [td for td in sources.findAll('td')]
print(len(sources_list))
```

The output is as follows:

```
Total number of tables are 3.
```

6. Use **findAll** function to find the data from the **data_table**'s **body** tag, using the following command:

```
data = data_table.tbody.findAll('tr', recursive=False)[1].findAll('td',
recursive=False)
```

7. Use the **findAll** function to find the data from the **data_table td** tag by using the following command:

```
data_tables = []
for td in data:
    data_tables.append(td.findAll('table'))
```

8. Find the length of **data_tables** by using the following command:

```
len(data_tables)
```

The output is as follows:

```
3
```

9. Check how to get the source names by using the following command:

```
source_names = [source.findAll('a')[0].getText() for source in sources_list]
print(source_names)
```

The output is as follows:

```
['International Monetary Fund', 'World Bank', 'United Nations']
```

10. Separate the header and data for the first source:

```
header1 = [th.getText().strip() for th in data_tables[0][0].findAll('thead')
[0].findAll('th')]
header1
```

The output is as follows:

```
['Rank', 'Country', 'GDP(US$MM)']
```

11. Find the rows from **data_tables** using **findAll**:

```
rows1 = data_tables[0][0].findAll('tbody')[0].findAll('tr')[1:]
```

12. Find the data from **rows1** using the **strip** function for each **td** tag:

```
data_rows1 = [[td.get_text().strip() for td in tr.findAll('td')] for tr in
rows1]
```

13. Find the DataFrame:

```
df1 = pd.DataFrame(data_rows1, columns=header1)
df1.head()
```

The output is as follows:

	Rank	Country	GDP(US$MM)
0	1	United States	19,390,600
1	2	China[n 1]	12,014,610
2	3	Japan	4,872,135
3	4	Germany	3,684,816
4	5	United Kingdom	2,624,529

Figure 5.35: DataFrame created from Web page

14. Do the same for the other two sources by using the following command:

```
header2 = [th.getText().strip() for th in data_tables[1][0].findAll('thead')
[0].findAll('th')]
header2
```

The output is as follows:

```
['Rank', 'Country', 'GDP(US$MM)']
```

15. Find the rows from **data_tables** using **findAll** by using the following command:

```
rows2 = data_tables[1][0].findAll('tbody')[0].findAll('tr')[1:]
```

16. Define **find_right_text** using the **strip** function by using the following command:

```
def find_right_text(i, td):
    if i == 0:
        return td.getText().strip()
    elif i == 1:
        return td.getText().strip()
    else:
        index = td.text.find("♠")
        return td.text[index+1:].strip()
```

17. Find the rows from **data_rows** using **find_right_text** by using the following command:

```
data_rows2 = [[find_right_text(i, td) for i, td in enumerate(tr.
findAll('td'))] for tr in rows2]
```

18. Calculate the **df2** DataFrame by using the following command:

```
df2 = pd.DataFrame(data_rows2, columns=header2)
df2.head()
```

The output is as follows:

	Rank	Country	GDP(US$MM)
0	1	United States	19,390,604
1		European Union[23]	17,277,698
2	2	China[n 4]	12,237,700
3	3	Japan	4,872,137
4	4	Germany	3,677,439

Figure 5.36: Output of the DataFrame

19. Now, perform the same operations for the third DataFrame by using the following command:

```
header3 = [th.getText().strip() for th in data_tables[2][0].findAll('thead')
[0].findAll('th')]
header3
```

The output is as follows:

['Rank', 'Country', 'GDP(US$MM)']

20. Find the rows from **data_tables** using **findAll** by using the following command:

```
rows3 = data_tables[2][0].findAll('tbody')[0].findAll('tr')[1:]
```

21. Find the rows from **data_rows3** by using **find_right_text**:

```
data_rows3 = [[find_right_text(i, td) for i, td in enumerate(tr.
findAll('td'))] for tr in rows2]
```

22. Calculate the **df3** DataFrame by using the following command:

```
df3 = pd.DataFrame(data_rows3, columns=header3)
df3.head()
```

The output is as follows:

	Rank	Country	GDP(US$MM)
0	1	United States	19,390,604
1		European Union[23]	17,277,698
2	2	China[n 4]	12,237,700
3	3	Japan	4,872,137
4	4	Germany	3,677,439

Figure 5.37: The third DataFrame

Solution of Activity 8: Handling Outliers and Missing Data

These are the steps to complete this activity:

1. Load the data:

```
import pandas as pd
import numpy as np
import matplotlib.pyplot as plt
%matplotlib inline
```

2. Read the .csv file:

```
df = pd.read_csv("visit_data.csv")
```

3. Print the data from the DataFrame:

```
df.head()
```

The output is as follows:

	id	first_name	last_name	email	gender	ip_address	visit
0	1	Knox	Ware	kware0@mysql.com	Male	135.36.96.183	1225.0
1	2	NaN	NaN	dhoovart1@hud.gov	NaN	237.165.194.143	919.0
2	3	Gar	Armal	garmal2@technorati.com	NaN	166.43.137.224	271.0
3	4	Ciarra	Nulty	cnulty3@newyorker.com	NaN	139.98.137.108	1002.0
4	5	NaN	NaN	sleaver4@elegantthemes.com	NaN	46.117.117.27	2434.0

Figure 6.10: The contents of the CSV file

As we can see, there is data where some values are missing, and if we examine this, we will see some outliers.

4. Check for duplicates by using the following command:

```
print("First name is duplicated - {}".format(any(df.first_name.
duplicated())))
print("Last name is duplicated - {}".format(any(df.last_name.
duplicated())))
print("Email is duplicated - {}".format(any(df.email.duplicated())))
```

The output is as follows:

```
First name is duplicated - True
Last name is duplicated - True
Email is duplicated - False
```

There are duplicates in both the first and last names, which is normal. However, as we can see, there is no duplicate in email. That's good.

5. Check if any essential column contains **NaN**:

```
# Notice that we have different ways to format boolean values for the %
operator
print("The column Email contains NaN - %r " % df.email.isnull().values.
any())
print("The column IP Address contains NaN - %s " % df.ip_address.isnull().
values.any())
print("The column Visit contains NaN - %s " % df.visit.isnull().values.
any())
```

The output is as follows:

```
The column Email contains NaN - False
The column IP Address contains NaN - False
The column Visit contains NaN - True
```

The column visit contains some None values. Given that the final task at hand will probably be predicting the number of visits, we cannot do anything with rows that do not have that information. They are a type of outlier. Let's get rid of them.

6. Get rid of the outliers:

```
# There are various ways to do this. This is just one way. We encourage you
to explore other ways.
# But before that we need to store the previous size of the data set and we
will compare it with the new size
size_prev = df.shape
df = df[np.isfinite(df['visit'])] #This is an inplace operation. After this
operation the original DataFrame is lost.
size_after = df.shape
```

7. Report the size difference:

```
# Notice how parameterized format is used and then the indexing is working
inside the quote marks
print("The size of previous data was - {prev[0]} rows and the size of the
new one is - {after[0]} rows".
format(prev=size_prev, after=size_after))
```

The output is as follows:

```
The size of previous data was - 1000 rows and the size of the new one is -
974 rows
```

8. Plot a boxplot to find if the data has outliers.

```
plt.boxplot(df.visit, notch=True)
```

The output is as follows:

```
{'whiskers': [<matplotlib.lines.Line2D at 0x7fa04cc08668>,
  <matplotlib.lines.Line2D at 0x7fa04cc08b00>],
 'caps': [<matplotlib.lines.Line2D at 0x7fa04cc08f28>,
  <matplotlib.lines.Line2D at 0x7fa04cc11390>],
 'boxes': [<matplotlib.lines.Line2D at 0x7fa04cc08518>],
 'medians': [<matplotlib.lines.Line2D at 0x7fa04cc117b8>],
 'fliers': [<matplotlib.lines.Line2D at 0x7fa04cc11be0>],
 'means': []}
```

The boxplot is as follows:

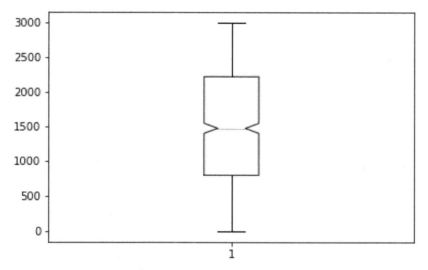

Figure 6.43: Boxplot using the data

As we can see, we have data in this column in the interval (0, 3000). However, the main concentration of the data is between ~700 and ~2300.

9. Get rid of values beyond 2900 and below 100 – these are outliers for us. We need to get rid of them:

```
df1 = df[(df['visit'] <= 2900) & (df['visit'] >= 100)]  # Notice the
powerful & operator
# Here we abuse the fact the number of variable can be greater than the
number of replacement targets
print("After getting rid of outliers the new size of the data is - {}".
format(*df1.shape))
```

After getting rid of the outliers, the new size of the data is **923**.

This is the end of the activity for this chapter.

Solution of Activity 9: Extracting the Top 100 eBooks from Gutenberg

These are the steps to complete this activity:

1. Import the necessary libraries, including **regex** and **beautifulsoup**:

```
import urllib.request, urllib.parse, urllib.error
import requests
from bs4 import BeautifulSoup
import ssl
import re
```

2. Check the SSL certificate:

```
# Ignore SSL certificate errors
ctx = ssl.create_default_context()
ctx.check_hostname = False
ctx.verify_mode = ssl.CERT_NONE
```

3. Read the HTML from the URL:

```
# Read the HTML from the URL and pass on to BeautifulSoup
top100url = 'https://www.gutenberg.org/browse/scores/top'
response = requests.get(top100url)
```

4. Write a small function to check the status of the web request:

```
def status_check(r):
    if r.status_code==200:
        print("Success!")
        return 1
    else:
        print("Failed!")
        return -1
```

5. Check the status of **response**:

```
status_check(response)
```

The output is as follows:

```
Success!
1
```

6. Decode the response and pass it on to **BeautifulSoup** for HTML parsing:

```
contents = response.content.decode(response.encoding)
soup = BeautifulSoup(contents, 'html.parser')
```

7. Find all the **href** tags and store them in the list of links. Check what the list looks like – print the first 30 elements:

```
# Empty list to hold all the http links in the HTML page
lst_links=[]
# Find all the href tags and store them in the list of links
for link in soup.find_all('a'):
    #print(link.get('href'))
    lst_links.append(link.get('href'))
```

8. Print the links by using the following command:

```
lst_links[:30]
```

The output is as follows:

```
['/wiki/Main_Page',
 '/catalog/',
 '/ebooks/',
 '/browse/recent/last1',
 '/browse/scores/top',
 '/wiki/Gutenberg:Offline_Catalogs',
 '/catalog/world/mybookmarks',
 '/wiki/Main_Page',
'https://www.paypal.com/xclick/business=donate%40gutenberg.org&item_
name=Donation+to+Project+Gutenberg',
 '/wiki/Gutenberg:Project_Gutenberg_Needs_Your_Donation',
 'http://www.ibiblio.org',
 'http://www.pgdp.net/',
 'pretty-pictures',
 '#books-last1',
 '#authors-last1',
 '#books-last7',
 '#authors-last7',
 '#books-last30',
 '#authors-last30',
 '/ebooks/1342',
 '/ebooks/84',
 '/ebooks/1080',
 '/ebooks/46',
```

```
    '/ebooks/219',
    '/ebooks/2542',
    '/ebooks/98',
    '/ebooks/345',
    '/ebooks/2701',
    '/ebooks/844',
    '/ebooks/11']
```

9. Use a regular expression to find the numeric digits in these links. These are the file numbers for the top 100 books. Initialize the empty list to hold the file numbers:

```
booknum=[]
```

10. Numbers 19 to 118 in the original list of links have the top 100 eBooks' numbers. Loop over the appropriate range and use a regex to find the numeric digits in the link (href) string. Use the **findall()** method:

```
for i in range(19,119):
    link=lst_links[i]
    link=link.strip()
    # Regular expression to find the numeric digits in the link (href)
string
    n=re.findall('[0-9]+',link)
    if len(n)==1:
        # Append the filenumber casted as integer
        booknum.append(int(n[0]))
```

11. Print the file numbers:

```
print ("\nThe file numbers for the top 100 ebooks on Gutenberg are shown
below\n"+"-"*70)
print(booknum)
```

The output is as follows:

```
The file numbers for the top 100 ebooks on Gutenberg are shown below
----------------------------------------------------------------------
[1342, 84, 1080, 46, 219, 2542, 98, 345, 2701, 844, 11, 5200, 43, 16328,
76, 74, 1952, 6130, 2591, 1661, 41, 174, 23, 1260, 1497, 408, 3207, 1400,
30254, 58271, 1232, 25344, 58269, 158, 44881, 1322, 205, 2554, 1184, 2600,
120, 16, 58276, 5740, 34901, 28054, 829, 33, 2814, 4300, 100, 55, 160,
1404, 786, 58267, 3600, 19942, 8800, 514, 244, 2500, 2852, 135, 768, 58263,
1251, 3825, 779, 58262, 203, 730, 20203, 35, 1250, 45, 161, 30360, 7370,
58274, 209, 27827, 58256, 33283, 4363, 375, 996, 58270, 521, 58268, 36,
815, 1934, 3296, 58279, 105, 2148, 932, 1064, 13415]
```

12. What does the soup object's text look like? Use the **.text** method and print only the first 2,000 characters (do not print the whole thing as it is too long).

You will notice a lot of empty spaces/blanks here and there. Ignore them. They are part of the HTML page's markup and its whimsical nature:

```
print(soup.text[:2000])
if (top != self) {
        top.location.replace (http://www.gutenberg.org);
        alert ('Project Gutenberg is a FREE service with NO membership
required. If you paid somebody else to get here, make them give you your
money back!');
        }
```

The output is as follows:

```
Top 100 - Project Gutenberg
Online Book Catalog
 Book   Search
-- Recent  Books
-- Top   100
-- Offline Catalogs
-- My Bookmarks
Main Page
...
Pretty Pictures
Top 100 EBooks yesterday —
  Top 100 Authors yesterday —
  Top 100 EBooks last 7 days —
  Top 100 Authors last 7 days —
  Top 100 EBooks last 30 days —
  Top 100 Authors last 30 days
Top 100 EBooks yesterday
Pride and Prejudice by Jane Austen (1826)
Frankenstein; Or, The Modern Prometheus by Mary Wollstonecraft Shelley
(1367)
A Modest Proposal by Jonathan Swift (1020)
A Christmas Carol in Prose; Being a Ghost Story of Christmas by Charles
Dickens (953)
```

```
Heart of Darkness by Joseph Conrad (887)
Et dukkehjem. English by Henrik Ibsen (761)
A Tale of Two Cities by Charles Dickens (741)
Dracula by Bram Stoker (732)
Moby Dick; Or, The Whale by Herman Melville (651)
The Importance of Being Earnest: A Trivial Comedy for Serious People by
Oscar Wilde (646)
Alice's Adventures in Wonderland by Lewis Carrol
```

13. Search the extracted text (using regular expression) from the soup object to find the names of top 100 eBooks (yesterday's rank):

```
# Temp empty list of Ebook names
lst_titles_temp=[]
```

14. Create a starting index. It should point at the text **Top 100 Ebooks yesterday**. Use the **splitlines** method of **soup.text**. It splits the lines of the text of the soup object:

```
start_idx=soup.text.splitlines().index('Top 100 EBooks yesterday')
```

15. Loop 1-100 to add the strings of the next 100 lines to this temporary list. Hint: use the **splitlines** method:

```
for i in range(100):
    lst_titles_temp.append(soup.text.splitlines()[start_idx+2+i])
```

16. Use a regular expression to extract only text from the name strings and append them to an empty list. Use match and span to find the indices and use them:

```
lst_titles=[]
for i in range(100):
    id1,id2=re.match('^[a-zA-Z ]*',lst_titles_temp[i]).span()
    lst_titles.append(lst_titles_temp[i][id1:id2])
```

17. Print the list of titles:

```
for l in lst_titles:
    print(l)
```

The output is as follows:

```
Pride and Prejudice by Jane Austen
Frankenstein
A Modest Proposal by Jonathan Swift
A Christmas Carol in Prose
Heart of Darkness by Joseph Conrad
Et dukkehjem
A Tale of Two Cities by Charles Dickens
Dracula by Bram Stoker
Moby Dick
The Importance of Being Earnest
Alice
Metamorphosis by Franz Kafka
The Strange Case of Dr
Beowulf
…
The Russian Army and the Japanese War
Calculus Made Easy by Silvanus P
Beyond Good and Evil by Friedrich Wilhelm Nietzsche
An Occurrence at Owl Creek Bridge by Ambrose Bierce
Don Quixote by Miguel de Cervantes Saavedra
Blue Jackets by Edward Greey
The Life and Adventures of Robinson Crusoe by Daniel Defoe
The Waterloo Campaign
The War of the Worlds by H
Democracy in America
Songs of Innocence
The Confessions of St
Modern French Masters by Marie Van Vorst
Persuasion by Jane Austen
The Works of Edgar Allan Poe
The Fall of the House of Usher by Edgar Allan Poe
The Masque of the Red Death by Edgar Allan Poe
The Lady with the Dog and Other Stories by Anton Pavlovich Chekhov
```

Solution of Activity 10: Extracting the top 100 eBooks from Gutenberg.org

These are the steps to complete this activity:

1. Import **urllib.request**, **urllib.parse**, **urllib.error**, and **json**:

   ```
   import urllib.request, urllib.parse, urllib.error
   import json
   ```

2. Load the secret API key (you have to get one from the OMDB website and use that; it has a 1,000 daily limit) from a JSON file, stored in the same folder into a variable, by using **json.loads()**:

   > **Note**
   >
   > The following cell will not be executed in the solution notebook because the author cannot give out their private API key.

3. The students/users/instructor will need to obtain a key and store it in a JSON file. We are calling this file **APIkeys.json**.

4. Open the **APIkeys.json** file by using the following command:

   ```
   with open('APIkeys.json') as f:
       keys = json.load(f)
       omdbapi = keys['OMDBapi']
   ```

   The final URL to be passed should look like this: http://www.omdbapi.com/?t=movie_name&apikey=secretapikey.

5. Assign the OMDB portal (http://www.omdbapi.com/?) as a string to a variable called **serviceurl** by using the following command:

   ```
   serviceurl = 'http://www.omdbapi.com/?'
   ```

6. Create a variable called **apikey** with the last portion of the URL (**&apikey=secretapikey**), where **secretapikey** is your own API key. The movie name portion is **t=movie_name**, and will be addressed later:

   ```
   apikey = '&apikey='+omdbapi
   ```

7. Write a utility function called **print_json** to print the movie data from a JSON file (which we will get from the portal). Here are the keys of a JSON file: 'Title', 'Year', 'Rated', 'Released', 'Runtime', 'Genre', 'Director', 'Writer', 'Actors', 'Plot', 'Language','Country', 'Awards', 'Ratings', 'Metascore', 'imdbRating', 'imdbVotes', and 'imdbID':

```
def print_json(json_data):
    list_keys=['Title', 'Year', 'Rated', 'Released', 'Runtime', 'Genre',
'Director', 'Writer',
                'Actors', 'Plot', 'Language', 'Country', 'Awards',
'Ratings',
                'Metascore', 'imdbRating', 'imdbVotes', 'imdbID']
    print("-"*50)
    for k in list_keys:
        if k in list(json_data.keys()):
            print(f"{k}: {json_data[k]}")
    print("-"*50)
```

8. Write a utility function to download a poster of the movie based on the information from the JSON dataset and save it in your local folder. Use the **os** module. The poster data is stored in the JSON key **Poster**. You may want to split the name of the **Poster** file and extract the file extension only. Let's say that the extension is **jpg**. We would later join this extension to the movie name and create a filename such as **movie.jpg**. Use the open Python command open to open a file and write the poster data. Close the file after you're done. This function may not return anything. It just saves the poster data as an image file:

```
def save_poster(json_data):
    import os
    title = json_data['Title']
    poster_url = json_data['Poster']
    # Splits the poster url by '.' and picks up the last string as file
extension
    poster_file_extension=poster_url.split('.')[-1]
    # Reads the image file from web
    poster_data = urllib.request.urlopen(poster_url).read()

    savelocation=os.getcwd()+'\\'+'Posters'+'\\'
    # Creates new directory if the directory does not exist. Otherwise,
just use the existing path.
```

```
    if not os.path.isdir(savelocation):
        os.mkdir(savelocation)

    filename=savelocation+str(title)+'.'+poster_file_extension
    f=open(filename,'wb')
    f.write(poster_data)
    f.close()
```

9. Write a utility function called **search_movie** to search a movie by its name, print the downloaded JSON data (use the **print_json** function for this), and save the movie poster in the local folder (use the **save_poster** function for this). Use a **try-except** loop for this, that is, try to connect to the web portal. If successful, proceed, but if not (that is, if an exception is raised), then just print an error message. Use the previously created variables **serviceurl** and **apikey**. You have to pass on a dictionary with a key, **t**, and the movie name as the corresponding value to the **urllib.parse.urlencode** function and then add the **serviceurl** and **apikey** to the output of the function to construct the full URL. This URL will be used for accessing the data. The JSON data has a key called **Response**. If it is **True**, that means that the read was successful. Check this before processing the data. If it was not successful, then print the JSON key **Error**, which will contain the appropriate error message that's returned by the movie database:

```
def search_movie(title):
    try:
        url = serviceurl + urllib.parse.urlencode({'t': str(title)})+apikey
        print(f'Retrieving the data of "{title}" now... ')
        print(url)
        uh = urllib.request.urlopen(url)
        data = uh.read()
        json_data=json.loads(data)

        if json_data['Response']=='True':
            print_json(json_data)
            # Asks user whether to download the poster of the movie
            if json_data['Poster']!='N/A':
                save_poster(json_data)
        else:
            print("Error encountered: ",json_data['Error'])

    except urllib.error.URLError as e:
        print(f"ERROR: {e.reason}"
```

10. Test the **search_movie** function by entering **Titanic**:

```
search_movie("Titanic")
```

The following is the retrieved data for **Titanic**:

```
http://www.omdbapi.com/?t=Titanic&apikey=17cdc959
-------------------------------------------------
Title: Titanic
Year: 1997
Rated: PG-13
Released: 19 Dec 1997
Runtime: 194 min
Genre: Drama, Romance
Director: James Cameron
Writer: James Cameron
Actors: Leonardo DiCaprio, Kate Winslet, Billy Zane, Kathy Bates
Plot: A seventeen-year-old aristocrat falls in love with a kind but poor
artist aboard the luxurious, ill-fated R.M.S. Titanic.
Language: English, Swedish
Country: USA
Awards: Won 11 Oscars. Another 111 wins & 77 nominations.
Ratings: [{'Source': 'Internet Movie Database', 'Value': '7.8/10'},
{'Source': 'Rotten Tomatoes', 'Value': '89%'}, {'Source': 'Metacritic',
'Value': '75/100'}]
Metascore: 75
imdbRating: 7.8
imdbVotes: 913,780
imdbID: tt0120338
-------------------------------------------------
```

11. Test the **search_movie** function by entering **"Random_error"** (obviously, this will not be found, and you should be able to check whether your error catching code is working properly):

```
search_movie("Random_error")
```

Retrieve the data of **"Random_error"**:

```
http://www.omdbapi.com/?t=Random_error&apikey=17cdc959
Error encountered:  Movie not found!
```

Look for a folder called **Posters** in the same directory you are working in. It should contain a file called **Titanic.jpg**. Check the file.

Solution of Activity 11: Retrieving Data Correctly from Databases

These are the steps to complete this activity:

1. Connect to the supplied **petsDB** database:

    ```
    import sqlite3
    conn = sqlite3.connect("petsdb")
    ```

2. Write a function to check whether the connection has been successful:

    ```
    # a tiny function to make sure the connection is successful
    def is_opened(conn):
        try:
            conn.execute("SELECT * FROM persons LIMIT 1")
            return True
        except sqlite3.ProgrammingError as e:
            print("Connection closed {}".format(e))
            return False
    print(is_opened(conn))
    ```

    The output is as follows:

    ```
    True
    ```

3. Close the connection:

    ```
    conn.close()
    ```

4. Check whether the connection is open or closed:

    ```
    print(is_opened(conn))
    ```

    The output is as follows:

    ```
    False
    ```

5. Find out the different age groups are in the **persons** database. Connect to the supplied **petsDB** database:

    ```
    conn = sqlite3.connect("petsdb")
    c = conn.cursor()
    ```

6. Execute the following command:

    ```
    for ppl, age in c.execute("SELECT count(*), age FROM persons GROUP BY age"):
        print("We have {} people aged {}".format(ppl, age))
    ```

The output is as follows:

```
We have 2 people aged 5
We have 1 people aged 6
We have 1 people aged 7
We have 3 people aged 8
We have 1 people aged 9
We have 2 people aged 11
We have 3 people aged 12
We have 1 people aged 13
We have 4 people aged 14
We have 2 people aged 16
We have 2 people aged 17
We have 3 people aged 18
We have 1 people aged 19
We have 3 people aged 22
We have 2 people aged 23
We have 3 people aged 24
We have 2 people aged 25
We have 1 people aged 27
We have 1 people aged 30
We have 3 people aged 31
We have 1 people aged 32
We have 1 people aged 33
We have 2 people aged 34
```

Figure 8.17: Section of output grouped by age

7. To find out which age group has the highest number of people, execute the following command:

```
sfor ppl, age in c.execute(
    "SELECT count(*), age FROM persons GROUP BY age ORDER BY count(*)
DESC"):
    print("Highest number of people is {} and came from {} age group".
format(ppl, age))
    break
```

The output is as follows:

```
Highest number of people is 5 and came from 73 age group
```

8. To find out how many people do not have a full name (the last name is blank/null), execute the following command:

```
res = c.execute("SELECT count(*) FROM persons WHERE last_name IS null")
for row in res:
    print(row)
```

The output is as follows:

```
(60,)
```

9. To find out how many people have more than one pet, execute the following command:

```
res = c.execute("SELECT count(*) FROM (SELECT count(owner_id) FROM pets
GROUP BY owner_id HAVING count(owner_id) >1)")
for row in res:
    print("{} People has more than one pets".format(row[0]))
```

The output is as follows:

```
43 People has more than one pets
```

10. To find out how many pets have received treatment, execute the following command:

```
res = c.execute("SELECT count(*) FROM pets WHERE treatment_done=1")
for row in res:
    print(row)
```

The output is as follows:

```
(36,)
```

11. To find out how many pets have received treatment and the type of pet is known, execute the following command:

```
res = c.execute("SELECT count(*) FROM pets WHERE treatment_done=1 AND pet_
type IS NOT null")
for row in res:
    print(row)
```

The output is as follows:

```
(16,)
```

12. To find out how many pets are from the city called "east port", execute the following command:

```
res = c.execute("SELECT count(*) FROM pets JOIN persons ON pets.owner_id =
persons.id WHERE persons.city='east port'")
for row in res:
    print(row)
```

The output is as follows:

```
(49,)
```

13. To find out how many pets are from the city called "east port" and who received treatment, execute the following command:

```
res = c.execute("SELECT count(*) FROM pets JOIN persons ON pets.owner_id =
persons.id WHERE persons.city='east port' AND pets.treatment_done=1")
for row in res:
    print(row)
```

The output is as follows:

```
(11,)
```

Solution of Activity 12: Data Wrangling Task – Fixing UN Data

These are the steps to complete this activity:

1. Import the required libraries:

```
import numpy as np
import pandas as pd
import matplotlib.pyplot as plt
import warnings
warnings.filterwarnings('ignore')s
```

2. Save the URL of the dataset and use the pandas **read_csv** method to directly pass this link and create a DataFrame:

```
education_data_link="http://data.un.org/_Docs/SYB/CSV/SYB61_T07_Education.
csv"
df1 = pd.read_csv(education_data_link)
```

3. Print the data in the DataFrame:

```
df1.head()
```

The output is as follows:

	T07	Enrolment in primary, secondary and tertiary education levels	Unnamed: 2	Unnamed: 3	Unnamed: 4	Unnamed: 5	Unnamed: 6
0	Region/Country/Area	NaN	Year	Series	Value	Footnotes	Source
1	1	Total, all countries or areas	2005	Students enrolled in primary education (thousa...	678,990	NaN	United Nations Educational, Scientific and Cul...
2	1	Total, all countries or areas	2005	Gross enrollement ratio - Primary (male)	104.8	NaN	United Nations Educational, Scientific and Cul...
3	1	Total, all countries or areas	2005	Gross enrollment ratio - Primary (female)	99.8	NaN	United Nations Educational, Scientific and Cul...
4	1	Total, all countries or areas	2005	Students enrolled in secondary education (thou...	509,100	NaN	United Nations Educational, Scientific and Cul...

Figure 9.3: DataFrame from the UN data

4. As the first row does not contain useful information, use the **skiprows** parameter to remove the first row:

```
df1 = pd.read_csv(education_data_link,skiprows=1)
```

5. Print the data in the DataFrame:

```
df1.head()
```

The output is as follows:

	Region/Country/Area	Unnamed: 1	Year	Series	Value	Footnotes	Source
0	1	Total, all countries or areas	2005	Students enrolled in primary education (thousa...	678,990	NaN	United Nations Educational, Scientific and Cul...
1	1	Total, all countries or areas	2005	Gross enrollement ratio - Primary (male)	104.8	NaN	United Nations Educational, Scientific and Cul...
2	1	Total, all countries or areas	2005	Gross enrollment ratio - Primary (female)	99.8	NaN	United Nations Educational, Scientific and Cul...
3	1	Total, all countries or areas	2005	Students enrolled in secondary education (thou...	509,100	NaN	United Nations Educational, Scientific and Cul...
4	1	Total, all countries or areas	2005	Gross enrollment ratio - Secondary (male)	65.7	NaN	United Nations Educational, Scientific and Cul...

Figure 9.4: DataFrame after removing the first row

6. Drop the column Region/Country/Area and Source as they will not be very helpful:

```
df2 = df1.drop(['Region/Country/Area','Source'],axis=1)
```

7. Assign the following names as the columns of the DataFrame: **['Region/Country/Area','Year','Data','Value','Footnotes']**

```
df2.columns=['Region/Country/Area','Year','Data','Enrollments
(Thousands)','Footnotes']
```

8. Print the data in the DataFrame:

```
df1.head()
```

The output is as follows:

	Region/Country/Area	Year	Data	Enrollments (Thousands)	Footnotes
0	Total, all countries or areas	2005	Students enrolled in primary education (thousa...	678,990	NaN
1	Total, all countries or areas	2005	Gross enrollement ratio - Primary (male)	104.8	NaN
2	Total, all countries or areas	2005	Gross enrollment ratio - Primary (female)	99.8	NaN
3	Total, all countries or areas	2005	Students enrolled in secondary education (thou...	509,100	NaN
4	Total, all countries or areas	2005	Gross enrollment ratio - Secondary (male)	65.7	NaN

Figure 9.5: DataFrame after dropping Region/Country/Area and Source columns

9. Check how many unique values the **Footnotes** column contains:

```
df2['Footnotes'].unique()
```

The output is as follows:

```
array([nan, 'Estimate.',
       'For statistical purposes, the data for China do not include those for the Hong Kong Special Administrative Region (Hong
Kong SAR), Macao Special Administrative Region (Macao SAR) and Taiwan Province of China.'],
      dtype=object)
```

Figure 9.6: Unique values of the Footnotes column

10. Convert the **Value** column data into a numeric one for further processing:

```
type(df2['Enrollments (Thousands)'][0])
```

The output is as follows:

```
str
```

11. Create a utility function to convert the strings in the Value column into floating-point numbers:

```
def to_numeric(val):
    """
    Converts a given string (with one or more commas) to a numeric value
    """
    if ',' not in str(val):
        result = float(val)
    else:
```

```
        val=str(val)
        val=''.join(str(val).split(','))
        result=float(val)
    return result
```

12. Use the **apply** method to apply this function to the **Value** column data:

```
df2['Enrollments (Thousands)']=df2['Enrollments (Thousands)'].apply(to_
numeric)
```

13. Print the unique types of data in the **Data** column:

```
df2['Data'].unique()
```

The output is as follows:

```
array(['Students enrolled in primary education (thousands)',
       'Gross enrollement ratio - Primary (male)',
       'Gross enrollment ratio - Primary (female)',
       'Students enrolled in secondary education (thousands)',
       'Gross enrollment ratio - Secondary (male)',
       'Gross enrollment ratio - Secondary (female)',
       'Students enrolled in tertiary education (thousands)',
       'Gross enrollment ratio - Tertiary (male)',
       'Gross enrollment ratio - Tertiary (female)'], dtype=object)
```

Figure 9.7:Unique values in a column

14. Create three DataFrames by filtering and selecting them from the original Data-Frame:

- **df_primary**: Only students enrolled in primary education (thousands)

- **df_secondary**: Only students enrolled in secondary education (thousands)

- **df_tertiary**: Only students enrolled in tertiary education (thousands):

```
df_primary = df2[df2['Data']=='Students enrolled in primary education
(thousands)']
df_secondary = df2[df2['Data']=='Students enrolled in secondary education
(thousands)']
df_tertiary = df2[df2['Data']=='Students enrolled in tertiary education
(thousands)']
```

15. Compare them using bar charts of the primary students' enrollment of a low-income country and a high-income country:

```
primary_enrollment_india = df_primary[df_primary['Region/Country/
Area']=='India']
primary_enrollment_USA = df_primary[df_primary['Region/Country/
Area']=='United States of America']
```

16. Print the **primary_enrollment_india** data:

```
primary_enrollment_india
```

The output is as follows:

	Region/Country/Area	Year	Data	Enrollments (Thousands)	Footnotes
3729	India	2003	Students enrolled in primary education (thousa...	125569.0	NaN
3744	India	2010	Students enrolled in primary education (thousa...	138414.0	NaN
3753	India	2014	Students enrolled in primary education (thousa...	137809.0	NaN
3762	India	2015	Students enrolled in primary education (thousa...	138518.0	NaN
3771	India	2016	Students enrolled in primary education (thousa...	145803.0	NaN

Figure 9.8: Data for the enrollment in primary education in India

17. Print the **primary_enrollment_USA** data:

```
primary_enrollment_USA
```

The output is as follows:

	Region/Country/Area	Year	Data	Enrollments (Thousands)	Footnotes
7858	United States of America	2005	Students enrolled in primary education (thousa...	24455.0	NaN
7865	United States of America	2010	Students enrolled in primary education (thousa...	24393.0	NaN
7872	United States of America	2014	Students enrolled in primary education (thousa...	24538.0	NaN
7879	United States of America	2015	Students enrolled in primary education (thousa...	24786.0	NaN

Figure 9.9: Data for the enrollment in primary education in USA

18. Plot the data for India:

```
plt.figure(figsize=(8,4))
plt.bar(primary_enrollment_india['Year'],primary_enrollment_
india['Enrollments (Thousands)'])
plt.title("Enrollment in primary education\nin India (in
thousands)",fontsize=16)
plt.grid(True)
plt.xticks(fontsize=14)
plt.yticks(fontsize=14)
plt.xlabel("Year", fontsize=15)
plt.show()
```

The output is as follows:

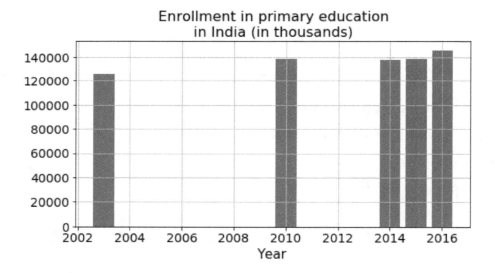

Figure 9.10: Bar plot for the enrollment in primary education in India

19. Plot the data for the USA:

```
plt.figure(figsize=(8,4))
plt.bar(primary_enrollment_USA['Year'],primary_enrollment_USA['Enrollments
(Thousands)'])
plt.title("Enrollment in primary education\nin the United States of America
(in thousands)",fontsize=16)
plt.grid(True)
plt.xticks(fontsize=14)
plt.yticks(fontsize=14)
plt.xlabel("Year", fontsize=15)
plt.show()
```

The output is as follows:

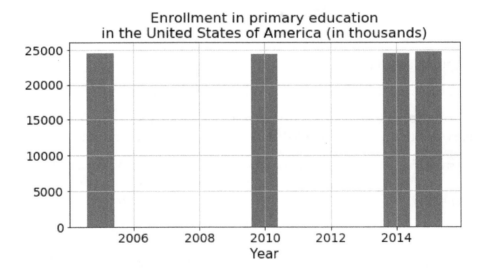

Figure 9.11: Bar plot for the enrollment in primary education in the USA

Data imputation: Clearly, we are missing some data. Let's say we decide to impute these data points by simple linear interpolation between the available data points. We can take out a pen and paper or a calculator and compute those values and manually create a dataset somehow. But being a data wrangler, we will of course take advantage of Python programming, and use pandas imputation methods for this task. But to do that, we first need to create a DataFrame with missing values inserted – that is, we need to append another DataFrame with missing values to the current DataFrame.

(For India) Append the rows corresponding to missing the years – 2004 - 2009, 2011 – 2013.

20. Find the missing years:

```
missing_years = [y for y in range(2004,2010)]+[y for y in range(2011,2014)]
```

21. Print the value in the **missing_years variable:**

```
missing_years
```

The output is as follows:

```
[2004, 2005, 2006, 2007, 2008, 2009, 2011, 2012, 2013]
```

22. Create a dictionary of values with **np.nan**. Note that there are 9 missing data points, so we need to create a list with identical values repeated 9 times:

```
dict_missing = {'Region/Country/Area':['India']*9,'Year':missing_years,
                'Data':'Students enrolled in primary education
(thousands)'*9,
                'Enrollments (Thousands)':[np.nan]*9,'Footnotes':[np.
nan]*9}
```

23. Create a DataFrame of missing values (from the preceding dictionary) that we can **append**:

```
df_missing = pd.DataFrame(data=dict_missing)
```

24. Append the new DataFrames to previously existing ones:

```
primary_enrollment_india=primary_enrollment_india.append(df_missing,ignore_
index=True,sort=True)
```

25. Print the data in **primary_enrollment_india**:

```
primary_enrollment_india
```

The output is as follows:

	Data	Enrollments (Thousands)	Footnotes	Region/Country/Area	Year
0	Students enrolled in primary education (thousa...	125569.0	NaN	India	2003
1	Students enrolled in primary education (thousa...	138414.0	NaN	India	2010
2	Students enrolled in primary education (thousa...	137809.0	NaN	India	2014
3	Students enrolled in primary education (thousa...	138518.0	NaN	India	2015
4	Students enrolled in primary education (thousa...	145803.0	NaN	India	2016
5	Students enrolled in primary education (thousa...	NaN	NaN	India	2004
6	Students enrolled in primary education (thousa...	NaN	NaN	India	2005
7	Students enrolled in primary education (thousa...	NaN	NaN	India	2006
8	Students enrolled in primary education (thousa...	NaN	NaN	India	2007
9	Students enrolled in primary education (thousa...	NaN	NaN	India	2008
10	Students enrolled in primary education (thousa...	NaN	NaN	India	2009
11	Students enrolled in primary education (thousa...	NaN	NaN	India	2011
12	Students enrolled in primary education (thousa...	NaN	NaN	India	2012
13	Students enrolled in primary education (thousa...	NaN	NaN	India	2013

Figure 9.12: Data for the enrollment in primary education in India after appending the data

26. Sort by **year** and reset the indices using **reset_index**. Use **inplace=True** to execute the changes on the DataFrame itself:

```
primary_enrollment_india.sort_values(by='Year',inplace=True)
primary_enrollment_india.reset_index(inplace=True,drop=True)
```

27. Print the data in **primary_enrollment_india**:

    ```
    primary_enrollment_india
    ```

    The output is as follows:

	Data	Enrollments (Thousands)	Footnotes	Region/Country/Area	Year
0	Students enrolled in primary education (thousa...	125569.0	NaN	India	2003
1	Students enrolled in primary education (thousa...	NaN	NaN	India	2004
2	Students enrolled in primary education (thousa...	NaN	NaN	India	2005
3	Students enrolled in primary education (thousa...	NaN	NaN	India	2006
4	Students enrolled in primary education (thousa...	NaN	NaN	India	2007
5	Students enrolled in primary education (thousa...	NaN	NaN	India	2008
6	Students enrolled in primary education (thousa...	NaN	NaN	India	2009
7	Students enrolled in primary education (thousa...	138414.0	NaN	India	2010
8	Students enrolled in primary education (thousa...	NaN	NaN	India	2011
9	Students enrolled in primary education (thousa...	NaN	NaN	India	2012
10	Students enrolled in primary education (thousa...	NaN	NaN	India	2013
11	Students enrolled in primary education (thousa...	137809.0	NaN	India	2014
12	Students enrolled in primary education (thousa...	138518.0	NaN	India	2015
13	Students enrolled in primary education (thousa...	145803.0	NaN	India	2016

Figure 9.13: Data for the enrollment in primary education in India after sorting the data

28. Use the **interpolate** method for linear interpolation. It fills all the NaN by linearly interpolated values. Check out this link for more details about this method: http://pandas.pydata.org/pandas-docs/version/0.17/generated/pandas.DataFrame.interpolate.html:

    ```
    primary_enrollment_india.interpolate(inplace=True)
    ```

29. Print the data in **primary_enrollment_india**:

```
primary_enrollment_india
```

The output is as follows:

	Data	Enrollments (Thousands)	Footnotes	Region/Country/Area	Year
0	Students enrolled in primary education (thousa...	125569.00	NaN	India	2003
1	Students enrolled in primary education (thousa...	127404.00	NaN	India	2004
2	Students enrolled in primary education (thousa...	129239.00	NaN	India	2005
3	Students enrolled in primary education (thousa...	131074.00	NaN	India	2006
4	Students enrolled in primary education (thousa...	132909.00	NaN	India	2007
5	Students enrolled in primary education (thousa...	134744.00	NaN	India	2008
6	Students enrolled in primary education (thousa...	136579.00	NaN	India	2009
7	Students enrolled in primary education (thousa...	138414.00	NaN	India	2010
8	Students enrolled in primary education (thousa...	138262.75	NaN	India	2011
9	Students enrolled in primary education (thousa...	138111.50	NaN	India	2012
10	Students enrolled in primary education (thousa...	137960.25	NaN	India	2013
11	Students enrolled in primary education (thousa...	137809.00	NaN	India	2014
12	Students enrolled in primary education (thousa...	138518.00	NaN	India	2015
13	Students enrolled in primary education (thousa...	145803.00	NaN	India	2016

Figure 9.14: Data for the enrollment in primary education in India after interpolating the data

30. Plot the data:

```
plt.figure(figsize=(8,4))
plt.bar(primary_enrollment_india['Year'],primary_enrollment_
india['Enrollments (Thousands)'])
plt.title("Enrollment in primary education\nin India (in
thousands)",fontsize=16)
plt.grid(True)
plt.xticks(fontsize=14)
plt.yticks(fontsize=14)
plt.xlabel("Year", fontsize=15)
plt.show()
```

The output is as follows:

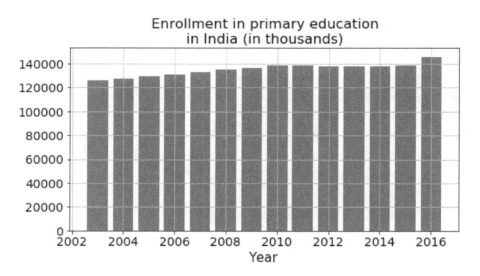

Figure 9.15: Bar plot for the enrollment in primary education in India

31. Repeat the same steps for the USA:

```
missing_years = [2004]+[y for y in range(2006,2010)]+[y for y in
range(2011,2014)]+[2016]
```

32. Print the value in **missing_years**.

```
missing_years
```

The output is as follows:

```
[2004, 2006, 2007, 2008, 2009, 2011, 2012, 2013, 2016]
```

33. Create **dict_missing**, as follows:

```
dict_missing = {'Region/Country/Area':['United States of
America']*9,'Year':missing_years, 'Data':'Students enrolled in primary
education (thousands)'*9, 'Value':[np.nan]*9,'Footnotes':[np.nan]*9}
```

34. Create the DataFrame fpr **df_missing**, as follows:

```
df_missing = pd.DataFrame(data=dict_missing)
```

35. Append this to the **primary_enrollment_USA** variable, as follows:

```
primary_enrollment_USA=primary_enrollment_USA.append(df_missing,ignore_
index=True,sort=True)
```

36. Sort the values in the **primary_enrollment_USA** variable, as follows:

```
primary_enrollment_USA.sort_values(by='Year',inplace=True)
```

37. Reset the index of the **primary_enrollment_USA** variable, as follows:

```
primary_enrollment_USA.reset_index(inplace=True,drop=True)
```

38. Interpolate the **primary_enrollment_USA** variable, as follows:

```
primary_enrollment_USA.interpolate(inplace=True)
```

39. Print the **primary_enrollment_USA** variable:

```
primary_enrollment_USA
```

The output is as follows:

	Data	Enrollments (Thousands)	Footnotes	Region/Country/Area	Value	Year
0	Students enrolled in primary education (thousa...	NaN	NaN	United States of America	NaN	2004
1	Students enrolled in primary education (thousa...	24455.00	NaN	United States of America	NaN	2005
2	Students enrolled in primary education (thousa...	24442.60	NaN	United States of America	NaN	2006
3	Students enrolled in primary education (thousa...	24430.20	NaN	United States of America	NaN	2007
4	Students enrolled in primary education (thousa...	24417.80	NaN	United States of America	NaN	2008
5	Students enrolled in primary education (thousa...	24405.40	NaN	United States of America	NaN	2009
6	Students enrolled in primary education (thousa...	24393.00	NaN	United States of America	NaN	2010
7	Students enrolled in primary education (thousa...	24429.25	NaN	United States of America	NaN	2011
8	Students enrolled in primary education (thousa...	24465.50	NaN	United States of America	NaN	2012
9	Students enrolled in primary education (thousa...	24501.75	NaN	United States of America	NaN	2013
10	Students enrolled in primary education (thousa...	24538.00	NaN	United States of America	NaN	2014
11	Students enrolled in primary education (thousa...	24786.00	NaN	United States of America	NaN	2015
12	Students enrolled in primary education (thousa...	24786.00	NaN	United States of America	NaN	2016

Figure 9.16: Data for the enrollment in primary education in USA after all operations have been completed

40. Still, the first value is unfilled. We can use the **limit** and **limit_direction** parameters with the interpolate method to fill that. How did we know this? By searching on Google and looking at this StackOverflow page. Always search for the solution to your problem and look for what has already been done and try to implement it:

```
primary_enrollment_USA.interpolate(method='linear',limit_
direction='backward',limit=1)
```

The output is as follows:

	Data	Enrollments (Thousands)	Footnotes	Region/Country/Area	Value	Year
0	Students enrolled in primary education (thousa...	24455.00	NaN	United States of America	NaN	2004
1	Students enrolled in primary education (thousa...	24455.00	NaN	United States of America	NaN	2005
2	Students enrolled in primary education (thousa...	24442.60	NaN	United States of America	NaN	2006
3	Students enrolled in primary education (thousa...	24430.20	NaN	United States of America	NaN	2007
4	Students enrolled in primary education (thousa...	24417.80	NaN	United States of America	NaN	2008
5	Students enrolled in primary education (thousa...	24405.40	NaN	United States of America	NaN	2009
6	Students enrolled in primary education (thousa...	24393.00	NaN	United States of America	NaN	2010
7	Students enrolled in primary education (thousa...	24429.25	NaN	United States of America	NaN	2011
8	Students enrolled in primary education (thousa...	24465.50	NaN	United States of America	NaN	2012
9	Students enrolled in primary education (thousa...	24501.75	NaN	United States of America	NaN	2013
10	Students enrolled in primary education (thousa...	24538.00	NaN	United States of America	NaN	2014
11	Students enrolled in primary education (thousa...	24786.00	NaN	United States of America	NaN	2015
12	Students enrolled in primary education (thousa...	24786.00	NaN	United States of America	NaN	2016

Figure 9.17: Data for the enrollment in primary education in the USA after limiting the data

41. Print the data in primary_enrollment_USA:

```
primary_enrollment_USA
```

The output is as follows:

	Data	Enrollments (Thousands)	Footnotes	Region/Country/Area	Value	Year
0	Students enrolled in primary education (thousa...	NaN	NaN	United States of America	NaN	2004
1	Students enrolled in primary education (thousa...	24455.00	NaN	United States of America	NaN	2005
2	Students enrolled in primary education (thousa...	24442.60	NaN	United States of America	NaN	2006
3	Students enrolled in primary education (thousa...	24430.20	NaN	United States of America	NaN	2007
4	Students enrolled in primary education (thousa...	24417.80	NaN	United States of America	NaN	2008
5	Students enrolled in primary education (thousa...	24405.40	NaN	United States of America	NaN	2009
6	Students enrolled in primary education (thousa...	24393.00	NaN	United States of America	NaN	2010
7	Students enrolled in primary education (thousa...	24429.25	NaN	United States of America	NaN	2011
8	Students enrolled in primary education (thousa...	24465.50	NaN	United States of America	NaN	2012
9	Students enrolled in primary education (thousa...	24501.75	NaN	United States of America	NaN	2013
10	Students enrolled in primary education (thousa...	24538.00	NaN	United States of America	NaN	2014
11	Students enrolled in primary education (thousa...	24786.00	NaN	United States of America	NaN	2015
12	Students enrolled in primary education (thousa...	24786.00	NaN	United States of America	NaN	2016

Figure 9.18: Data for the enrollment in primary education in USA

42. Plot the data:

```
plt.figure(figsize=(8,4))
plt.bar(primary_enrollment_USA['Year'],primary_enrollment_USA['Enrollments
(Thousands)'])
plt.title("Enrollment in primary education\nin the United States of America
(in thousands)",fontsize=16)
plt.grid(True)
plt.xticks(fontsize=14)
plt.yticks(fontsize=14)
plt.xlabel("Year", fontsize=15)
plt.show()
```

The output is as follows:

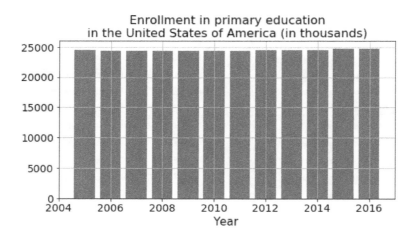

Figure 9.19: Bar plot for the enrollment in primary education in the USA

Activity 13: Data Wrangling Task – Cleaning GDP Data

These are the steps to complete this activity:

1. GDP data for India: We will try to read the GDP data for India from a CSV file that was found in a World Bank portal. It is given to you and also hosted on the Packt GitHub repository. But the Pandas **read_csv** method will throw an error in we try to read it normally. Let's look at a step-by-step guide on how we can read useful information from it:

    ```
    df3=pd.read_csv("India_World_Bank_Info.csv")
    ```

    The output is as follows:

    ```
    ---------------------------------------------------------------------
    ParserError                             Traceback (most recent call last)
    <ipython-input-45-9239cae67df7> in <module>()
    …..

    ParserError: Error tokenizing data. C error: Expected 1 fields in line 6,
    saw 3
    ```

    We can try and use the **error_bad_lines=False** option in this kind of situation.

2. Read the India World Bank Information `.csv` file:

```
df3=pd.read_csv("India_World_Bank_Info.csv",error_bad_lines=False)
df3.head(10)
```

The output is as follows:

	Data Source World Development Indicators
0	Last Updated Date\t11/14/2018\t\t\t\t\t\t\t\t\t\t...
1	Country Name\tCountry Code\tIndicator Name\t19...
2	India\tIND\tBattle-related deaths (number of p...
3	India\tIND\tTravel services (% of commercial s...
4	India\tIND\tTransport services (% of commercia...
5	India\tIND\tHigh-technology exports (% of manu...
6	India\tIND\tHigh-technology exports (current U...
7	India\tIND\tCommercial service exports (curren...
8	India\tIND\tExport value index (2000 = 100)\t\t...
9	India\tIND\tMerchandise exports to low- and mi...

Figure 9.20: DataFrame from the India World Bank Information

Note:

At times, the output may not found because there are three rows instead of the expected one row.

3. Clearly, the delimiter in this file is tab (**\t**):

```
df3=pd.read_csv("India_World_Bank_Info.csv",error_bad_
lines=False,delimiter='\t')
df3.head(10)
```

The output is as follows:

	Data Source	World Development Indicators	Unnamed: 2	Unnamed: 3	Unnamed: 4	Unnamed: 5	Unnamed: 6	Unnamed: 7	Unnamed: 8	Unnamed: 9	...	Unnamed: 51	Unnamed: 52	Unna
0	NaN	NaN	NaN	NaN	NaN	NaN	NaN	NaN	NaN	NaN	...	NaN	NaN	
1	Last Updated Date	11/14/2018	NaN	NaN	NaN	NaN	NaN	NaN	NaN	NaN	...	NaN	NaN	
2	NaN	NaN	NaN	NaN	NaN	NaN	NaN	NaN	NaN	NaN	...	NaN	NaN	
3	Country Name	Country Code	Indicator Name	1960.0	1961.0	1962.0	1963.0	1964.0	1965.0	1966.0	...	2.008000e+03	2.009000e+03	2.010
4	India	IND	Presence of peace keepers (number of troops, p...	NaN	NaN	NaN	NaN	NaN	NaN	NaN	...	NaN	NaN	
5	India	IND	Intentional homicides (per 100,000 people)	NaN	NaN	NaN	NaN	NaN	NaN	NaN	...	3.842386e+00	3.773790e+00	3.774
6	India	IND	Intentional homicides, male (per 100,000 male)	NaN	NaN	NaN	NaN	NaN	NaN	NaN	...	4.672067e+00	4.441221e+00	4.477
7	India	IND	Intentional homicides, female (per 100,000 fem...	NaN	NaN	NaN	NaN	NaN	NaN	NaN	...	2.948596e+00	3.054638e+00	3.016
8	India	IND	Internally displaced persons, total displaced ...	NaN	NaN	NaN	NaN	NaN	NaN	NaN	...	NaN	5.000000e+05	6.500
9	India	IND	Internally displaced persons, new displacement...	NaN	NaN	NaN	NaN	NaN	NaN	NaN	...	6.662000e+06	5.304000e+06	1.411

10 rows × 61 columns

Figure 9.21: DataFrame from the India World Bank Information after using a delimiter

4. Use the **skiprows** parameter to skip the first 4 rows:

```
df3=pd.read_csv("India_World_Bank_Info.csv",error_bad_
lines=False,delimiter='\t',skiprows=4)
df3.head(10)
```

The output is as follows:

	Country Name	Country Code	Indicator Name	1960	1961	1962	1963	1964	1965	1966	...	2008	2009	2010	2011	2012
0	India	IND	Presence of peace keepers (number of troops, p...	NaN	NaN	NaN	NaN	NaN	NaN	NaN	...	NaN	NaN	NaN	NaN	NaN
1	India	IND	Intentional homicides (per 100,000 people)	NaN	NaN	NaN	NaN	NaN	NaN	NaN	...	3.842386e+00	3.773790e+00	3.774227e+00	3.819646e+00	3.758949e+00	3.
2	India	IND	Intentional homicides, male (per 100,000 male)	NaN	NaN	NaN	NaN	NaN	NaN	NaN	...	4.672067e+00	4.441221e+00	4.477722e+00	4.468965e+00	4.431416e+00	4.
3	India	IND	Intentional homicides, female (per 100,000 fem...	NaN	NaN	NaN	NaN	NaN	NaN	NaN	...	2.948596e+00	3.054638e+00	3.016158e+00	3.119986e+00	3.034514e+00	2.
4	India	IND	Internally displaced persons, total displaced ...	NaN	NaN	NaN	NaN	NaN	NaN	NaN	...	NaN	5.000000e+05	6.500000e+05	6.500000e+05	1.000000e+06	5.
5	India	IND	Internally displaced persons, new displacement...	NaN	NaN	NaN	NaN	NaN	NaN	NaN	...	6.662000e+06	5.304000e+06	1.411000e+06	1.503000e+06	9.110000e+06	2
6	India	IND	Internally displaced persons, new displacement...	NaN	NaN	NaN	NaN	NaN	NaN	NaN	...	NaN	3.300000e+04	1.070000e+05	5.300000e+04	5.000000e+05	6.
7	India	IND	Battle-related deaths (number of people)	NaN	NaN	NaN	NaN	NaN	NaN	NaN	...	1.076000e+03	1.115000e+03	1.029000e+03	4.330000e+02	4.090000e+02	3.
8	India	IND	Travel services (% of commercial service exports)	NaN	NaN	NaN	NaN	NaN	NaN	NaN	...	1.119735e+01	1.204084e+01	1.242864e+01	1.283755e+01	1.239164e+01	1.
9	India	IND	Transport services (% of commercial service ex...	NaN	NaN	NaN	NaN	NaN	NaN	NaN	...	1.211740e+01	1.214528e+01	1.138684e+01	1.283318e+01	1.207117e+01	1.

10 rows × 61 columns

Figure 9.22: DataFrame from the India World Bank Information after using skiprows

5. Closely examine the dataset: In this file, the columns are the yearly data and rows are the various types of information. Upon examining the file with Excel, we find that the column **Indicator Name** is the one with the name of the particular data type. We filter the dataset with the information we are interested in and also transpose (the rows and columns are interchanged) it to make it a similar format as our previous education dataset:

```
df4=df3[df3['Indicator Name']=='GDP per capita (current US$)'].T
df4.head(10)
```

The output is as follows:

	981
Country Name	India
Country Code	IND
Indicator Name	GDP per capita (current US$)
1960	81.2848
1961	84.4264
1962	88.9149
1963	100.049
1964	114.315
1965	118.063
1966	89.0536

Figure 9.23: DataFrame focusing on GDP per capita

6. There is no index, so let's use **reset_index** again:

```
df4.reset_index(inplace=True)
df4.head(10)
```

The output is as follows:

	index	981
0	Country Name	India
1	Country Code	IND
2	Indicator Name	GDP per capita (current US$)
3	1960	81.2848
4	1961	84.4264
5	1962	88.9149
6	1963	100.049
7	1964	114.315
8	1965	118.063
9	1966	89.0536

Figure 9.24: DataFrame from the India World Bank Information using reset_index

7. The first 3 rows aren't useful. We can redefine the DataFrame without them. Then, we re-index again:

```
df4.drop([0,1,2],inplace=True)
df4.reset_index(inplace=True,drop=True)
df4.head(10)
```

The output is as follows:

	index	981
0	1960	81.2848
1	1961	84.4264
2	1962	88.9149
3	1963	100.049
4	1964	114.315
5	1965	118.063
6	1966	89.0536
7	1967	95.3308
8	1968	98.8312
9	1969	106.496

Figure 9.25: DataFrame from the India World Bank Information after dropping and resetting the index

8. Let's rename the columns properly (this is necessary for merging, which we will look at shortly):

```
df4.columns=['Year','GDP']
df4.head(10)
```

The output is as follows:

	Year	GDP
0	1960	81.2848
1	1961	84.4264
2	1962	88.9149
3	1963	100.049
4	1964	114.315
5	1965	118.063
6	1966	89.0536
7	1967	95.3308
8	1968	98.8312
9	1969	106.496

Figure 9.26: DataFrame focusing on Year and GDP

9. It looks like that we have GDP data from 1960 onward. But we are interested in 2003 - 2016. Let's examine the last 20 rows:

```
df4.tail(20)
```

The output is as follows:

	Year	GDP
38	1998	409.194
39	1999	437.586
40	2000	438.865
41	2001	447.014
42	2002	466.201
43	2003	541.135
44	2004	621.318
45	2005	707.008
46	2006	792.026
47	2007	1018.17
48	2008	991.485
49	2009	1090.32
50	2010	1345.77
51	2011	1461.67
52	2012	1446.99
53	2013	1452.2
54	2014	1576
55	2015	1606.04
56	2016	1717.47
57	2017	1939.61

Figure 9.27: DataFrame from the India World Bank Information

10. So, we should be good with rows 43-56. Let's create a DataFrame called **df_gdp**:

```
df_gdp=df4.iloc[[i for i in range(43,57)]]
df_gdp
```

The output is as follows:

	Year	GDP
43	2003	541.135
44	2004	621.318
45	2005	707.008
46	2006	792.026
47	2007	1018.17
48	2008	991.485
49	2009	1090.32
50	2010	1345.77
51	2011	1461.67
52	2012	1446.99
53	2013	1452.2
54	2014	1576
55	2015	1606.04
56	2016	1717.47

Figure 9.28: DataFrame from the India World Bank Information

11. We need to reset the index again (for merging):

```
df_gdp.reset_index(inplace=True,drop=True)
df_gdp
```

The output is as follows:

	Year	GDP
0	2003	541.135
1	2004	621.318
2	2005	707.008
3	2006	792.026
4	2007	1018.17
5	2008	991.485
6	2009	1090.32
7	2010	1345.77
8	2011	1461.67
9	2012	1446.99
10	2013	1452.2
11	2014	1576
12	2015	1606.04
13	2016	1717.47

Figure 9.29: DataFrame from the India World Bank Information

12. The year in this DataFrame is not of the **int** type. So, it will have problems merging with the education DataFrame:

```
df_gdp['Year']
```

The output is as follows:

```
0       2003
1       2004
2       2005
3       2006
4       2007
5       2008
6       2009
7       2010
8       2011
9       2012
10      2013
11      2014
12      2015
13      2016
Name: Year, dtype: object
```

Figure 9.30: DataFrame focusing on year

13. Use the **apply** method with Python's built-in **int** function. Ignore any warnings that are thrown:

```
df_gdp['Year']=df_gdp['Year'].apply(int)
```

Solution of Activity 14: Data Wrangling Task – Merging UN Data and GDP Data

These are the steps to complete this activity:

1. Now, merge the two DataFrames, that is, **primary_enrollment_india** and **df_gdp**, on the **Year** column:

```
primary_enrollment_with_gdp=primary_enrollment_india.merge(df_
gdp,on='Year')
primary_enrollment_with_gdp
```

The output is as follows:

	Data	Enrollments (Thousands)	Footnotes	Region/Country/Area	Year	GDP
0	Students enrolled in primary education (thousa...	125569.00	NaN	India	2003	541.135
1	Students enrolled in primary education (thousa...	127404.00	NaN	India	2004	621.318
2	Students enrolled in primary education (thousa...	129239.00	NaN	India	2005	707.008
3	Students enrolled in primary education (thousa...	131074.00	NaN	India	2006	792.026
4	Students enrolled in primary education (thousa...	132909.00	NaN	India	2007	1018.17
5	Students enrolled in primary education (thousa...	134744.00	NaN	India	2008	991.485
6	Students enrolled in primary education (thousa...	136579.00	NaN	India	2009	1090.32
7	Students enrolled in primary education (thousa...	138414.00	NaN	India	2010	1345.77
8	Students enrolled in primary education (thousa...	138262.75	NaN	India	2011	1461.67
9	Students enrolled in primary education (thousa...	138111.50	NaN	India	2012	1446.99
10	Students enrolled in primary education (thousa...	137960.25	NaN	India	2013	1452.2
11	Students enrolled in primary education (thousa...	137809.00	NaN	India	2014	1576
12	Students enrolled in primary education (thousa...	138518.00	NaN	India	2015	1606.04
13	Students enrolled in primary education (thousa...	145803.00	NaN	India	2016	1717.47

Figure 9.31: Merged data

2. Now, we can drop the **Data**, **Footnotes**, and **Region/Country/Area** columns:

```
primary_enrollment_with_gdp.drop(['Data','Footnotes','Region/Country/
Area'],axis=1,inplace=True)
primary_enrollment_with_gdp
```

The output is as follows:

	Enrollments (Thousands)	Year	GDP
0	125569.00	2003	541.135
1	127404.00	2004	621.318
2	129239.00	2005	707.008
3	131074.00	2006	792.026
4	132909.00	2007	1018.17
5	134744.00	2008	991.485
6	136579.00	2009	1090.32
7	138414.00	2010	1345.77
8	138262.75	2011	1461.67
9	138111.50	2012	1446.99
10	137960.25	2013	1452.2
11	137809.00	2014	1576
12	138518.00	2015	1606.04
13	145803.00	2016	1717.47

Figure 9.32: Merged data after dropping the Data, Footnotes, and Region/Country/Area columns

3. Rearrange the columns for proper viewing and presentation to a data scientist:

```
primary_enrollment_with_gdp = primary_enrollment_with_
gdp[['Year','Enrollments (Thousands)','GDP']]
primary_enrollment_with_gdp
```

The output is as follows:

	Year	Enrollments (Thousands)	GDP
0	2003	125569.00	541.135
1	2004	127404.00	621.318
2	2005	129239.00	707.008
3	2006	131074.00	792.026
4	2007	132909.00	1018.17
5	2008	134744.00	991.485
6	2009	136579.00	1090.32
7	2010	138414.00	1345.77
8	2011	138262.75	1461.67
9	2012	138111.50	1446.99
10	2013	137960.25	1452.2
11	2014	137809.00	1576
12	2015	138518.00	1606.04
13	2016	145803.00	1717.47

Figure 9.33: Merged data after rearranging the columns

4. Plot the data:

```
plt.figure(figsize=(8,5))
plt.title("India's GDP per capita vs primary education
enrollment",fontsize=16)
plt.scatter(primary_enrollment_with_gdp['GDP'],
            primary_enrollment_with_gdp['Enrollments (Thousands)'],
            edgecolor='k',color='orange',s=200)
plt.xlabel("GDP per capita (US $)",fontsize=15)
plt.ylabel("Primary enrollment (thousands)",fontsize=15)
plt.xticks(fontsize=14)
plt.yticks(fontsize=14)
plt.grid(True)
plt.show()
```

The output is as follows:

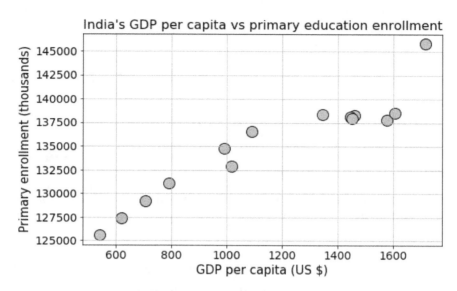

Figure 9.34: Scatter plot of merged data

Activity 15: Data Wrangling Task – Connecting the New Data to a Database

These are the steps to complete this activity:

1. Connect to a database and writing values it. We start by importing the **sqlite3** module of Python and then use the connect function to connect to a database. Designate **Year** as the **PRIMARY KEY** of this table:

```
import sqlite3
with sqlite3.connect("Education_GDP.db") as conn:
    cursor = conn.cursor()
    cursor.execute("CREATE TABLE IF NOT EXISTS \
                    education_gdp(Year INT, Enrollment FLOAT, GDP FLOAT,
PRIMARY KEY (Year))")
```

2. Run a loop with the dataset rows one by one to insert them in the table:

```
with sqlite3.connect("Education_GDP.db") as conn:
    cursor = conn.cursor()
    for i in range(14):
        year = int(primary_enrollment_with_gdp.iloc[i]['Year'])
        enrollment = primary_enrollment_with_gdp.iloc[i]['Enrollments
(Thousands)']
        gdp = primary_enrollment_with_gdp.iloc[i]['GDP']
        #print(year,enrollment,gdp)
        cursor.execute("INSERT INTO education_gdp (Year,Enrollment,GDP)
VALUES(?,?,?)", (year,enrollment,gdp))
```

If we look at the current folder, we should see a file called **Education_GDP.db**, and if we can examine that using a database viewer program, we can see the data transferred there.

In these activities, we have examined a complete data wrangling flow, including reading data from the web and a local drive, filtering, cleaning, quick visualization, imputation, indexing, merging, and writing back to a database table. We also wrote custom functions to transform some of the data and saw how to handle situations where we may get errors upon reading the file.

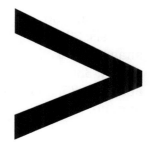

Index

About

All major keywords used in this book are captured alphabetically in this section. Each one is accompanied by the page number of where they appear.

A

algorithm: 336
analysis: 326, 328
analytics: 325, 332,
    334, 336
apache: 325, 333-334
append: 327, 329

B

balancer: 334

C

calculator: 327
cluster: 334
column: 328-329, 331
components: 335
compute: 327
convert: 328

D

database: 327-328,
    331-332, 334-335
dataframe: 327-330
dataframes: 329, 331
dataset: 325-328, 330-331
datasets: 325-326,
    328, 330
delimiter: 330
deluge: 336
docker: 333
domain: 335-336

F

features: 333
footnotes: 328, 331

framework: 332-334
full-stack: 332
function: 328-331

G

github: 328-329, 332
graphx: 334

H

hadoop: 325, 333

I

imputation: 327, 329, 331
impute: 326-327, 329
indexing: 331
inplace: 329
insert: 331

K

kdnuggets: 336

L

libraries: 335-337
linear: 327, 329-330

M

map-reduce: 333
matplotlib: 335

N

notebook: 327, 331

P

pandas: 327-330, 337
pipeline: 332, 334
postgresql: 331
pydata: 330
python: 326-327,
    331, 334-337
pytorch: 337

R

rearrange: 331
rohrer: 336

S

scraping: 335
seaborn: 335
skiprows: 328, 330
sqlite: 331
supervised: 337

T

tensorflow: 337
tolerance: 334

W

workflow: 335
worldbank: 329
wrangle: 328, 335
wrangling: 325-329,
    331-332, 334-337

Z

zookeeper: 333

Printed in the USA
CPSIA information can be obtained
at www.ICGtesting.com
LVHW080016220224
772455LV00007B/680

9 781789 800111